Race, Nation, and Market

Race, Nation, and Market

Economic Culture in Porfirian Mexico

RICHARD WEINER

The University of Arizona Press

Tucson

The University of Arizona Press
© 2004 The Arizona Board of Regents
First printing
♾ This book is printed on acid-free, archival-quality paper.
Manufactured in the United States of America

09 08 07 06 05 04   6 5 4 3 2 1

Library of Congress Cataloging-in-Publication Data
Weiner, Richard, 1957–
Race, nation, and market : economic culture in Porfirian Mexico / Richard Weiner.
p. cm.
Includes bibliographical references and index.
ISBN 0-8165-2326-6 (Cloth: alk. paper)
1. Mexico—Economic policy. 2. Capitalism—Mexico—History. 3. Political culture—Mexico—
History—19th century. 4. Political culture—Mexico—History—20th century. 5. Economics—
Mexico—History—19th century. 6. Economics—Mexico—History—20th century. 7. Mexico—
Economic conditions—19th century. 8. Mexico—Economic conditions—20th century.
9. Mexico—Politics and government—1867–1910. 10. Liberalism—Mexico—History—19th
century. I. Title.
HC135.W435 2004
330.12'2'097209034—dc22
2003015696

British Library Cataloguing-in-Publication Data
A catalogue record for this book is available from the British Library.

To Rosy and Eric

Contents

Preface

This work began a decade ago as a doctoral dissertation on Porfirian economic ideology. After I had written a substantial amount of material, I elected to refocus my study and concentrate specifically on the symbolic significance of the market. Following in the footsteps of Albert Hirschman and Ricardo Salvatore, I decided to treat dialogues about the market as a form of sociopolitical discourse that played a pivotal role in the construction of Mexican identity. While this new approach required extensive reworking, I was much more satisfied with the final product. Although I have done additional research and revisions for this book, my focus on the market has remained. Throughout the text, the translations of Spanish materials are mine unless otherwise indicated.

Chapter 1 begins by providing a theoretical and methodological background to the concept of market symbolism. It then places the study in a nineteenth-century historical context and explains why the market became a dominant symbol in Porfirian national discourse. Finally, it provides background on the groups examined in the study: liberals, social Catholics, and the Mexican Liberal Party.

Chapter 2 examines the liberals' discourse about the market's effects on political and economic behavior. It first covers the issue of the market's impact on the political conduct of the middle and upper classes and then studies the market's influence on the economic actions of Indians and hacendados.

Chapter 3 continues to study liberals but takes on a distinct issue: the international market's impact on Mexican politics and society. First, the chapter explores liberals' conceptions of the international economy. It then examines their discourse about foreigners' economic role in Mexico. Finally, it studies rhetoric about the state's economic function. A version of chapter 3 was published in the *Journal of Latin American Studies* in 2000.

Chapter 4 examines the discourse of Trinidad Sánchez Santos, Mexican social Catholicism's leading publicist. It surveys his discourse about the societal effects of the market and includes sections on workers, the family, and the community. In 2001 a version of chapter 4 was published in *Mexican Studies/Estudios Mexicanos*.

The Mexican Liberal Party's market rhetoric is examined in chapter 5, which is divided chronologically. The first part surveys the party's discourse about the market's impact on the labor force, land distribution, and the Mexican nation during the period 1900–1906. The second part, which studies the 1907–11 era, covers these topics as well as ideas about the destruction of market society and the construction of a collectivist order.

I spent a year and a half in Mexico City doing research for this study. The bulk of my research was done at the Hemoreteca Nacional, the largest repository of periodicals in Mexico. I also spent significant amounts of time at the Archivo General de la Nación, the Centro de Estudios de Historia de México Condumex, and Biblioteca Miguel Lerdo de Tejada. The library at Colegio de México also proved useful. Grants and scholarships helped support my research. An initial examination of Mexican archives was funded by a graduate research fellowship awarded by the School of Humanities at the University of California, Irvine. Return visits were supported by dissertation fellowships and dissertation grants awarded by the School of Humanities at the University of California, Irvine, as well as a dissertation research grant provided by the University of California Consortium on Mexico and the United States (UCMEXUS). More recently, I was able to carry out additional research at Harvard University's Widener Library with the support of a library scholars grant provided by Harvard's David Rockefeller Center for Latin American Studies. A summer research grant from Indiana University provided me with time to make revisions.

I have benefited from contact with many scholars, but I will limit my acknowledgments to the people who had the greatest impact on my research. Over the years I have had countless discussions with Bob Duncan, who has been very generous with his time and extensive knowledge of nineteenth-century Mexico. During the later stages of writing I benefited from conversations with Raúl

Galoppe. At the Hemoreteca Nacional, I had the fortunate opportunity to discuss my research regularly with Israel Arroyo and Juan Roman Monroy de la Rosa. Carlos Marichal commented on my work, introduced me to scholars in Mexico, and gave me access to the stacks at Colegio de México's library. Jaime Rodríguez, a member of my dissertation committee, provided a wise critique. Ron Chilcote, another committee member, gave very useful advice. Ted Beatty has been more than generous with his time, knowledge, and insights. We discussed my work at length, and he made extensive comments on my book manuscript. Jonathan Brown, too, ably critiqued the manuscript. Anonymous reviewers for the University of Arizona Press provided intelligent and useful suggestions for revision. Steven Topik, my dissertation advisor, was tremendously helpful. Not only did he put an immense amount of time and energy into my work, but he also had an uncanny knack of providing the right mix of support and criticism. He made comments on more drafts than I care to remember, and we had an ongoing dialogue for years. He was extremely generous with his time, knowledge, and friendship. His impact was profound, and I am deeply grateful.

This work would not have been possible without behind-the-scenes aid from friends and family. My lifelong friend John Fahey has been an important source of encouragement throughout. My mother and late father raised me in a rich intellectual environment and provided economic and moral support while I was a graduate student. My brother Dave and sister-in-law Judy generously gave financial help (on numerous occasions) and encouragement over the years. My siblings Steve, Rachel, Mike, and late brother Ken all took an interest in this project. My in-laws in Mexico (Ale, Alex, Angelina, Eva, Laura, Mary, and Tania) played a crucial role by providing a loving and supportive home environment while I was doing research in Mexico City and a tranquil abode in the countryside that proved superb for writing. My son, Eric, has been not only a study in patience and understanding but also a source of joy and inspiration. The love, support, and encouragement of my wife, Rosy, have been indispensable. I couldn't have done it without her.

Race, Nation, and Market

1 Market as Symbol in Porfirian Mexico

The Symbolic Significance of the Market

At a meeting of the Rio Group in Cochabamba, Bolivia, in September 1996, Mexican president Ernesto Zedillo (1994–2000) contended that "the free market without limits" was the answer to poverty in Latin America. Zedillo, by utilizing the term *market* as a rhetorical tool, was building upon a tradition that has a long history in Mexico, for during the Porfiriato (1876–1910) the market was a dominant symbol in Mexican national discourse. But it was a controversial sign: Porfirian contemporaries both demonized the market as an agent of social destruction and praised it as an instrument of national evolution. Since the market became a primary symbol, it was intimately linked to Porfirian political groups' self-definition.

The market's symbolic importance, however, has been ignored by scholars. This oversight is ironic, for specialists agree that the emergence of the market transformed Porfirian Mexico. Economic historians maintain that a traditional economy became modern. Labor historians chronicle the (albeit incomplete) proletarianization of the peasantry. Social historians document a shift from a caste to a class society. Agrarian historians maintain that market expansion was a cause of the Mexican Revolution.[1] Scholars, however, have neglected the immense influence that discourses about the market had on the formation of political groups in late Porfirian Mexico, an age marked by political mobilization. My study fills this lacuna in the literature by documenting the ways in which liberals, radicals, and conservatives employed market rhetoric to establish their political identities and map out their courses of action.

My work fills another gaping hole in the literature, for a study of market discourse necessarily examines economic thought. Given the Díaz regime's emphasis on material progress, it is ironic that while there have been studies about political and social thought, the field of economics has been neglected.[2] Not surprisingly, there seems to be a scholarly consensus that Porfirian economic thought is a significant but understudied topic. Reflecting this assumption, Charles Hale, in his now-classic study of Porfirian political ideas, defends himself for studying politics instead of economics: "My initial pursuit of political ideas therefore led me into philosophical and social topics rather than into economic thought and policy, which many would regard as the more pertinent direction for the historian of Porfirian Mexico to take. In making this choice, I in no way denigrate the importance of economics, but rather I hope to bring into relief other aspects of the period that may be of roughly equal importance."[3]

Not only do I examine a vital and little-explored topic, but conventional wisdom on the subject, which assumes the Porfirian regime was guided by a laissez-faire philosophy, is in need of revision.[4] By examining the influences of corporatist trends in the discipline of Western economics and the impact of positivism, racial determinism, and social Darwinism on Porfirian economic ideas, I demonstrate that Porfiristas countered basic tenets of classic liberalism.[5] Opposing liberal notions like individualism, economic man, and laissez-faire, Porfiristas' economic thought stressed the collective, racial hierarchy, and the state. Given this emphasis, it is not surprising that nationalism, not a celebration of free markets, reigned.

If my work serves as a corrective in regard to economic thought, it also counters recent trends in the literature vis-à-vis culture. Modern scholarship on Latin America examines the economy in a vacuum, for it ignores the cultural milieu in which the economy operated.[6] And even works that do examine ideas primarily view discussions about the market as economic, for they treat economic dialogue as pertinent solely to "development" and thus overlook the broader cultural relevance of economic discourse.[7] Porfiristas of all political persuasions, in contrast, conceived of the development of the market as not only an economic endeavor but also a cultural project. Social Catholics, for example, identified the central economic problem as the dominance of an individualist-materialist ethic and sought to undermine it by instilling a Catholic economic philosophy. Liberals, in contrast, maintained that the principal stumbling block to material progress was the absence of a materialist ethos. They were social engineers who advocated introducing foreign elements into Mexican culture to rectify the problem. Anarchists conceived the project of building a new economic order not only as destroying capitalism but also as inculcating Mexicans with a collective worker consciousness. Thus, Porfiristas had cultural-economic agendas. Consequently, perhaps more than profits and productivity, contemporaries' market discourses focused on social themes such as Indians' traits and characteristics, the nature of the Mexican citizenry, foreigners' place in national life, men's and women's roles in society, and the function that institutions (particularly the Church, the state, and the educational system) played in the formation of economic culture.

Emphasizing the symbolic significance of the market, as I have done, is a new approach to studying the economic realm. It builds upon the work of a small group of anthropologists, historians, and economists who treat economic doctrine as a form of discourse, rhetoric, or ideology as opposed to a science.[8] Despite varied orientations, this scholarship is unified in its rejection of a positivist approach that interprets theoretical developments in the field of economics as a story of progress in the sense that as the discipline evolves "errors" are corrected and a more accurate economic science is created.[9]

In this new scholarship the market, the central construct in economics, has been singled out for special attention. In fact, four recent edited volumes have been dedicated to it.[10] I examine a little-explored theme in this scholarship that analyzes the relationship between market discourse and the formation of identity.[11] The link between these two subjects is significant because the social order has been a dominant theme in writings about the market. Historian Ricardo Salvatore theorizes why the market has been a significant symbol in discourses about politics and society: "As a central rhetorical construct that conveys meaning to a series of other signifiers (autocratic or seignorial power, mercantilism, freedom of conscience, etc.), the market produces ideal visions of social order and politics." Salvatore underscores the importance of market rhetoric to the formation of political identity: "It was in relation to the market, constructed as a force able to erode community values, to destroy traditional ways of life, and to impart an unsavory materialism on social relations that important social movements of the nineteenth century built their identity and political strategy."[12] From Salvatore's theoretical orientation, the market is not a physical place where goods are exchanged but a symbolic site where the identities and programs of social movements are constructed.

Salvatore's work was inspired by Albert Hirschman's groundbreaking book *The Passions and the Interests: Political Arguments for Capitalism before Its Triumph*, which demonstrated that the eighteenth-century economic works of Montesquieu and other precursors to modern political economy lauded commerce not only on economic but also political grounds. The French Encyclopedists contended that humans' desire for economic gain held their more barbaric and violent passions in check.[13] Thus commerce was a civilizing force. Stressing this point, Hirschman labeled commerce *doux*, or sweet. He followed this monograph with a companion work that examines the nineteenth and twentieth centuries.[14] It shows that the market became a contradictory social and political symbol, for along with doux commerce, contemporaries also contended that the market was an agent of social destruction.

One does not need to read between the lines to analyze the market from Salvatore's and Hirschman's perspectives, for its impact on the realms of politics, culture, and society has been a central theme in Western discourse. As Salvatore suggests, a variety of nineteenth-century social movements—anarchists, socialists, communists, and social Catholics—depicted the market as the agent behind the "social problem" and organized mass movements against it.[15] By the late nineteenth century even some liberals came to condemn the social consequences of laissez-faire.[16] If one strand in Western thought has emphasized the negative social consequences of the market, another has depicted it as a positive social force. According to the classical political economists, the self-regulating market governs social relations. The political significance of classical economic discourse cannot be overlooked, for laissez-faire rhetoric helped undermine a mercantilist order and institute a system of free trade in nineteenth-century Europe.[17]

Today the market is also a dominant symbol in political discourse, and, true to the past, it is a controversial sign. In the former Soviet bloc, the symbol of the "free" market has been associated with political freedom and thus has legitimated the dismantling of the socialist state.[18] More recently, Washington politicians who supported granting China most favored nation trade status stressed the positive political impact of free trade. On another border of the political landscape, market demonization—from social, political, cultural, economic, and environmental perspectives—has been the principal rhetoric in mass mobilizations. Environmentalists, workers, indigenous groups, gays, and academics have found a common cause in their fight against globalization.[19] Thus nowadays, with the demise of communism, the market is a dominant symbol in political and social discourse. Given the intense debate over globalization today, one would be hard-pressed to dispute Fredric Jameson's contention that "the fundamental level on which political struggle is waged is that of the struggle over the legitimacy of concepts and ideologies" and that the concept of the market is at the center of this war of words.[20]

The central questions of my study are informed by a conception of the market as a political symbol: what sociopolitical powers did Porfirian liberals, radicals, and conservatives ascribe to the market, and what impact did their discourses have on the formation of their identities, platforms, programs, and policies? In addition to addressing these questions, I also explore the related themes of dialogues between market discourses, the ways in which counterdiscourses attempted to undermine dominant narratives about the market, and the ideological obstacles that may have prevented specific accounts of the market from gaining widespread appeal.[21] I analyze discourse, which is not the same thing as engaging in discourse analysis. Discourse analysis, according to one student of the topic, "refers to attempts to study the organization of language."[22] In contrast, I take the term *discourse* to mean a lengthy discussion on a particular subject. Thus, I analyze discussions about the market. I do not study linguistics.

I examine public discourse. I focus not on the texts and teachings of academic political economy but rather on the quotidian articulation of its terms in relatively widely distributed periodical literature (financial, agricultural, and industrial press; semiofficial newspapers and opposition press), official publications such as government reports and presidential messages, and notable pamphlets, essays, and books. Even though the press was heavily censored in Mexico, there were lively debates over economic issues such as taxing uncultivated lands, nationalizing foreign enterprises, Porfirian material progress, the labor question, and policies on immigration, mining, and agriculture. *El País*, the leading social Catholic daily, debated regularly with *El Imparcial*, the premier semiofficial daily, and Mexico's most significant financial journals, *Semana Mercantil* and *El Economista Mexicano*. Even if the liberal and radical opposition press was severely constricted by censorship, it was also able to voice opinions on economic issues.[23]

While the market was a multifarious signifier in the sense that contemporaries maintained that it had numerous social consequences, the signification of the term *market* in the Porfirian context also varied. Given the abstract nature of the concept, it is unsurprising that contemporaries did not define it in a precise or homogeneous way. Scholarship on markets, too, has noted the ambiguous nature of the term. Historian Jean Agnew maintains that there is no universal definition: "What is a market? Is it a place? a process? a principle? a power? History yields no definitive answers to [these] question[s]."[24] This absence of a set definition has led anthropologist James Carrier to advocate "models" of the market as opposed to "the market" in a sweeping sense.[25] The editors of a historical work on market culture follow this strategy by discussing influential "conceptions" as opposed to a single form.[26] In keeping with this insight, I eschew absolutes. Rather than superimposing my own definition, I adhere to the models articulated in Porfirian Mexico. The discourses of all the groups I study, albeit to different degrees, examined the privatization of communal lands, the construction of a labor force, the investment of capital, the domestic and international circulation of goods, and foreigners' impact on the national economy. I conceptualize dialogues about these topics as discourses about distinct markets: land, labor, capital, commodity, and international markets, respectively. Following the nuances of Porfirian discourse also requires more general conceptions of the market. This type of approach is in keeping with Hirschman, who conceives the market broadly by making it a synonym for capitalism.[27] In this vein, I interpret writings that focus on capitalism and material progress (*progreso material*) as market discourses. Thus, I study several Porfirian market models. I also make distinctions between them, for I analyze the strength and consequences that contemporaries ascribed to particular markets and note that certain groups emphasized types of markets that others ignored.

The Porfirian Political Context

The late Porfiriato is a promising era in which to examine the links between economic discourse and political identity, for mobilization against the government increased during the last decade of Porfirio Díaz's reign. This unrest contrasted with the early Porfiriato, an era when Díaz forged political peace. He integrated conservatives back into the regime by not implementing anticlerical reform laws and thus creating a reconciliation between Church and state.[28] He also created a degree of unity between liberal factions by easing the tensions that put them at odds with Porfiristas. This harmony was relatively short-lived, however. Not only did tensions within the ruling elite increase, but conservative, liberal, and radical opposition groups emerged. My study explores political mobilization from the vantage point of economic symbols.

Since there were no organized political parties, Porfirian elites banded together in informal political interest groups, or camarillas. The *científicos* formed the most powerful camarilla in late Porfirian Mexico and held influential positions in the national government, strongly influencing Porfirian policy and ideology. While they clearly made an impact during the 1890s, they became a more dominant force during the last decade of the Porfiriato. One of the científicos' influential competitors, Matías Romero, died in 1898. When the position of vice president was created in 1904, the post was filled by Ramón Corral, a científico sympathizer. The Reyistas, led by Bernardo Reyes, posed the greatest threat to the científicos during the last decade of the Porfiriato. Reyes had support within the military and, unlike the científicos, had a popular political base. After a conflict with the científicos in 1902, he was dismissed from his post as minister of war and installed as governor of Nuevo León. At the very end of the Porfiriato, when Díaz's power was waning and there was greater support for political democracy, Díaz again perceived Reyes as a political threat and assigned him to a mission in Europe, a move that was akin to political exile.

If tensions within the government became more conspicuous after 1900, an independent liberal opposition to the Porfirian regime also became more visible.[29] In 1900, under the leadership of Camilo Arriaga, a liberal engineer from a wealthy and prestigious family in San Luis Potosí, liberal opposition to the regime increased. Arriaga called for the formation of liberal clubs to oppose Díaz, and many, mostly in northern Mexico, responded. Among them was Ricardo Flores Magón, who had founded an opposition paper, *Regeneración*, in 1900. The effectiveness of the liberal opposition movement was severely limited, for it was repressed by the Díaz government. Flores Magón and other members of the movement were jailed. *Regeneración* and other opposition papers were shut down by the government. The government's oppression forced leaders of the movement into exile in the United States in 1904. In 1905, in the United States, Flores Magón formed the Partido Liberal Mexicano (PLM). Remaining in exile, Flores Magón staged attacks on the Porfirian regime from the United States. In 1906, 1908, and 1911 the PLM inspired revolts against the regime, but they were suppressed.[30] Deeming Flores Magón a revolutionary, U.S. forces apprehended and incarcerated him. He died in a U.S. jail in 1922.

The ideology of the opposition movement led by Ricardo Flores Magón and Camilo Arriaga changed over time. In 1900 liberalism dominated. Harking back to the liberals of the Reforma (1855–61), Arriaga and others complained about the regime's lax enforcement of the reform laws and the Church's increasing power in Porfirian society. The absence of political liberties and democracy were other concerns. Finally, articulating a form of social liberalism, opposition liberals maintained that modern capitalism generated social ills. When the movement went into exile in the United States it began to radicalize, largely due to the fact that Ricardo Flores Magón became the dominant figure in the PLM. The PLM's 1906 manifesto harshly attacked capitalism, and in 1907 anarchist rhetoric entered the PLM's discourse. The PLM's 1911 manifesto explicitly articulated anarchist dogma.

The radicalization of the PLM alienated some liberals from the movement.

Francisco Madero is an influential case in point. The Maderos were a wealthy family based in Coahuila that had investments in mining, cattle, and banking. While they had economic power, they were political outsiders, unconnected to the Porfirian regime. Showing interest in political reforms, Francisco Madero provided economic support to Ricardo Flores Magón when he first went into exile in 1904. As the PLM became more radical, however, he stopped supporting it. In 1908 he waged his own political attack on the Porfirian regime, an antireelectionist campaign that proved to be immensely successful. Díaz's attempts to suppress the movement failed. He resigned in the spring of 1911. After an interim ruler, Madero became president. His reign was short-lived, however; he was assassinated by conservative opponents in 1913. But Madero had many enemies, among them the PLM, which maintained that his focus on political reform and his inattention to the problems generated by capitalism meant that there was really no difference between him and the former president, Díaz.

Social Catholics were the central voice in a conservative opposition movement that also gained momentum at the turn of the century.[31] Social Catholicism, an international movement, was a religious response to the social question, which became more pronounced with the emergence of industrial capitalism and the formation of a working class in Europe. The movement's defining feature was its effort to address the problem of world poverty. Social Catholics promoted social reform on behalf of the masses. They organized social and educational programs, workers organizations, and civic groups.[32] While these general assertions can be made about social Catholicism, it was not a monolithic movement.[33]

Pope Leo XIII's 1892 encyclical, *Rerum Novarum*, provided strength and momentum to social Catholicism.[34] It harshly condemned the individualist and materialist currents in liberalism and embraced a neo-Thomist corporate order to ameliorate social ills. The encyclical was very influential in Mexico and paved the way for the strengthening of Mexican social Catholicism, which became the dominant strand in Mexican Catholicism during the last decade of the Porfiriato. It contrasted significantly with liberal Catholicism, which had reigned in Mexico during the 1890s. In keeping with the regime's focus on reconciliation, liberal Catholicism sought to adapt to the liberal order rather than challenge it. By accepting liberal tenets such as freedom and equality, liberal Catholicism found ways to reconcile Catholicism with the economic, political, and social doctrines of liberalism. Social Catholicism, in contrast, took a much more defiant stance toward the liberal order. Given their antagonism toward liberalism, it is not surprising that social Catholics chastised liberal Catholicism's comfortable relationship with the Díaz regime. Contrary to liberal Catholics' acceptance of some aspects of liberalism, social Catholics were heavily influenced by neo-Thomist corporate thought, which came back into vogue during the second half of the nineteenth century.[35]

Between 1903 and 1909 Mexican social Catholics held a series of highly publicized Catholic congresses that discussed social and economic problems such as low wages, exploitative labor conditions, and problems with the credit system.[36] They also developed a national and regional press that emphasized the social problem.[37] Social Catholics raised awareness about social problems in study groups and Catholic schools.[38] In addition to discussing problems, social Catholics took some active steps to ameliorate them. They championed the family wage and organized Catholic labor unions, which mostly represented artisans.[39]

Even though social Catholics, the liberal opposition, and the radical opposition all became more visible at the turn of the twentieth century, the Díaz regime did not respond to the three movements consistently. Whereas Díaz severely repressed the liberal and radical opposition, he did not hamper the activities of social Catholics. Perhaps Díaz did not repress social Catholicism because he did not see it as a direct threat to his regime. After all, it was public knowledge that one of the main goals of the liberal and radical opposition was to oust Díaz from power, albeit by different means. In contrast, the social Catholics did not single out the president, for they had a less specific opponent, namely, the liberal order.

Even if social Catholicism was not openly repressed, it did have many critics. A salient issue for both the liberal and radical opposition was reducing the Church's power in secular society. Reflecting concern about this issue, liberals, radicals, and Protestants attacked the Díaz regime for not implementing reform laws that would restrict the Church's power.[40] This goal directly clashed with social Catholics' overarching design: increasing the Church's role in civil society. After all, social Catholicism focused on contemporary material issues as opposed to spiritual themes. It is unsurprising that liberals and radicals rejected social Catholicism, but some segments of the Catholic Church also failed to embrace it. Some of the clergy resisted the movement and continued to adhere to the philosophy of liberal Catholicism.[41] In addition, spiritual currents in Mexican Catholicism did not focus on social issues.[42] Social Catholicism had more impact in central Mexico than in other regions of the country.[43]

The Symbol of the Market in Nineteenth-Century Mexico

If the market became a dominant symbol in late Porfirian Mexico, this had not been the case for most of the nineteenth century. While economic dilemmas received attention during the first half-century of independence, political and military problems were deemed more serious. Furthermore, economics did not play a significant role in elites' solutions to Mexico's problems. Thus, the market was represented as a weak agent of political and social change during the first half-century of independence and did not play an important role in the formation of identity or political strategy until the Porfiriato.

Hale outlined two positions vis-à-vis the market during the first three decades of independence: doctrinaire and pragmatic.[44] The doctrinaire position, whose principal proponent was José María Luis Mora, was similar to classic economic liberalism. It embraced individualism, supported free trade, attacked secular and religious corporate property, and envisioned Mexico as an agricultural and mining nation. Influenced by Adam Smith and other liberal economists, the doctrinaire position attacked Spanish mercantilism as the source of Mexico's economic woes. Without rejecting the primacy of agriculture and mining, the pragmatic position, whose chief representative was Lucas Alamán, sought also to develop Mexico's industrial base with the aid of state intervention. In contrast to the doctrinaire view, pragmatists embraced the corporate order. During the Reforma (1855–61), classic economic liberal rhetoric, which embraced laissez-faire, dominated.[45] Economic liberalism continued to reign for the rest of the nineteenth century and even until the Mexican Revolution. By the late Porfiriato, however, doctrinaire liberalism and a celebration of free markets were rejected, for the state came to have an increasingly important role in Porfirian economic ideology. Porfirian economist Alberto Carreño maintained, for example, that by the late Porfiriato the popularity of Leroy Beaulieu, the French proponent of laissez-faire, had waned, and French economist Charles Gide, who was a corporatist, had become more influential.[46] In 1909 Porfirian economist Enrique Martínez Sobral asserted that he followed Gide's ideas, particularly his text *Curso de economía política*. Martínez Sobral maintained that Gide was not a "liberal economist" but a "cooperative socialist or a solidarist."[47]

Since Mexico's tariffs were low during the 1820s, aspects of the doctrinaire view were implemented. Beginning in 1829, however, components of the pragmatic program became policy. In that year a protectionist tariff was implemented.[48] In 1830 a government development bank to foment industry, Banco de Avío, was founded.[49] The closing of the bank in 1842 signaled the waning influence of the pragmatic program. After 1846 levels of protection in the form of tariffs diminished. During the 1850s a new generation of liberals who were influenced by Mora's doctrinaire ideology came to power. During the Reforma they implemented a liberal economic program, the most significant aspect of which was Ley Lerdo, which strengthened private property by prohibiting ecclesiastical and civil corporate property. Embracing individualism, liberals also attacked the corporate order by outlawing special privileges and proclaiming equality before the law. Despite liberal rhetoric, pragmatic concerns limited the implementation of free national and international trade. The *alcabala,* an internal tax, remained, and so, too, did tariffs to protect national industry.[50] Despite conservatives' hopes that Maximilian, who ruled Mexico during the French occupation of the 1860s, would renounce the reform laws, he did not. His economic program did not differ significantly from those of the Reforma liberals.[51]

During the early Porfiriato, more liberal economic reforms were implemented. A new commercial code was implemented in 1884 that created a more secure basis for commercial relations. Revisions to the mining code in 1884 and 1892 strengthened individual property rights.[52] Revisions in patent law in 1890 and 1903 strengthened private property rights.[53] The alcabala was finally abolished in 1896. There were, however, statist tendencies that countered classic economic liberalism in Porfirian policy.[54] Despite a focus on Mexico's agricultural and mining industries, Porfirian policy also promoted industrialization. The primary instruments to achieve this goal were tariffs and government support to industry in the form of a new industries program.[55] Conceiving the international realm as dominated by trusts and monopolies as opposed to free markets led to state intervention. The nationalization ("Mexicanization") of foreign railroads began in 1903.[56]

Since state building was viewed as more of a political project than an economic endeavor during the new nation's first half-century of existence, political themes dominated the national discourse from the 1820s to the 1870s.[57] This focus on politics is unsurprising given the instability that plagued the fledgling nation. During independent Mexico's first half-century of existence the presidency changed hands more than fifty times. The guiding mechanism for transitions in power was the *pronunciamiento,* or military rebellion, as opposed to the ballot box. Bitter conflicts broke out not only between liberals and conservatives but also between centralists and federalists. Consistent with its analysis of Mexico's problems, the national discourse championed political solutions. During the early republic, before intense conflict emerged, liberals, adhering to "constitutional determinism," maintained that an effective constitution would place the new nation on a proper course.[58] Liberals of the Reforma had a different political solution. They proposed strengthening the national government (via a unicameral legislature and a powerful president) as a solution to political instability. This promotion of a strong central government contrasted with their liberal predecessors, who championed federalism.[59] It must be acknowledged that some did depict the market as a solution to specific political problems, but it appears that this was not a dominant theme.[60]

Sovereignty, too, was conceived mostly in political and military terms, despite the fact that nationalist rhetoric was employed by promoters of national industry. Alamán stressed that national industry would end Mexico's dependence on Europe.[61] Even after the Mexican War, this nationalist theme continued, as proponents of national industry invoked the threat of economic "vassalage" and "conquest."[62] But economic nationalism paled compared to political nationalism.[63] Not economic conquest but rather territorial conquest via foreign military intervention was the overriding concern. This emphasis is not surprising, since Mexico was invaded repeatedly during the nineteenth century. Shortly after independence was established in 1821, Mexico had to repel Spanish forces, and during the 1830s the new nation successfully defended itself against French aggression in the "pastry war." Given Mexico's powerful internal divisions, it is not surprising that the country was not always effective in maintaining sovereignty. The most devastating defeat was in the Mexican War of 1846–48, when Mexico lost half its territory. The French established a Second Empire (the short-lived First Empire had been pronounced by Iturbide in 1822) in Mexico by military force during the 1860s, but a persistent and unrelenting national resistance movement dissuaded France of its imperial ambitions. Both the causes for imperialism and the explanations for Mexico's limited success (in the cases of the Mexican War and the French Intervention) were defined in political terms. Perceiving conquest in political terms was in keeping with the age, for it was not until the end of the nineteenth century that economic analyses of imperialism emerged. Prior to that, imperialism had been conceived as a political and territorial conquest.[64] Reforma liberals underscored a lack of political unity (particularly the problem of independent regional caudillos and rebellious conservatives) in Mexico's loss to the United States.[65] The liberal-conservative split was paramount during the French Intervention, despite the fact that the national debt was also a factor.

In discussions of Indian citizenship, the market did not figure prominently. This assertion holds despite the fact that liberals maintained that the market—in the form of private property—was an agent of progress. During the early republic, some maintained that privatizing communal property and turning Indians into smallholders would turn Indians into "true citizens."[66] But this was not a dominant theme, for liberals rarely discussed Indians.[67] Reforma liberals made the same claim when they discussed privatizing communal property. But again, during the Reforma, this was not an important issue, for liberals usually did not identify precisely who would inhabit the privatized communal lands.[68] Similarly, during Maximilian's Second Empire the rhetoric that associated private property with Indian citizenship continued to be a marginal theme.[69] Throughout the nineteenth century, immigration and education, much more than private property, were deemed the agents of citizenship.[70]

Even if political themes took precedence over economics, the social realm, albeit in isolated discourses, proved an exception to the depiction of the market as a weak agent of change. Artisans who championed protectionism in the 1820s maintained that the influx of foreign goods caused a social crisis by putting them out of work.[71] Similarly, promoters of national industry (Hale's "pragmatists") contended that national industry would serve a social function by creating jobs for the indigent and inexpensive goods for the poor.[72]

Why, in contrast, did the market become a dominant symbol in Mexican national discourse during the late Porfiriato? A series of converging political, economic, social, and ideological developments accounted for the market's high visibility. One key catalyst was Díaz's ability to establish political stability and national sovereignty, which marked a stark contrast from the past. The Porfiriato was unprecedented, since it was a departure from the age of pronunciamiento (despite the fact that it was initiated in this fashion) and foreign military intervention. Dubbing the Porfiriato an age of "peace," contemporaries emphasized how the period marked a break with the past. Resolving issues on political fronts enabled greater attention to be placed on economic issues. Predictably, there was a proliferation of economic journalism during the Porfiriato.[73]

The Porfiriato was an unprecedented age not only in the political realm but also in the material sphere, for it was an era of unparalleled economic modernization. This modernity was largely fueled by changes in the international economy. This age witnessed increased industrialization in western Europe and the United States, the use of mass-production technologies, and the emergence of finance capital. These developments made Mexico an attractive place for England, France, Germany, and the United States (to mention the most significant nations) in which to invest capital and sell industrial technology and consumer goods and from which to extract resources.[74] The Porfiriato witnessed an astounding increase in foreign investment, the construction of a national railroad network, the revival of extractive industries, an incipient industrialization, and booming exports.

Even if it celebrated moral, social, and racial progress, Porfirian positivist ideology, expressed in the slogan "order and progress," emphasized material progress. This focus on the material realm intensified during the 1890s because achievements of the early Porfiriato were highlighted and because the científicos, who strongly influenced official ideology, ascended to power at this time. Porfirian "progress" was glorified in national discourse articulated in official publications and the progovernment political and financial press. The narrative was a triumphant success story. It boasted about railroads, ports, industries, investments, imports, exports, and banks.

But there was also a critical side to the official rhetoric's tale of progress, though it has been largely overlooked by scholars. Since the official discourse evaluated Mexico largely in economic terms, not only were the nation's successes accentuated but also its deficiencies. Acutely aware of economic developments in the United States and Europe, this analysis emphasized Mexico's limited "economic evolution." Some even spoke of "regression" as opposed to "progress." Commentators stressed the shortcomings of the Indians, the perennial shortage of workers, the inability to attract foreign immigrants, the need for new technology, the inadequacy of Mexico's resources, the declining international value of silver, and the sorry state of Mexican agriculture. By the late Porfiriato, perhaps because Mexico had achieved so much, a critique emerged that stressed how far the nation still had to go.

A strand of social Darwinism that emerged in the 1890s increased attention to Mexico's economic woes. Influenced by the economic determinism that characterized the age, this brand of social Darwinism conceived of the international struggle for survival between nations as a war waged on the economic front. Not only did this scenario place Mexico's economic shortcomings in relief, it also made the quest for economic progress imperative, for sovereignty was at stake. Greater visibility of foreign economic interests in late Porfirian Mexico heightened nationalist apprehensions. Indeed, foreign investment was at an all-time high by the late Porfiriato, and the inflow of foreign capital increased with Mexico's 1905 monetary reform. U.S. capital especially was a source of concern, for it came to predominate over British, French, and German economic interests during the first decade of the new century. And anxieties that the turn-of-the-century U.S. merger movement would cross America's southern border into Mexico in the form of powerful trusts escalated concerns. Finally, the fact that the American colony both increased in size and became more isolated from Mexican society during the last decade of the Porfiriato was another source of anxiety.[75] It is no wonder that the subject of foreign economic domination became a central topic in official discourse during the last decade of the Porfiriato.

It is common knowledge that official rhetoric stressed the economy, but scholars have not appreciated the degree to which liberal, radical, and conservative opposition groups' discourses focused on economics. Contemporaries, in contrast, underscored it. Social Catholics' concentration on economics was so strident that it drew attention. *El Imparcial*, commenting on a 1903 Catholic congress in Puebla, stated that, judging from the topics covered ("credit, capital investment, and interest"), "one would believe it was a monetary conference."[76] The financial press, too, noted social Catholics' attention to financial themes.[77] These observations were accurate. Conservative social Catholics' discourse overlooked political issues but stressed the negative consequences of the market on the laboring classes. Since radical anarchists were economic determinists, they, too, disregarded politics and emphasized the market. In addition to highlighting the plight of workers, they also underscored the dilemma of Indians. Thus, radicals championed a pressing issue that social Catholics ignored: land redistribution. Even if segments of the liberal opposition mobilized around the political issues of reelection and the Church's place in society, fractions of it, articulating a form of social liberalism, emphasized the negative social impact of the market.[78] Ironically, despite political opposition to Díaz's long tenure in office, economic rather than political themes dominated in late Porfirian Mexico. The fact that three main socioeconomic themes in revolutionary discourse—exploitative labor conditions, inequitable land distribution, and foreign economic domination—were central issues in the national debate during the late Porfiriato is a testament to the visibility and enduring significance of Porfirian economic discourse.

Opposition groups focused on the economy in part because the terms of their rhetoric were set by the dominant discourse.[79] An editorial in *Regeneración* conceptualized material progress as a form of ideology that legitimated the Porfirian regime. Discrediting the idea that material progress had been achieved was a strategy the editor utilized to undermine the government. In 1901 *Regeneración* put it this way:

> [Porfirio Díaz] has [had] twenty-five years holding chains. How can he defend his rule? Will not the idea of rule based in slavery undermine his dignity? Material progress—this irritable superstition with which we are made to believe that General Díaz's autocracy is healthy and made to admire the stupid political program of the Man of Necessity. . . . Material progress—the myopia of the lackeys who attempt to excuse the autocracy with material progress, to which they dedicate nauseous hymns.[80]

This was not an isolated critique. Throughout the last decade of the Porfiriato, the liberal, radical, and conservative opposition countered the dominant discourse by contending that material progress had not been achieved. Redefining progress as the distribution of wealth as opposed to its accumulation, they contended that Porfirian progress had been a dismal failure.[81] This critique inspired a debate in the press, as supporters of the Porfirian economic program maintained that the conditions of the poor had improved during the era of Porfirian modernization.[82]

This criticism of Porfirian progress was part of a larger critique of capitalism that emerged in nineteenth-century Western discourse. Mexican opposition groups' emphasis on the market was a consequence of this Western critique as well as a manifestation of it. Anthropologist Joel Kahn emphasizes the centrality of antimarket themes in Western thought. He maintains that critiques of the market emerged in the West, not in traditional societies.[83] The rise of the "social question" in nineteenth-century Western discourse confirms Kahn's claim. Three prominent strands in Mexican antimarket rhetoric—social liberalism, social Catholicism, and anarchism—were part of this larger Western antimarket thought.

Developments in late Porfirian Mexico provided fertile soil in which to plant cultural and social criticism of the market. The labor question emerged as a national issue during the last decade of the Porfiriato, particularly after labor unrest and a wave of strikes broke out in 1906. This strike activity marked a break with the past, for there had been a lull in worker protest since the 1880s. Even if strikes had been common during the 1870s and early 1880s, the nature of the worker movement of the 1900s was distinct. During the 1870s artisan production was the rule, but by the 1900s modern industrial production began to eclipse artisan production, a shift that was, in part, a consequence of late Porfirian government policy that promoted national manufacturing.[84] Although the modern industrial workforce was only about one tenth of the nation's labor force, it played a significant role in the unrest of the 1900s. Labor protest in the modern textile industry was very visible, for textile workers organized a militant union, the Gran Círculo de Obreros Libres (Great Circle of Free Workers). Agitation in the modern industrial sector as well as labor unrest in the mine of Cananea, Sonora, in June 1906 were also instrumental in raising the labor question.[85]

A Catholic publication specifically linked labor agitation to the industrial age.[86] Nevertheless, exploitative working conditions in rural settings also brought increased attention to the plight of laborers. This was especially the case for Yucatán, a region that the Porfirian establishment defined as a great symbol of Mexican progress, since the members of a national planter bourgeoisie from the peninsula were successful henequen exporters. Henequen plantations were famous among liberal and radical opposition groups for another reason, however: planters exploited and coerced the Maya and Yaqui Indian labor force.[87]

If conflicts between workers and owners in urban and rural settings could be used to spark the labor question, other hardships created a favorable climate in which to raise the intimately related but broader social question. The Porfiriato witnessed class formation, a process of change that upset patterns of existence. Indigenous peoples and artisans were displaced, for the export boom required extensive land, and industrial production undermined crafts production. Economic decline during the last decade of the Porfiriato, especially after the 1907 recession, had adverse effects on the quality of life of the majority of Mexicans. Real wages decreased throughout the decade. Despite hardships, the government did not provide relief. The regime's focus on exports, which resulted in dependence on foreign imports of basic necessities such as corn, added to the dilemma. Social problems came to a crisis in 1908 and 1909, a period that witnessed the outbreak of food riots. Critics of the regime emphasized social problems, which suggested that economic modernization had dire social costs.[88]

Developmentalist Liberals, Social Catholics, and Anarchists

Paradoxically, even though scholars acknowledge the Porfirian regime's emphasis on the economic sphere, no in-depth study of the economic thought or ideology of the business class and government has been undertaken. What makes studying this topic even more pressing is that conventional wisdom needs revising, and not only in regard to the erroneous assumption that the Díaz regime adhered to laissez-faire, which was mentioned above. This faulty portrayal was but one component of a broader interpretation that emerged in the 1970s that depicted nineteenth-century Latin American economic ideas as imitative and impoverished. E. Bradford Burns's work *The Poverty of Progress* was very influential in this scholarship. Latin American elites, according to this portrayal, employed foreign blueprints that were ill suited to Latin American conditions. The problem with this interpretation is that it oversimplifies history by creating two static and isolated categories, foreign and indigenous. This suggests that if one adopts foreign assumptions or values, then one necessarily ignores the local context. The Porfirian regime was not guilty of this. This is not to say that the regime and business class did not place foreign economic models on a pedestal and denigrate Mexico. They did. But they did so in a way that created a dynamic interaction between the foreign and the local that is overlooked in Burns's interpretation. Porfirian ideologues' orientation was the Mexican national context. They stressed the ways that local conditions would be altered by foreign influences (technologies, capital, goods, and immigrants). In Burns's model, in contrast, the foreign supplants the local. Some Porfirian elites did desire this, but they did not have their heads in the clouds. In other words, they realized that the local context and conditions had to be the necessary starting point. Studying Porfirian economic thought not only sheds light on the past but also speaks to present issues. Current Mexican policies are labeled "neo-Porfirian" by critics. Thus, interpreting the Porfiriato is not only a scholarly enterprise but also a matter of contemporary polemics.

To study the economic discourse of the Porfirian regime and business class, I focus on a wide range of governmental and business publications. I rely most heavily on the press—financial journals and semiofficial newspapers. I also examine official publications such as governmental reports from the Ministries of Development and Finance, financial bulletins, agricultural journals, and economic studies. Finally, I study books, articles, and pamphlets written by individuals with ties to the government but not published in an official capacity. Most of the writers I examine share some broad similarities. Most of these men had links to the Porfirian government, albeit in different capacities (as politicians, bureaucrats, and publicists). Most of them were born during the 1850s and 1860s; thus, they were children during the Reforma and the French Intervention. They all wrote about economic issues, although some specialized in economics more than others. In this age of the *pensador,* the intellectual who did not limit himself to a specific field, one did not have to specialize in economics to be considered an authority. Reflecting this lack of specialization, contemporary Alberto Carreño maintained that there was only a handful of true "economists" during the Porfiriato.[89] Even Carlos Díaz Dufoo, who was noted by contemporaries and historians for his expertise in economics, studied theater as well.

I have not limited my study to a specific camarilla, although the científicos do loom large, for they shaped Porfirian ideology and policy. But studying this camarilla is problematic. There is no scholarly agreement regarding who belonged to it, since it was an informal group. Even its name was created by its critics. In 1892 the Liberal Union was formed to support Díaz's reelection and promote constitutional reforms. The group was labeled "científicos" by its detractors. Some contemporaries even questioned whether a group called the científicos even existed.[90] Hale, however, has a productive approach to defining the científicos. He stresses that membership in the camarilla changed over time. The broadest and least precise definition was created during the era of the revolution, when critics associated the term *científico* almost indiscriminately with members of the Porfirian regime. During the last decade of the Porfiriato, the term referred to a specific Porfirian camarilla that was at odds with the Reyista camarilla. The final definition was the most specific: the científicos promoted constitutional reform in the early 1890s.[91] Since my study places greatest emphasis on the last decade of the Porfiriato, it corresponds with Hale's second definition in regard to time frame. Nevertheless, my interpretation of the camarilla is distinct. I do not focus on the científicos' conflicts with rival camarillas. Rather, I stress their pivotal role in the formation of Porfirian market rhetoric. Thus, my approach to the científicos also departs from Hale's other two definitions. Unsurprisingly, members of the camarilla who held influential posts in the government and who published extensively are featured. Justo Sierra, José Yves Limantour, and Francisco Bulnes are especially prominent. Given my focus on national discourse, I also emphasize científicos who played a role in the press, even if they may not have been famous members of the camarilla. Thus, Rafael Reyes Spíndola, Carlos Díaz Dufoo, and José Castellot (though to a lesser degree) are also highlighted. It is important to note that individuals who were not científicos (such as Alberto Carreño) and even belonged to rival camarillas (such as Reyista Otto Peust) are also prominent.

Even though I do not limit my study to any particular camarilla, my account of the market symbolism of the Porfirian regime emphasizes similarities much more than differences. This is not to say that there were not divisions within the Porfirian government. There were bitter conflicts, but they were more political than economic. Competing camarillas vied for political power. Differences between camarillas, however, did not manifest themselves in competing economic visions. Thus, within the government, overarching conceptions of the economy were in congruence. (Even Francisco Madero, a political outsider, was largely in agreement with the Porfirian economic program. He attempted to discredit Díaz not by questioning or challenging the notion of material progress but by contending that the president could not claim credit for this positive development since he was not the engine behind it.)[92] Similarly, the economic worldview expressed in the business press was not fundamentally at odds with the vision of the Porfirian regime. Of course, there were differences and debates over specific issues both within the government and the private sector and between the two.[93] Some of these conflicts will be examined. But my focus on market symbolism reveals more commonalities than conflicts.

Employing a term coined by Alan Knight, I call the form of liberalism adhered to by the Díaz regime and the business class during the late Porfiriato "developmentalist liberalism."[94] Even though Knight explored this variant of liberalism only briefly, I think he has aptly labeled it, for developmentalist liberalism reflects the Porfirian regime's focus on material progress. It needs to be stressed that this is a term invented by historians. During the Porfiriato no group was called developmentalist liberal. Nevertheless, I find the label useful because it makes a distinction between late-nineteenth-century liberalism and its earlier counterparts. Knight contrasts developmentalist liberalism with constitutional and institutional liberalism. Constitutional liberalism, which was influential during the early republic, focused on the business of creating a representative constitutional government. Institutional liberalism, which emerged during the 1830s and only became dominant with the expulsion of the French in 1867, advocated institutional changes to create a secular liberal state, such as reducing the power of the Church in civil society, restricting special privileges, and abolishing corporations, which were deemed vestiges of conservative Spanish colonialism.

Developmentalist liberalism, which appeared during the Porfiriato, contrasted with its earlier counterparts by emphasizing the economic realm. Material progress became the central goal. Not only was there greater focus on economics, but the emphasis was also distinct. The egalitarian strands in the discourse of the Reforma (creating a nation of smallholders) were absent from developmentalist liberalism, which stressed the creation of wealth as opposed to the distribution of riches. Reflecting this obsession with the economic realm, the Reforma's strident anticlerical themes were also muted in developmentalist liberalism. By favoring political stability as opposed to democracy and civil liberties, developmentalist liberalism contrasted with earlier forms of liberalism. True, Hale demonstrates that there was a constitutionalist element to Porfirian politics that suggests a continuity with liberalism during the early republic.[95] But he contends that it had receded by the last decade of the Porfiriato, the era on which I focus. Order, not constitutionalism, predominated. Furthermore, despite Hale's focus on politics, he describes the "scientific politics" he examines as "analogous" to Knight's developmentalist liberalism and thus acknowledges the Porfirian regime's authoritarian tendencies and stress on material progress.[96]

Chapter 2 examines developmentalist liberals' discourse about the market's impact on political and economic behavior. It focuses on writings about the political actions of the middle class and elites and the economic practices of Indians and hacendados. The degree of strength that liberals assigned to the market to affect behavior was mostly determined by their conceptions of race and human nature. The chapter also surveys discussions about the roles that the state and foreigners played in shaping political and economic values.

Chapter 3 studies developmentalist liberals' arguments about the impact that the international market—that is, the international flow of capital, labor, and goods—had on Mexico. Social Darwinism, evolutionary thought, and economic determinism strongly influenced liberals' rhetoric about the international economy. In keeping with the previous chapter, the topics of racial groups and the state's function in society are prominent themes.

The mobilization of opposition groups is a central theme in the historiography of late Porfirian Mexico, for the liberal and radical opposition to Díaz has been examined extensively.[97] In contrast, the topic of chapter 4, the social Catholic movement in late Porfirian Mexico, has been largely ignored by scholars. This lack of attention to social Catholic mobilization during Díaz's reign is particularly surprising given the intense battles between Church and state that were fought during the revolutionary period.[98] Manuel Ceballos Ramírez's study reveals that the Church's political mobilization began during the last decade of Díaz's rule.[99] Furthermore, themes in Porfirian social Catholic thought were echoed in Catholic ideology during the revolution and beyond.[100] Thus, the late Porfiriato is an important but understudied episode in the history of Catholic mobilization in Mexico. My study complements Ceballos's work, for while he focuses on everyday activities of the movement, I emphasize its public rhetoric.

I study the discourse of Trinidad Sánchez Santos, social Catholicism's leading publicist in Porfirian Mexico.[101] Given his importance, it is ironic that in-depth historical studies of his life and thought have not been undertaken.[102] *El País*, the periodical he edited, was named the official organ of social Catholicism.[103] He founded the daily in 1899 and continued publishing it until his death in 1912. Even though he was only forty when he founded the paper, he had already had nearly two decades of experience working in journalism. Not only had he written for several periodicals, but he had also served as editor for *El Nacional, La Voz de México*, and *El Heraldo*.

El País had a very wide readership. Sánchez Santos had his sights on challenging Rafael Reyes Spíndola's periodical, *El Imparcial*, which, with the aid of financial support from the Porfirian government, was the most widely distributed paper in Mexico. While *El País* never reached the circulation of *El Imparcial*, its distribution was nevertheless very impressive. It not only eclipsed *El Tiempo* and *La Voz de México*, the other Catholic dailies based in Mexico City, in importance but also became one of the most influential papers of the era.[104] It started with a circulation of 8,000 in 1899, and by 1910 it had expanded to 30,000.[105] According to one of Sánchez Santos's biographers, during the first two years of the revolution the paper's circulation expanded significantly. By early 1911 circulation had reached 100,000, and in 1912, the year Sánchez Santos died, circulation had reached 200,000.[106] While the paper was most heavily distributed in Mexico City, it also circulated in more remote regions.[107]

Perhaps it was the flamboyant way in which Sánchez Santos delivered his message that made his paper so popular. Sánchez Santos espoused social Catholic doctrine in lengthy and passionate editorials, which were prominently featured on the front page. *El País* debated with notable Porfirian periodicals such as *El Imparcial* and *Semana Mercantil*. Further, Sánchez Santos engaged in polemical exchanges with Francisco Bulnes and Justo Sierra, two famous members of the científico clique. After Madero came to power, Sánchez Santos had serious conflicts with him. Sánchez Santos debated with *La Nueva Era*, a Maderista periodical, and was eventually jailed for his attacks on Madero's government.[108] It appears that Sánchez Santos held influence not only with people of power but also with the masses. When the Díaz government fell and huge demonstrations were held in Mexico City, a biographer of Sánchez Santos reports that 100,000 people gathered outside his office and cheered him.[109] He was clearly a political force to be reckoned with.

Chapter 4 surveys Sánchez Santos's discourse about the market's social impact. In keeping with that of developmentalist liberals, his rhetoric was strongly affected by his conceptions of human nature. In contrast, racial themes were absent from his writings, and he did not emphasize the state's role in society. Finally, in contrast to liberals' stress on the nation, discussed in chapter 3, Sánchez Santos highlighted the worker, family, and community.

Ricardo Flores Magón and the PLM, the subject of chapter 5, have received much scholarly attention.[110] Nevertheless, given the theme of my study, the PLM could not be overlooked. Furthermore, by placing the PLM's market imagery within a broader Mexican symbolic context, this chapter provides an uncommon vantage point from which to examine the ongoing controversy over the PLM's significance in the Mexican Revolution.[111] Chapter 5 evaluates the strength the PLM assigned to the market to shape the social and political spheres. The evolution of the PLM's philosophy strongly affected its rhetoric. As the PLM's ideology radicalized, the party assigned greater power to the market. In keeping with developmentalist liberalism, the themes of race and human nature loomed large, but, in contrast, the theme of nation did not. Rather, consistent with Sánchez Santos, the plight of the workers was prominent.

2 "Material and Political Movements Depend on Character"

The Market's Impact on Economic and Political Behavior

This chapter examines the strength that developmentalist liberals attributed to the market to shape political and economic behaviors in late Porfirian Mexico. (Unless otherwise noted, I use the term *liberals* to refer specifically to *developmentalist liberals*.) For them, the political and economic attitudes and practices of Mexicans were essential matters, but, in contrast to aspects of Western market rhetoric that emphasized freedom, they stressed discipline and control.[1] In the political realm, they were mostly concerned not about democracy but about stability, a characteristic that had been absent from Mexico's political order during the first half-century of independence. (Even though political peace had been established during the early Porfiriato, stability remained a liberal preoccupation, albeit a less pressing one than in previous decades.) Economics was far more than a concern. It was an obsession, with the principal focus not on the distribution of wealth but on increased production. There was an intertwined fixation: forging a labor force. Given the Porfirian export boom, this emphasis on workers and production is not surprising. Liberals directed each of these anxieties at distinct segments of the population. Their political preoccupations were mostly focused on the middle class and elites, that is, the socioeconomic groups that had historically instigated political unrest. Their economic concerns concentrated on the group they termed *Indians* and, to a lesser degree, hacendados, a fraction of the elite.[2]

What role did liberals envision for the market in forging political peace and manufacturing a workforce? A few of them maintained that the market played an important part in constructing political stability, but virtually none of them deemed it a powerful enough agent to build a labor force. Thus, the market's strength was limited, for it shaped political behavior but not economic actions (at least when it came to the indigenous population and hacendados). Liberals' notions of race and human nature go a long way toward explaining why they came to different conclusions about the market's impact on the political and economic realms. Científicos, the main cluster of liberals who argued that market expansion generated political stability, based their claims about the political efficacy of the market on an economic conception of human nature. From their vantage point, the political discontent of the middle class and the elite stemmed from economic hardship. Thus, expanding the market and the economy would result in political peace. Liberals' notions of race and racial hierarchy led them to minimize the market's ability to shape the economic behavior of Indians. In contrast to their conceptions of the middle class and elite, liberals did not conceive of Indians as economic beings. Furthermore, they were pessimistic about Indians' ability to acquire a capitalist work ethic. No wonder they maintained that market forces were insufficient to transform the mores, values, and practices of the indigenous population.

The liberals' positions on the market supported the scope and policies of the regime. The assertion that market expansion created political stability fit nicely with the government's emphasis on material progress. Inverting the watchwords of the era, progress created order. Given their negative ideas about the indigenous population, it is to be expected that liberals' labor policies would eschew laissez-faire by championing state intervention. Not market forces but rather education, immigration, and coercion were deemed necessary to transform the "lazy" natives into capitalist workers. Liberals, then, were social engineers, not free-market ideologues. The debate about the market also affected national identity. By denigrating Mexicans and placing foreigners (especially northern Europeans and Americans) in high esteem, liberals constructed a nation on foreign ideological foundations.

Material Progress and Political Behavior

Before discussing the strength that liberals ascribed to the market in creating political peace, it must be conceded that it was not a dominant theme in their creed, even if it may have been a major concern. To the contrary, during the last two decades of the Porfiriato, liberal rhetoric celebrated the peace that had been achieved by Díaz. Fittingly, the era was dubbed the "paz Porfiriana." This peaceful characterization of the Díaz era was strengthened by the regime's desire to instill confidence in foreign investors. To dispel the idea that Mexico was a wartorn and violent country, Díaz launched an extensive international public relations campaign that included Mexico's participation in international expositions, permanent exhibitions in foreign nations, and bribing the national and international press to ensure they would depict Mexico in a favorable light.[3]

Since the regime emphasized the Porfirian peace, the dominant ideology did not promote the market's role in forging political stability.[4] Nevertheless, there was a visible element in the liberals' discourse that did just that. It credited the market with creating political harmony. Members of the científico camarilla, especially, lauded the market for its positive influence on the political realm, claiming it had a soothing effect not only on disorderly individuals but also on dissident regions. The científicos' adherence to economic determinism explains why they attributed these political powers to the market. Historian François Chevalier stresses this determinism, maintaining that the científicos viewed economic development as the answer to all dilemmas: "Instead of 'Liberty, Order, and Progress' of the first Mexican positivists, their [científicos'] slogan should have been 'Progress before Everything Else,' something like the modern *desarrollistas* [developmentalists] who see in economic development the solution to all problems."[5]

Economic determinism, the sense that developments in the economic realm shape events in other spheres, was evident in the assertions of leading científicos. Justo Sierra (1848–1912), a prominent member of the científico clique, contended: "The moral and social state of the large human groups depends on their economic state."[6] Sierra's views were influential, for he was a writer, publisher, and prominent national politician. He had been the editor of *La Libertad* during the late 1870s.[7] After serving as a deputy in Congress during the 1880s he was appointed to the Supreme Court. During the last decade of Díaz's reign he served as secretary of public education. In 1902 he edited *México, su evolución social*, an impressive historical work that consisted of three large volumes. In addition to a Spanish edition, it was also published in English and French.

Científico Rafael Reyes Spíndola (1860–1922) also stressed the economy's impact on other realms. A 1903 reelectionist pamphlet that he signed maintained that the most pressing problems to resolve were economic "because they are related to the material well-being of the nation, and on the solution to that [problem] others depend."[8] *El Imparcial*, the highly influential Mexico City daily owned by Reyes Spíndola, made a similar, albeit more general, claim, asserting that economics "are the grand forces that move humanity in the twentieth century."[9] Científico Carlos Díaz Dufoo (1861–1941) also played a significant role in the paper, which was founded in 1896. At the inexpensive price of one centavo, it became the most widely distributed paper in Mexico. Since it received a government subsidy, it was widely viewed as an organ of the government.[10]

Prominent científico Francisco Bulnes (1847–1924) made a similar declaration: "To judge a nation's future it is best to focus on her predicted economic performance, which is revealed in present economic conditions."[11] Given Bulnes's background, it makes sense that he stressed economics. As a member of the national Congress (he served as both a deputy and a senator), he served on numerous committees dedicated to banking, mining, and financial legislation. In addition, he wrote extensively on economics and even published a book on the English debt. His education had prepared him for this focus; he had received a civil and mining engineering degree from the national school of mines. Bulnes had worked with Sierra on *La Libertad* and had been a member of the Liberal Union.

Bulnes applied economic determinism to the political realm. He boldly stated that economics determined politics and claimed that other científicos shared this view: "Those called científicos, among whom I am to be counted, are convinced that economic organization irresistibly controls political organization, and that to modify this [politics] it is indispensable to transform that [economics]." Bulnes's ideas about the proper role of government flowed from this assumption. He stated: "Their [the científicos'] principles can be reduced to desiring and sustaining a government . . . that develops the public wealth as quickly as possible."[12]

Bulnes's understanding of the economic and political spheres as separate realms was grounded in conceptions developed during the eighteenth and nineteenth centuries, when economics became a scientific discipline divorced from politics, morality, and culture.[13] Similarly, his claims about the political significance of economics were rooted in his notion of human nature, a perception influenced by developments in political economy that can be dated back to the works of Adam Smith and David Ricardo published during the late eighteenth and early nineteenth centuries, an era when the "economic man," or *Homo economicus*, emerged. Ricardo, especially, developed this notion. To create an explanatory economic model, he represented humans as one-dimensional and universal, depicting them as material beings whose principal desire was to maximize profit.[14] This concept of humanity differed from a seventeenth- and eighteenth-century portrayal that interpreted material desire as just one passion among many.

The concept of economic man altered the relationship between economics and politics in the social debate. The Encyclopedists viewed commerce as an agent of peace: the desire for wealth checked violent and barbarian impulses and thus was an agent of social harmony. With the birth of political economy, the idea of commerce as an agent of peace was altered: fulfilling humans' material desires—that is, their only desires—made them content.[15] Following precedents set in political economy, Bulnes divorced economics from other spheres and argued that man was an economic being: "Man, before being a religious, moral, or political animal, is an economic animal."[16] Bulnes underscored the political significance of economic man. He asserted that humans were not interested in political ideologies, for conservative, liberal, and Jacobin principles did not interest Mexicans. Emphasizing the irrelevance of political ideology, he contended, "We are tired of principles that do not represent the economic conscience of society."[17] For Bulnes, then, political differences were insignificant, for they did not reflect society's true nature, which was economic. In Bulnes's rhetoric, the idea of *Homo economicus* had a pivotal political impact: it signified the end of factional politics, a position that was in keeping with some of Bulnes's European contemporaries.[18] The quest for money reigned supreme.[19]

Bulnes took his argument to the next logical step. If human desire could be reduced to material needs, then fulfilling those needs was the key factor in establishing political stability. Bulnes cited the Porfirian peace as a case in point. He contended that it demonstrated that political peace was a consequence of economic development, not vice versa.[20] The revolutionary class, which he declared was the middle class, could only be appeased by economic development. Economic prosperity would quell revolutionary sentiments because, Bulnes insisted, they were ignited not by "principle" but by "hunger."[21] At a later date, Bulnes expanded on the relationship between economics and political stability, maintaining that governments forged peace by meeting the economic demands of the elite and middle class. He cited the slogan associated with Díaz's ruling style, "Pan o palo" [bread or stick], emphasizing *pan,* as a case in point, asserting that Díaz used the treasury effectively to establish political peace. He also suggested that Mexico's economic growth promoted peace by creating jobs in commerce and industry for the middle class.[22]

Bulnes applied his thesis to all of Latin America. He claimed that a number of Latin American nations were headed for a future "barbarism" and "civil war" for lack of economic development.[23] He identified the middle class and elite as the principal threats to political order. If the middle class could not expand and maintain its level of wealth, it would become a political threat.[24] Further, he contended that if the state could not satisfy the material desires of powerful families, then they would turn into subversive bands that would attempt to over-throw the state.[25] Bulnes, then, championed economic development as the pana-cea to the political instability that plagued much of Latin America during the nineteenth century.

Other científicos also claimed that economic progress resulted in political peace. Díaz Dufoo, in an article on Mexican industry he contributed to Sierra's multivolume *México, su evolución social*, quoted a passage from Bulnes that as-serted that the peace established during Díaz's reign was a consequence of com-merce and industry.[26] Díaz Dufoo formulated a similar claim: "The new middle class, which is a product of modern industrialization, is linked to all the interests that lend a proper life to society and the state. Here is the seat of the prosperous homeland, peace, and national solidarity."[27] Similarly, the Liberal Union's 1892 manifesto (critics of the manifesto labeled its authors "científicos") stated that economic progress resulted in political stability: it asserted that "peace based in interest" would make "revolt and civil war an accident."[28] The document linked the expansion of commerce and the establishment of free markets to political stability: "We desire free national commerce by suspending internal taxes . . . and reducing tariffs to a simple fiscal recourse . . . [as well as] commercial treaties to put us in intimate contact with the centers that can provide us with capital and emigration, the elements that will mobilize our riches [and] that still lie dormant. *Only in this way will peace be prepared for future generations.*"[29] A reelectionist pamphlet signed by científico Rafael Reyes Spíndola also associated the expan-sion of the economy with political stability. After recounting impressive economic developments in Porfirian Mexico, the document contended that these economic accomplishments provided the solution not only to economic problems but also to political ones.

Despite this similarity to Bulnes, the pamphlet altered his thesis slightly. The political peace that resulted from economic development, according to the pamphlet, was not solely a consequence of fulfilling Mexicans' material desires. Emphasizing daily labor, it asserted that "habits of order were instilled in the social masses by working." The order that resulted from work countered the destructive "germs" of "anarchy and dissolution." The pamphlet also argued that material prosperity resulted in political peace because it gave Mexicans a stake in the system: "The workers who toil will not risk the revolutionary action of other epochs [or] the fruits of their toil and weariness, acquired by constant labor and many years of abnegation and sacrifice."[30]

The científicos' arguments about the positive political consequences of ma-terial progress served to legitimate Díaz's economic and political agendas. At a time when social Catholics and liberal opposition groups were claiming that Porfirian material progress had negative social consequences, Bulnes made it appear that there were no social costs that accompanied economic modernization. To the contrary, there were only benefits.[31] Bulnes's assertions also provided a rationale for the famous Porfirian slogan "Poca política y mucha administración." From the vantage point of economic determinism, the fact that politics were not being focused on directly did not mean that they were being neglected. To the contrary, economics had political significance.

Commerce and State Building

The científicos applied their thesis that market expansion resulted in political stability not only to recalcitrant groups and individuals but also to dissident regions. They maintained that the expansion of national commodity markets harmonized and integrated different regions of Mexico into the national state. Given the powerful regional challenges to state formation in nineteenth-century Mexico, it is not surprising that they focused on the relationship between commerce and state formation. Their analysis of the links between commerce and regional integration illustrates the eclectic nature of their economic thought, for both liberalism and positivism informed their discourse.

The científicos explained the relationship between commerce and state building in a detailed way in their position on abolishing the alcabala. The alcabala, an internal tax charged on goods when they crossed state lines, had been established in the colonial era. While liberals had condemned it earlier in the nineteenth century, it was not abolished until 1896.[32] José Yves Limantour (1854–1935), the leader of the científico clique, was the Federal District representative on a commission that discussed abolishing the alcabala. Limantour's background prepared him for this task. In the 1870s Limantour was a professor of political economy and served on a commission that studied commercial treaties with the United States. In the 1880s he studied the problem of silver depreciation for the government. From 1891 to 1911 he was Mexico's minister of finance. He played a decisive role in Mexico's 1905 monetary reform and was also a significant actor in the Mexicanization of the railroads. Limantour utilized both positivist and liberal concepts to make his claim that the alcabala had negative political effects. He charged that it caused "a spirit of economic hostility between entities."[33] Four years later he made the same point, asserting that the tax posed a "grave danger to national integrity."[34]

Científico Pablo Macedo (1851–1918), a deputy in Congress who served on government economic commissions and wrote extensively on economic matters, echoed Limantour's claims.[35] He quoted Manuel Dublán, Mexico's finance minister during the 1880s, to make his point, declaring that the alcabala fomented "perpetual war and hostility."[36] Macedo's own analysis developed this point. He maintained that having different "tribute systems" within the same "social organism" resulted in "chaos."[37] Díaz Dufoo linked the alcabala to the political problem of regionalism.[38] He published his analysis in the financial weekly he edited from 1901 to 1911, *El Economista Mexicano*, a publication that had close ties to the Porfirian regime.[39] He explicitly charged that the alcabala fostered regionalism and thus hindered state consolidation, maintaining that "the [alcabala] system admirably cultivates . . . the feudal organization of the territory." In keeping with this contention, he went on to complain about the problems of "state sovereignty" and cacique rule, which were impediments to national "cohesion."[40] The científicos, then, defined the alcabala not as an economic problem but as a political dilemma. Despite their liberal economic goal, the científicos departed from liberal theory, for they located social foundations not in the free individual but in the "social organism," which consisted of different parts, or "entities."

Macedo celebrated the act of abolishing the alcabala as a milestone for national integration. He maintained that for the cause of national unification it was the economic equivalent of the grand political act of repelling the French in 1867, which had resulted in political unification. Emphasizing the close relationship between establishing the market and political harmony, he stated that after abolishing the alcabala "our interests are only one, from the United States to Guatemala and from the Atlantic to the Pacific."[41] In keeping with Smithian rhetoric, the market, then, symbolized harmony. Paradoxically, this assertion was based in positivist doctrine. Harmony was realized by creating a homogeneous national market, which unified the interests of the different "entities" of the "social organism." This clashed with a liberal construct in which individuals unintentionally promote the common good by pursuing their own interests. In the científicos' argument, the liberal god of self-interest was condemned, and a homogeneous national interest that could only be realized by state regulation was promoted.

The association between commerce and national unity was also made by científicos and other bureaucrats who were members of a commission created to examine Mexico's merchant marine. The commission partly used the political impact of commerce to justify its call to expand the merchant marine. The commission explained the centrifugal effects associated with the absence of commerce: "We will see weakened and compromised her [Mexico's] autonomous unity, because the absence of communication between diverse parts of her territory will make it impossible to realize the formation of a common interest that only commerce can create."

In keeping with the earlier debate surrounding the alcabala, the commission emphasized the way commerce served to integrate diverse regions and thereby create a unified state. This formulation was also in accord with another aspect of the alcabala debate: it associated the market not with a harmony generated by competition and individualism but with a unity forged by harmonizing regional interests.[42] Reflecting a positivist influence, the científicos supported market expansion from a collectivist position. In contrast, as chapter 4 shows, social Catholics attacked the market from a collectivist angle, arguing that market expansion undermined cohesion by stressing the individual over the community. The científicos, guided by a positivist-liberal philosophy, came to the opposite conclusion: market expansion increased social cohesion.

In keeping with the científicos' position on the effects of the market on individuals, their dialogue on the alcabala also supported Porfirian policy. It legitimated the Porfirian economic modernization program by lauding the political consequences of market expansion. By portraying the state's hegemony over regions as a benevolent force, it also supported state building. Forcing recalcitrant states into a homogeneous national commercial order was not a form of coercion but a peaceful mission undertaken in the name of national harmony. Thus, the alcabala debate can be read as an attack on federalism.

The Market's Impact on Indians' Behavior

In contrast to the liberals' claims about the powerful impact that the market had on the political behavior of members of the middle class and the elite was their contention that it had no influence on the economic actions of Indians. Since they believed economic incentives were lost on Indians, they championed forms of coercion and indoctrination to forge a labor force. Their writings on labor deviated in another way: by the last decade of the Porfiriato the necessity to realize political stability was not a central issue, but creating a labor force was. Since the demand for workers increased during the Porfirian export boom, forging a workforce was a major concern.

When it came to the indigenous population, liberals rejected the concept of economic man. Their position was not unique, for some Europeans and Latin Americans, implicitly and explicitly, also disavowed the Ricardian concept, albeit from distinct perspectives.[43] In stark contrast to Porfirian discourse, the creation of a labor force was not problematized by Ricardo, for his economic man always sought to work to maximize profit. This idea applied to less developed regions of the world, for Ricardo's solution for these areas was only increased capital investment, implying that there was no difference between workers from different nations, races, and regions of the world.[44] This was in keeping with Ricardo's overarching conceptualization of workers, for he depicted labor as unchanging, egalitarian, universal, and individualist.[45] Thus, albeit for different reasons, he embraced the same horizontal social body espoused by political liberalism. During the late nineteenth century, an intellectual age marked by racialist and evolutionary thought, Mexican liberals did not follow Ricardo's notion of economic man. Not the universal worker but a hierarchy of labor formed the foundation of their platform.

Nevertheless, many of the views articulated by liberals about Indians had their roots in the early nineteenth century. For example, the liberals' denigration of the indigenous population and their calls for Indian education and European immigration to rectify the labor problem can be traced back to the early nineteenth century.[46] Despite these continuities, Porfirian elites had distinct views about Indians. First, the liberals ascribed even less transformative power to the market to shape Indians' behaviors than their forerunners had. Second, they discussed the "Indian problem" much more extensively than their predecessors had. Finally, they had a vision of Indians' role in society different from that of their precursors. While creating the "good worker" was one early model, it became the only model during the Porfiriato. A central explanation for this disparity is that even if Mexican liberals during the first half-century of independence did not embrace the concept of economic man in the case of Indians, they nevertheless adhered more closely to classic economic and political liberalism than their late-nineteenth-century counterparts had.[47]

Disapproving of a corporate notion of the social body that constructed Indians as a special group with its own rights and obligations, José Mora and other early-nineteenth-century liberals rejected the term *Indian*, replacing it with *citizen*.[48] This horizontal conception of the social order deemphasized race. In keeping with this liberal conception of society, Mora and others depicted the colonial heritage as a force that blocked the Indians' progress and modernity. It followed, then, that dismantling the corporate order and constructing a liberal economic and political order would play a role in the Indians' progress. Indians were citizens like all other Mexicans; however, the corporate status they had experienced during the colonial era had inhibited their growth and individualism.

A component of the liberals' attack on the colonial order was their effort to dismantle the Indians' communal property and replace it with private property.

From the early nineteenth century through the 1860s the liberals praised the effects that private property would have on the mores and values of the indigenous population, claiming a modern individualist spirit would be awakened in the Indians when they became property owners. The influential liberal José María Luis Mora argued this point in the 1830s and was echoed by Francisco Pimentel, who carried out extensive investigations of Mexico's indigenous population in the 1860s. Thus, liberal rhetoric celebrated the market—in the form of private property—as an agent of the Indians' modernization.[49] (It is worth noting that liberals did not make great efforts to put their ideas into practice, however.)[50] Beatríz Urías Horcasitas's study supports the assertion that liberals during the early republic viewed market expansion as a solution to the "Indian problem." But instead of private property as an agent of change, she focuses on the development of the labor market. She argues that liberals maintained that laziness did not explain why Indians did not work. Rather, they were jobless because of high levels of unemployment. Thus, it follows that development of the market would solve the problem.[51] One small part of the liberal rhetoric depicted Indians as materialistic beings.

It needs to be stressed, however, that liberals hardly discussed Indians during the early republic. This lack of attention to such a fundamental issue can be explained in part by liberals' attempts to do away with the "Indian" category and replace it with "citizen."[52] The limited need for labor during this era of economic stagnation probably resulted in decreased interest in the Indian labor force. Furthermore, liberals hoped that foreign immigrants would fill Mexico's labor needs.

During the Porfiriato, in contrast, liberals discussed Indians extensively. The Mexican discourse was not unique, for race was a dominant theme in Western thought during the second half of the nineteenth century. During the nineteenth century lineage-based notions of race were countered by the ideas that races were fixed types and that there was a hierarchy of races.[53] This notion of race contradicted the liberal idea that the individual was the basis of social order. Further challenging this liberal conception, race was often conflated with nation. Thus, instead of a nation of individuals, there were "national races." These notions of race influenced liberals' analysis of the Indians. They conceived of Indians as a racial group with specific traits and characteristics that made them distinct rather than as individuals or citizens.

Despite maintaining that specific races had distinct traits, most liberals were not biological determinists. Rather, when discussing the indigenous population, they regarded biology as a factor in behavior but not the only determinant. Other explanations for behavior they cited included diet, climate, education, and the colonial heritage.[54] Another significant theme in their racial thought that contested the notion of fixed racial types was evolutionism. Races could evolve or regress over historical time. This depiction is in keeping with scholarship, for a revisionist literature has effectively challenged the view that Porfirian elites were biological determinists. However, this scholarship has overlooked the fact that Porfiristas did subscribe to racial determinism, albeit of a flexible variant.[55] Whether determined by biology, diet, climate, and/or evolution, races had specific traits. This conception of Indians as a specific race with distinct traits was a far cry from the liberals' predecessors, who, at least in theory, attempted to do away with the "Indian" category. The upshot of liberals' reconceptualization of race was an increased attention focused on the Indian "race."

Their overriding preoccupation with labor also led them to focus more on Indians than had their liberal predecessors. A number of factors resulted in an increased attention to the workforce. First, Porfirian political stability prompted a shift in economic strategy, which resulted in a greater emphasis on generating wealth through the production process as opposed to the realm of finance.[56] Second, owing to the falling international value of silver from the 1880s onward, liberals increasingly came to believe that agriculture needed to replace mining as Mexico's primary export, which, in turn, led them to focus on the quality of the rural agricultural labor force.[57] A third factor was intimately related to the second: during the Porfiriato, liberals articulated theories about the basis of wealth that placed more emphasis on the quality of the workforce.[58] Rejecting the notion that resources were the basis of wealth, they stressed the importance of labor and technology in creating value.[59] Finally, and perhaps most importantly, the booming Porfirian economy created a greater demand for workers.

By the late Porfiriato there was not only a greater stress on the labor force but also a belief that the indigenous population needed to fill the nation's labor needs. While earlier in the century and even during the early Porfiriato, for that matter, liberals had imagined that foreign immigrants would fill this role, by the late Porfiriato this was no longer the case. Thus, during the late Porfiriato, improving the quality of the indigenous labor force was deemed an imperative task. But this was no easy mission, for liberals conceptualized Indians as an inferior race divorced from modern society.[60] Writer Maqueo Castellanos, for example, complained that the Indians practiced an "imperfect and absurd socialism."[61] Adolfo Duclos Salinas (c. 1855–1915), a Porfirian journalist who wrote on politics and economics, made a similar complaint. Racial determinism clearly influenced his analysis. He protested that the Indians "will not separate themselves from their tribal customs to join in the general movement of progress and civilization and the uniting of their races with the more intelligent one."[62]

Liberals' principal preoccupation concerning the Indians' lack of integration into modern Mexico was economic, not political, social, or cultural. Indeed, their chief complaint was that rather than produce for the growing internal and external markets, Indians remained wedded to their self-sufficient communal existence.[63] The agricultural journal *Boletín de la Sociedad Agrícola Mexicana*, the organ of the Mexican Agricultural Society, an organization that heavily promoted agriculture exports and was first presided over by Matías Romero (1837–98), blamed Mexico's limited exports on Indians' unwillingness to produce for the external market: "Our commerce with foreign nations cannot pass certain limits; we hardly produce more than we consume. The 4 million Indians that exist . . . are not producers."[64]

Liberals used racial explanations to account for Indians' inadequacy as workers. The Indian race produced little because it was low on the evolutionary scale. Genaro Raigosa (1847–1906), a congressman who served on economic commissions, attributed low productivity to racial factors in a chapter written for *México, su evolución social*: "Owing to a depressive selection . . . the rural labor force has been restricted to the population most resistant to the enticements of modern progress, . . . the indigenous population, whose regressive evolution has not yet come to a standstill."[65] *Semana Mercantil*, a Mexico City financial weekly owned and edited by Everado Hegewisch, also articulated a racial explanation for Indians' low productivity: "The Indian, our only agricultural worker, sticks to his birthplace, like the other [the turtle] to his shell, and because of his atavism he does not produce all he is capable of, even in that region."[66] As the official organ of the industrial confederation and the chamber of commerce, the weekly financial journal represented industrial and commercial interests.[67]

Certain assumptions perpetuated this negative view of Indian workers. First, liberals defined "work" as production for national and international commodity markets. Thus, Indians' subsistence production was not considered "work." This was a far cry from earlier positive depictions of Indian production.[68] Second, the way "Indians" were defined was also a factor. Liberals generally employed a social definition of race, depicting people who lived in traditional communities and retained customs associated with the pre-Columbian era as Indians. In contrast, people who integrated into modern Mexico were no longer "Indians." Consequently, despite the fact that many "Indians" integrated into modern Mexican society, there were few Indian success stories. This social definition of race, ironically, perpetuated the notion that Indians were intransigent.

Unlike their predecessors, liberals, virtually unanimously, placed no faith in the market as an agent to transform the mores and practices of Indians. It was evident that they did not envision the market as a revolutionary force because they virtually never advocated market forces as an agent to modernize the Indians.[69] No longer did they hail private property as an agent of progress. Alberto María Carreño (1875–1962), a scholar and diplomat who wrote extensively on economics in *El Economista Mexicano* and other publications, argued that turning Indians into private property owners would be to the "detriment" of the nation, for, owing to their "indolence," the "productive capacity of the soil" would decrease. Indians' "natural tendency" was to produce the minimum necessary for their own survival.[70] Emphasizing this point, Carreño asserted that Francisco Pimentel's claim that private property would civilize Indians was erroneous.[71]

How do we explain liberals' lack of faith in the market? Racial determinism was surely a factor. The fact that the Reforma had occurred about half a century earlier perhaps strengthened the notion that it was not the absence of the market but instead racial factors that explained Indians' resistance to modernity. Indeed, had not the Reforma initiated the process of dismantling corporate society and replacing it with a modern bourgeois order? Thus, from the liberals' vantage point, notwithstanding Mexico's economic modernization, Indians had not changed. Indeed, científico Miguel Macedo (1856–1929) stated that despite the legal dismantling of Indians' communal existence, conditions remained the same. He complained that Indians "have continued . . . sitting in their huts cultivating and exploiting by the most primitive procedures their lands and forests."[72]

German sociologist Otto Peust, a bureaucrat in Mexico's Ministry of Development, wrote extensively on Mexico's Indians in journals, pamphlets, and government studies. In 1903 he became director of the ministry's department of agriculture and carried out studies on Indians' productivity.[73] He explicitly argued that modern economic culture did not have the strength to shape or influence Indians' behaviors. In fact, he contended that the case of Mexico's Indians disproved European theories that economics shaped behavior: "The racial inferiority of our workers is the . . . cause [of agricultural backwardness]. . . . The sickly situation that has existed in our large-scale agriculture, which is based on Indian labor, proves the stupidity of the theories of certain European economists, who say that development and the economic environment determine the march of nations, when the contrary is true: the nation's material and political movements depend on their [Indians'] character."[74] Peust was a biological determinist. Challenging what he explained as Darwin's notion of the "perfectibility of races," he maintained that "the constitution of each race is inalterable."[75] Peust's racial hierarchy emphasized economics. He contended that inferior races were less economically active than superior races.[76]

Peust's claim that economic modernization did not alter Indians' economic behavior indicated his belief that the market was not an agent of change. He made this assertion even more explicitly in his discussion of wages, maintaining that increased wages would result in Indians working less, not more. "The indolence of the [Indian] race," Peust explained, has "reduced the number of individuals interested in making a living with their work and conquering progress and material advancement. Of the 12 to 13 million rural inhabitants only 1 million are occupied in agricultural industry. The rest are inert and only cultivate what is indispensable for their own consumption. High salaries do not make them more active; to the contrary, they make Indians work less, because they acquire the little they need faster."[77] Even if Peust's biological determinism was not representative, his claim that the market was an insufficient force to alter the mores and practices of the indigenous population was. Liberals, for example, echoed his argument regarding the negative effects that increased wages had on Indians' productivity.[78]

Liberals' depictions of Indians as a little-evolved race that could not be propelled forward into modernity by market forces had significant consequences for government policy. This negative depiction of Indians opened up the possibilities of coercion. If economic forces could not transform them, then more drastic measures were necessary. The fact that liberals were generally silent on the issue of forced labor suggests that they deemed coercion necessary to create a capitalist workforce.[79] Indeed, despite the fact that the Porfiriato was notorious for different forms of labor coercion (debt peonage, *enganche* [impressment], and neoslavery), liberals rarely criticized it.[80] In contrast, opposition liberals and social Catholics condemned coercive labor systems extensively, as will be shown in chapters 4 and 5.[81] Not only did liberals remain silent about the issue of forced labor, but they also championed legal forms of coercion such as vagrancy laws, mandatory consumption, and employing labor contractors.[82]

The form of coercion liberals advocated most strongly was education. Educating the indigenous population, Sierra contended, was essential to its transformation. Even though there were opponents who claimed that educating Indians was worthless, the call for Indian education strengthened during the late Porfiriato.[83] In fact, legislation was passed that made universal education obligatory (the law, however, was never implemented). Liberals contended that education, unlike the market, had the power to modernize Indians. Indeed, the education solution, clearly not "Indianist," did not celebrate Indians' non-Western traditions.[84]

To the contrary, liberals maintained that "backward" Indians needed to be changed into rational economic agents, and they used terms like *transformation* and *regeneration* to emphasize this metamorphosis.[85] The idea was liberal and reformist, for it posited that there was a remedy to Indians' deviant economic behavior. These educational concepts, then, were "corrective" or "disciplinary," for Indians' "backward" behaviors were to be curbed and "modern" and "materialist" practices encouraged.

Liberals envisioned education as a tool to integrate Indians into capitalist society. Not only would education teach Indians the Spanish language, it would also instill bourgeois cultural practices, consumption patterns, and personal hygiene habits. The secularization of education was particularly important to this task. It would shift Indians' alliances from the Church and a spiritual existence to modern bourgeois materialist culture. Bulnes complained about the Church's influence over the rural population and warned about the negative impact of Catholic education, contending that "to give the children to the Church is to give it civilization and to cut off the head of the future."[86] He suggested that the secularization of education could, at least to a degree, free rural society from the Church's clutches.[87] Castellanos's educational plan also sought to integrate Indians into modern society, albeit in a different fashion. His plan focused on consumption practices and promoted consumerism by demonstrating the advantages of modern housing (which, he explained, required purchasing materials for upkeep), dress styles (shoes, etc.), and eating habits (meat, not corn). This educational plan, as Castellanos put it, would "create necessities."[88]

Most importantly, education was conceptualized as a tool to create a capitalist workforce, not to emancipate Indians from ignorance or to turn them into citizens. Some liberals' concern with a labor force was so strong that they viewed the Reforma's plan to turn Indians into smallholders as erroneous because it would shrink the size of the labor pool and thus create a shortage of workers.[89] Reflecting this stress on education as a means to create a labor force, technical education was emphasized. Not only was it the focus of adult education, but it was also a key component of primary education.[90] The press, too, stressed it. The daily and business press discussed it, and journals dedicated to technical education such as *El Consultor* were founded.[91] This focus was in keeping with Díaz's presidential messages, which lauded advancements in Mexico's technical schools.

Liberals' social engineering project had a biological component: foreign immigration. Given their lack of confidence in the power of the market, their negative views about the indigenous labor force, the influence of racial determinism, and successful immigration examples in North and South America (the United

States, Brazil, and Argentina), it is not surprising that liberals represented state-sponsored immigration as a solution to Mexico's "worker shortage," a position consistent with other Latin American nations. The Díaz government placed so much stock in immigration that it financed and promoted official immigration until the early 1890s. Rhetoric, too, stressed immigration. The rationale for land survey and division policies was that they would attract foreigners.[92] Even when state-sponsored immigration ended during the 1890s, liberals still supported the policy in principle.[93] Indeed, the policy was attacked with pragmatic instead of ideological reasoning. Citing successful cases in other nations, officials maintained that not state-sponsored immigration but rather the level of national economic progress was the determining factor in immigration. As Mexico progressed economically it would create opportunities that would serve as a far more powerful magnet than any immigration policy.[94]

Given their eclectic brand of racial determinism, it is not surprising that some liberals supported both immigration and education. Sierra was a case in point. Clearly influenced by a form of biological racial determinism, he argued that the infusion of European blood into Mexican stock would improve the quality of the Mexican race.[95] Sierra's dual strategy reflected the eclectic nature of his beliefs, for it was influenced by scientific racism and the liberal notion of reform via education.

Sierra's racial determinism was representative of the liberal position. Race explained not only why Mexican Indians were inferior workers but also why foreigners were superior laborers. *Semana Mercantil*, for example, complained that Indians had a "low economic level" due to "antiquated customs," and it promoted immigration to remedy the problem.[96] Similarly, in 1907 Castellanos emphasized foreign supremacy, claiming that "if instead of the 11 million Indians spread out in woods and mountains we had the same number of foreign immigrants from all or any nationality, we would be a country thirty times richer, more respected, and stronger."[97] When advocating immigration, Roberto Gayol (1857–1936), an engineer, author, and professor who specialized in irrigation and immigration, emphasized Europeans' superior economic traits: "Their [Europeans'] vigorous mentality, their robust physical constitution, and their habits of work and economy are capable of generating progress in new countries."[98] Díaz Dufoo, repeating an argument made by Romero about worker productivity on looms, fine-tuned Gayol's generalizations when he made distinctions between the productive capacities of Europeans from different nations. Yet he agreed with Gayol when he placed Mexicans far below all Europeans. He contended that a Frenchman could manage four looms, a Belgian five, and an Englishman "even six to eight." In sad contrast, "a Mexican arrives at two as a *maximum*."[99] Bulnes lauded Argentineans, most likely because they were the most Europeanized Latin Americans: Argentina had high levels of European immigration and a relatively small indigenous population. He declared that the 5 million inhabitants of Argentina were more valuable than Mexico's 14 million.[100]

The Market's Impact on the Behavior of the Hacendados

There had been ideological attacks on the hacienda system throughout the nineteenth century, but they had always been expressed by a minority.[101] Labeled a form of private property, the hacienda had escaped the liberal attacks on landholdings—attacks that had resulted in the privatization of indigenous communal lands and Church property.[102] In regard to the hacienda, the Porfiriato did not break with the past, for the division of large landholdings came later, during the age of revolution. Historical scholarship, which depicts the Porfirian government as maintaining the status quo, supports this.[103] In contrast, it emphasizes the liberal and radical oppositions' attack on the hacienda. This scholarship, however, overlooks a critique of the hacienda that was articulated by elements within the Porfirian regime and the business press. Liberals criticized not only the Indians' communal holdings but also the hacienda system.

The liberals' attack on hacendados was not nearly as powerful as their criticism of the Indians, however. Indeed, while liberals unanimously agreed that Indians were a serious problem, they were divided when it came to hacendados. Despite the fact that their critique of hacendados was weaker than their assault on Indians, there were important similarities between the two. In both cases, liberals depicted the market as an impotent force to change the mores and practices of the populace. In addition, in both instances they relied on racial arguments to explain why the market had no impact. Finally, in both cases they promoted coercion as the preferred tool to alter behavior.

Elements in liberals' racialist thought about Indians were present in their critique of hacendados. The notion of evolution was particularly strong. Raigosa maintained that hacendados were an atavistic group, a product of "depressive selection."[104] Evolutionary thought was a component of racial determinism. Liberals portrayed hacendados as a little-evolved racial group, namely, feudalistic Spaniards who were relics from the age of conquest. Further revealing their emphasis on race, liberals depicted hacendados as a homogeneous race; that is, certain character traits and behaviors held for the entire group.

Boletín de la Asociación Financiera Internacional, a financial journal edited by

José Castellot (1856–1938), a científico who specialized in banking and finance, attacked the hacienda.[105] The journal, which strongly promoted foreign investment, depicted hacendados as feudal lords from a bygone epoch.[106] The financial periodical invoked a feudal image by emphasizing hacendados' strong interest in land but limited concern with production: "We have often called attention to the unfortunate mania, possessed by many Mexicans, for large holdings of lands which they never think of cultivating to any appreciable extent and never attempt to sell any portion of in lots so that they might have money to cultivate the remainder."[107] *Semana Mercantil*, quoting another source to support its position, made the same charge, contending that "hacendados [were] very preoccupied with expansion" but little interested in "production."[108] *Boletín de la Sociedad Agrícola Mexicana* reprinted a foreign study that made a similar claim: "Hacendados are something like feudal barons from the Middle Ages. They only cultivate a limited part of their land, leaving the rest to pastures."[109]

A component of the feudal critique focused on hacendados' resistance to technological change. This attack, too, depicted them as throwbacks from an earlier epoch who were antagonistic to modern capitalism. Leopoldo Palacios, a government agronomist, stated in a 1909 report that "it takes tremendous work to introduce the smallest innovation in agriculture. . . . Even if the benefits are demonstrated with numbers the answer is always the same: 'Let someone else do it first.'"[110] Similarly, *El Progreso Latino*, a Mexico City–based weekly financial journal owned and edited by Roman Rodríguez Peña, complained about "the systematic resistance of hacendados to abandon their old practices known to be deficient and adopt new techniques already in practice used by intelligent and expert agriculturalists in Europe and the United States."[111] (Since it was a business journal that focused on Mexican industry and international trade and was independent of the government, it had similarities with *Semana Mercantil*. Its prolabor stance, however, made it distinct, for, unlike *Semana Mercantil*, it did not solely represent the interests of capital.)[112]

Ironically, liberals' critique of the hacienda was echoed by Andrés Molina Enríquez (1868–1940), the famous agrarian critic of the Porfirian regime.[113] True, his critique, which was articulated in his 1909 publication *Los grandes problemas nacionales*, was more detailed than that of the liberals. (Before it was published as a book, sections of it were printed in serial form in *El Tiempo*.) Nevertheless, his analysis also emphasized hacendados' feudal traits. Stressing similarities between the Porfirian regime and Molina Enríquez is not totally at odds with scholarship, for some historians have shown that he, too, was influenced by positivism, social Darwinism, and racial determinism.[114]

Molina Enríquez portrayed hacendados as artifacts from the age of feudalism and the Spanish Conquest of Mexico.[115] He made this link by depicting them as the direct descendants of conquistadores. He argued that land directly tied them to the conquistadores; families had held onto the same land from the Conquest to the present.[116] Further developing his feudal characterization of hacendados, he claimed that their land was controlled by their blood. It did not circulate on the market.[117] Not only were their roots in an earlier epoch, Molina Enríquez argued, but so were their worldviews. They lacked a materialist ethic. The main attack leveled by Molina Enríquez (and by other liberals, for that matter) related to hacendados' attitudes about land. They valued land, he argued, for social prestige, not for profit.[118] Thus, they accrued enormous holdings but did not cultivate them. Molina Enríquez made this point emphatically, maintaining repeatedly that haciendas were "not a business."[119] He supported this assertion by claiming that indigenous communities produced more than hacendados. (It is worth noting that this "feudal" depiction of Mexican hacendados has been overturned by recent scholarship, which has shown that haciendas were business enterprises and that hacienda property changed hands quite frequently.)[120]

Since hacendados were an atavistic group, a throwback from the era of feudalism, modern materialist incentives were lost on them. They were relics of a premodern age in which production was not the key to wealth and power. Molina Enríquez, for example, argued that the hacendados' lust for land was so great that even when they were forced to part with it for economic necessity, they would not. This critique gained credence because it appeared to be a reasonable explanation for Mexico's limited agricultural production.

The liberals' market rhetoric shaped their political strategy. Since the market proved unable to shape hacendados' actions, more drastic measures were necessary. A fraction of liberals supported a stiff tax on uncultivated lands.[121] The tax, according to its proponents, would compel hacendados either to abandon their noncapitalist practices and outlook or to face economic ruin. According to the assumptions of liberal critics, coercion was totally justified, for hacendados' anticapitalist practices were forms of deviance that needed to be eradicated. The quest for increased productivity, not the sanctity of private property, reigned supreme.

Some liberals who advocated the tax were not solely or even principally interested in reforming hacendados. Rather, they envisioned the tax as a way to break the dominance of the hacienda in the countryside and increase the number of medium- and small-scale capitalist producers. Some renditions of this thesis had a racist element that echoed the liberals' position on Indians, since they called for replacing hacendados with foreign immigrants. Bulnes criticized Mexico's agricultural system, labeling it "aristocratic agriculture," which he defined as a system in which land was in "very few hands, which were very torpid to manage them well." Only foreigners could turn this around: "Colonization is the only way we can democratize our agriculture and produce a mass of men that conserve their wealth."[122] Thus, from this perspective, it was impossible to inculcate hacendados with a capitalist ethic by any means. Hacendados, like Indians, were low on the evolutionary scale; they needed to be displaced by foreigners. Thus, a fraction of the liberals denigrated not only Mexico's pre-Columbian past but also the colonial era. They lamented Mexico's historical roots and sought to erect a nation upon modern northern European foundations.

Liberals divided over the land tax proposal.[123] It was debated hotly in the press during the last decade of the Porfiriato, albeit in fits and starts. It is worth noting that Americans, who were proponents of the tax, played a small but significant role in the debate by starting a rumor that the tax was impending.[124] Opponents of the tax attacked proponents' principal argument, namely, that hacendados' economic vision needed to be reformed. According to opponents, limited production was not rooted in hacendados' mentality. Not mindset but material factors prevented hacendados from cultivating their land. *El Economista Mexicano* put it this way: "The absence of cultivation on many rural properties is not necessarily due to the indolence of the owners but to other causes that a tax will not remedy: inadequate information about markets, a worker shortage, scarcity of water, etc., etc."[125]

Proponents of the tax clearly lost the day; in fact, the tax never made it past the public debate stage. Official sources remained silent throughout the debate. At the very end of the Porfiriato, however, when pressures for land reform heightened, the government directly opposed the tax. Falling back on the defense of the hacienda employed by its predecessors, the government upheld the principle that private property was sacred. Instead, the government promoted less interventionist policies to implement land reform.[126]

Education was a less controversial method of coercion. Liberals also championed education to modernize hacendados, although not as strongly as they promoted Indian education. All liberals could embrace this strategy, for it did not threaten the integrity of the hacienda. Palacios hailed education as a tool to inculcate a capitalist ethic in hacendados. Palacios believed that race and climate accounted for hacendados' limited productivity. Indeed, he complained about the "apathy . . . inherent in our climate and race" but explained that "there is nothing better to combat this than the diffusion of knowledge about irrigation."[127]

This educational position, which lauded the benefits of modern and scientific production procedures, was articulated through public and private channels. Educator Rafael de Zayas Enríquez emphasized the government's efforts in this realm, citing that it published teaching materials and organized agricultural expositions to convince agriculturalists to adopt modern production methods.[128] Further, governmental and quasi-governmental publications, particularly *Boletín de la Secretaría de Fomento*, and technical journals that focused on agriculture, for instance, *Boletín de la Sociedad Agrícola Mexicana*, *Haciendas y Ranchos*, and *El Heraldo Agrícola*, all promoted reform via education.

This chapter has illustrated that in regard to shaping Mexicans' mores, values, and behaviors, the market was an inconstant power. While a fraction of liberals, the científicos, acclaimed the market because it could pacify the political sphere, liberals unanimously agreed that it was unable to create *Homo economicus*. Liberals' concepts of race and human nature explain why they assigned greater power to the market to shape political behavior than economic actions. From the vantage point of racial determinism, it would take more than market forces to reform the nonmaterialist economic attitudes of Indians and hacendados, two segments of society that liberals depicted as atavistic. Conversely, liberals portrayed the middle and upper classes primarily as economic beings. Thus, it followed that political peace was a consequence of satisfying their material needs.

Market discourse impacted policy. Científicos, who maintained that creating a national market fostered regional peace, employed market rhetoric to support abolishing the alcabala. Depicting the market as an impotent force to change the economic behaviors of Indians and hacendados, too, supported policy. Immigration, education, vagrancy, and taxation were all justified by depicting the market as a weak agent of change. Liberals' market rhetoric also converged more broadly with agendas of the Porfirian regime. Científico Francisco Bulnes's writings supported the government's nondemocratic tendencies. According to Bulnes, humans were economic beings who solely desired to fulfill their material needs. Political aspirations did not exist. Thus, democracy was an irrelevant concept. Bulnes's notion that humans were economic beings also supported the regime's economic program. Since material progress guaranteed political peace, científicos' rhetoric supported the regime's stress on economics. The liberal position that depicted the market as an impotent agent bolstered the idea of state intervention, for it set the stage for the Porfirian social engineering project. The design of breaking down local markets in the name of national political integration provided implicit support for strengthening the center at the expense of the regions.

Liberals' discourse affected national identity. It denigrated the historical racial foundations of Mexico. It attacked not only Mexico's pre-Columbian population but also Spaniards, the group that merged with the indigenous population during Mexico's colonial era. These groups were so atavistic that they remained resistant to the power of the market. Thus, liberals depicted foreigners as playing a leading role in forging modern Mexico.

Even if liberals' contention that economic progress resulted in harmony was in keeping with a Smithian position, they nevertheless departed significantly from classic economic liberalism. Unlike that of Smith, liberals' rhetoric did not feature competition but rather cooperation. Cooperation was consistent with their organic conception of society, another aspect of their ideology that countered classic liberalism, for it rejected individualism. Adhering to a racial hierarchy of workers, liberals, too, eschewed classic liberalism's universalism, which manifested itself in the notion of homogeneous economic man. By subscribing to the notion of a ranking of workers, liberals problematized an aspect of the economy that Smith and Ricardo did not even consider: forging a labor force.

3 A "Battle for Existence"

The Power of the International Market

This chapter examines the liberals' position on the political impact that the international market (i.e., the global flow of capital, labor, and goods) had on Mexico. This issue cannot be overlooked. After all, this was not only an age when formal and informal economic imperialism were in their heyday, it was also an epoch when foreign economic activity in Mexico had reached unprecedented levels. This, in Eric Hobsbawm's words, was the "age of empire."[1] What political powers did liberals attribute to the international market during the age of empire?

Conventional wisdom holds that the Porfirian regime subscribed to the theory of comparative advantage.[2] From the standpoint of this theory, the international market is a positive force. Comparative advantage posits that there is a form of economic reciprocity between nations, albeit within the context of competition. Thus, the international economic order fosters interdependence and harmony between nations. Consequently, all nations stand to gain by participating in the global economy.

I will demonstrate that in direct contrast to this harmonious international order, liberals conceived of the international economic arena as a zero-sum game. There were winners and losers, and the stakes were high, for not only economic prosperity was at stake but, more important, national sovereignty. The world was engaged in a Darwinian struggle for survival that was waged on an economic battlefield.

Engagement in a struggle for survival did not bode well, for liberals depicted Mexico as a poor nation and thus in a subordinate economic position vis-à-vis the economic strongholds in Europe and the United States. There was a racial component to this formulation. According to liberals, economic superiority stemmed in part from racial superiority. They deemed Mexico racially inferior and thus especially vulnerable. They were not fatalists, however. They protested bitterly against foreign economic domination. Thus, there were powerful nationalist strains in their economic discourse.[3] Nonetheless, they did not espouse a form of economic isolationism; rather, they were profoundly ambivalent about opening Mexico to the international economy. Embracing foreign ideas about the superiority of Europe and the United States, liberals maintained that infusing Mexico with foreign blood, money, and technology would bring economic prosperity and thus strengthen the country's position in the international economic war. Yet they were also in constant fear that foreign economic penetration would result not in national prosperity but foreign domination. Consequently, they conceived of the state as a vital force to regulate foreign economic power and thus protect sovereignty.[4]

Liberals, then, depicted the international market as an almighty political force. This contrasts sharply with their position outlined in the previous chapter. They portrayed the Mexican market—in the incarnations of material progress, commerce, and free internal trade—as a relatively weak agent of change. Despite this difference, there are some overarching similarities between the two positions, especially in regard to ideas about laissez-faire, the role of the state, and the significance of race. Liberals also distrusted laissez-faire in the international market, spurning the notion that the market was the divine regulator and instead championing state intervention in the economy. They also criticized Mexico's Indians while placing foreigners on a pedestal. By advocating the regulation and even nationalization of foreign industry on political grounds, liberal arguments about the international market, too, informed policy. The discourse examined in this chapter, however, had a distinct impact on national identity. Paradoxically, rhetoric about the international market denigrated Mexicans but was also intensely nationalist.

The International Economic Order

Social Darwinism was only loosely derived from Charles Darwin's ideas, and it was Herbert Spencer, the man who coined the phrase "survival of the fittest," who was most responsible for popularizing the movement. In Mexico, as in other parts of the Western Hemisphere, social Darwinism was very popular. Indeed, phrases like "the struggle for life" were fairly common in Mexico at the turn of the century.[5]

While social Darwinism had a unified theme in that it stressed a struggle for existence between competitors, there were numerous variations. Social Darwinists discussed competition between individuals, sexes, firms, classes, nations, and economic systems.[6] The most prominent concept in Mexican social Darwinism stressed the issue of national sovereignty, depicting a struggle for existence taking place between nations.

It is not surprising that liberals articulated a nationalist variant of social Darwinism, for a number of factors facilitated such an articulation. The influence of positivism led them to focus on the collective rather than the individual. Following a theme in the racial ideology of the era, they conflated race with nation: races/nations competed for existence.[7] The numerous foreign interventions Mexico had experienced since independence made Mexicans acutely aware of the fragility of sovereignty. The fact that Mexico shared a border with the United States also brought attention to the issue of national existence.

This was a dangerous world order. Only the strongest nations endured. José Yves Limantour explained that weak nations perished in this battle: "In this work of adaptation, the weak ones [human societies], the poorly prepared ones, those that lack elements to victoriously consummate their evolution have to succumb, leaving the field to the more vigorous [societies], or, because of the characteristics that enable [societies to] win and dominate, they can transmit to their descendants the qualities to which they owe their supremacy. By this terrible law . . . the phenomena of life are ordered."[8] Científico Pablo Macedo depicted this struggle taking place on the economic front. Citing Mexico's balanced budget in the 1894–95 fiscal year, he maintained that healthy state finances were essential to Mexico's existence: "Economic independence . . . ensures a level of respect and consideration from friends and strangers and above all in one's own conscience a respect and esteem without which there is no force and energy for the eternal battle for existence or to resolve the frightful problems that confront nations that do not wish to perish."[9]

Certain biological metaphors employed by Macedo to describe the economy reinforced this link between economic modernization and sovereignty. He contended that development of the economic realm brought life to the social organism and thus metaphorically equated the economy with the birth and growth of the nation. Macedo emphasized the role the railroads played in bringing life to the nation:

Without roads or navigable rivers our social organism was compressed like those Egyptian mummies, but the insatiable scientific curiosity of our days has drawn it out of its tomb. . . . Once the ligatures were untied, the arteries through which previously a trickle of poor and discolored blood circulated became enlarged and full of life. With the whistle of the locomotive that crossed our territory, the nation has awakened from its long sleep. . . . It has spread the movement, . . . activity, and warmth characteristic of healthy organisms. It is therefore not in vain that we sons of the land are saying that with the railways we have been born to the life of civilized nations.[10]

Given Macedo's equation of the economy with national existence, it is little wonder that foreign economic domination was an overriding concern. Liberals did not view all members of the international economy as equally dangerous, however. Rather, they maintained that the U.S. economy was the principal threat. This is hardly surprising, since the United States had come to be the dominant foreign economic force in Mexico by the turn of the century.

Fear of the United States was nothing new. Depicting the principal threat that the United States posed to Mexico as economic rather than military was novel, however. In 1906 *El Progreso Latino* explicitly made this point. The journal stated that Mexico had entered a new era in which not the American army or political system but rather the U.S. economy posed the greatest danger: "The true danger that is now felt is not in the White House or the armored and large armies the United States can bring against us; it is in the absorption of our mines, of our land, of the country's industry, of our maritime commerce; it is their railroad and merchant marine, which monopolize our markets in Europe and Asia and in the American union. We can say . . . [that] American industrialism . . . is the enemy!"[11] Emphasizing that the Porfiriato was a new age in which threats to sovereignty were economic as opposed to military, *El Progreso Latino* contended that "in Mexico there is no longer the danger of other epochs."[12]

In 1902 Justo Sierra articulated a similar argument in an essay he contributed to *México, su evolución social*. He depicted a struggle for existence between Mexico and the United States taking place on the economic plane. Discussing the historical period after Mexico had repelled the French, he contended that the very existence of the "social organism" (i.e., Mexico) was threatened by U.S. economic expansion: "The giant [the United States] that grows at our side and keeps coming closer, due to industrial and agricultural growth of the frontier states and the growth of the railroads, will absorb and dissolve us if it finds us weak."[13] In keeping with *El Progreso Latino*, Sierra made a distinction between military and economic realms and contended the latter was the sphere in which the battle was being waged, for he contended that Mexico's only national defense in this Darwinian struggle was "passing from the military to the industrial phase." Clearly, for Sierra, the weapons in this international struggle were economic. Accordingly, he contended that the most pressing need for Mexico's defense was economic development.[14]

By downplaying military threats and emphasizing economic dangers, Sierra and *El Progreso Latino* were echoing arguments that had been made in the 1890s. In the wake of American military intervention in Cuba in 1898, científico Francisco Bulnes maintained that Mexicans need not fear U.S. military intervention.[15] Bulnes echoed an argument made by Matías Romero, who held key positions in the government first as minister of finance and ultimately as foreign minister to the United States and who also published extensively on economic matters. His 1890 book, *Estudio sobre la anexión de México a los Estados Unidos* (originally published in 1889 in the *North American Review*), argued that the threat of American military annexation of Mexico no longer existed.[16] The book was inspired in part by Romero's desire to increase economic ties between the two nations. In a Mexican intellectual climate that stressed economic perils and minimized military menaces, it is unsurprising that *El Tiempo*, the Catholic Mexico City daily, attacked Romero's work from an economic vantage point. The daily criticized Romero for overlooking the threat of American economic "conquest" of Mexico.[17]

The debate about American economic domination was widespread. Carlos Pereyra (1871–1942), a writer, journalist, and historian who collaborated with Justo Sierra, noted that it was a popular concern that manifested itself in the phrase "peaceful conquest," a saying that referred to the idea that the United States was conquering Mexico economically instead of militarily: "Mexico is a field of economic expansion for Americans. And many Mexicans who have not forgotten that this has been a land of conquest call economic expansion a peaceful conquest, believing that the veins of [Sam] Houston are in every North American capitalist and prospector."[18] The liberal and conservative opposition to the Díaz regime, too, regularly employed the phrase.[19]

Given the repeated military interventions that Mexico experienced during the nineteenth century, it may seem surprising that Mexicans defined the principal threat as economic. Yet when one considers Mexico's international relations during the Porfiriato, this focus on the economic sphere appears more logical. The Porfiriato was an era of unprecedented peace on the military front, for the repeated foreign military interventions that had plagued the nation during its first half-century of independence had finally ended. But it was also a period in which powerful foreign economic interests were attaining a global reach, resulting in an unprecedented level of foreign economic expansion into Mexico. Furthermore, the fact that liberals adhered to economic determinism, a topic discussed in the previous chapter, helps explain why they defined the economic threat as so powerful.

Given Mexico's subordinate position in the world economy, the outcome of this international economic struggle did not bode well. Moreover, the way that liberals (especially científicos) depicted Mexico reinforced the idea that the nation was economically weak. Given the context of the Porfirian export boom, which had generated the highest levels of growth in the history of independent Mexico, this portrayal of Mexico as economically undeveloped was ironic. Liberals' representation of Mexico as undeveloped stemmed in part from their redefinition of wealth. They rejected a mercantilist conception that stressed resources and trade and instead emphasized the realm of production, particularly the central roles of capital, technology, and labor in generating wealth.

Reflecting this new definition of wealth, liberals turned the historic notion that Mexico was an extremely rich nation owing to its immense natural resources, an idea that had been popularized during the late colonial period in Alexander von Humboldt's famous work, *Political Essay on the Kingdom of New Spain*, on its head.[20] Countering Humboldt, they maintained that resources and geography were obstacles to prosperity. It is not surprising that liberals attacked the notion of Mexico's abundant resource wealth, for the international value of silver was declining, which led them to promote a shift from a silver-based to an agricultural-based export economy.[21] Mexico's arable agricultural lands were extremely limited. No wonder liberals contended that nature was a hindrance to economic growth.

Díaz Dufoo, in an essay in Sierra's multivolume work, attacked the notion that Mexico's natural resources made it a wealthy nation. Quoting Sierra, Díaz Dufoo identified the source of this erroneous association between nature and wealth. He claimed that the "greatest error" of Augustín Iturbide, the first leader of the independent Mexican nation, was his assertion to the Mexican people: "You are the richest people in the world."[22] This pronouncement, according to Díaz Dufoo, reflected the faulty popular myth that Mexico was wealthy because of its abundant natural resources. To combat this view, he documented the ways nature was a roadblock to Mexico's industrialization, emphasizing the lack of navigable rivers, the poor quality of the ore and agricultural soil, and a score of other physical handicaps. He concluded: "Natural obstacles oppose . . . the Republic's industrial evolution."[23] Overturning the notion of Mexico as a land rich in natural resources, Díaz Dufoo, contrasting the dearth of resources in

Mexico with their abundance in England and the United States, suggested that Mexico had a comparative disadvantage in natural resources.[24]

Díaz Dufoo was not alone in this opinion. Macedo underscored the way the physical environment, which, he explained, was divided up by mountain chains and lacked a river system that could be exploited commercially, was a severe impediment to national and international commerce.[25] Manuel Fernández Leal (1831–1909), Mexico's minister of development from 1891 to 1900, made the same point, emphasizing the fact that Mexico's mountain chains and absence of navigable rivers were barriers to commerce.[26]

Implicit in this discussion of Mexico's natural resources was the concept that not nature but rather capital and labor were the source of Mexico's wealth.[27] Indeed, the possibility of increased agricultural production via capital investment was stressed. Capital investment could transform Mexico's unproductive land into models of productivity. Genaro Raigosa, in his study of Mexican agriculture that was published in Sierra's multivolume work, maintained that capital improvements could make even inadequate land productive: "Agriculture today, so transformed by the inestimable conquests of science, only asks nature for normal meteorological conditions and enough land for sowing and planting." He detailed the transformation of the "American desert [Arizona, New Mexico, Texas, and Colorado], up to now classed as absolutely arid," into an area of "profitable cultivation" as a case in point.[28] Díaz Dufoo, too, represented human intervention as a force that could overcome the roadblocks to wealth that were created by nature. He described the "destruction of the obstacles" to wealth created by nature, citing "large material works, development of energies, amassment of capitals, [and] scientific education" as "forces that were remov[ing] these hindrances that spontaneously arise in front of the development of the national welfare."[29]

Thus, there were analyses of the economy that emphasized the importance of capital, labor, and technology to the creation of wealth. In addition, there were rare explicit theoretical formulations that made this same argument. Historian and national deputy Genaro García (1867–1920), in his 1902 textbook on political economy, maintained that humans, not nature, were the source of value: "Primitively, nature is more an agent of ruin than production. . . . [Man] arrives to dominate nature more and more and make it his docile collaborator in the production process."[30] Moreno Cora (1837–1922), a writer and scholar who studied the field of jurisprudence, also stressed labor in the form of capital. He explained that the "national territory had lost much of its importance as an element of domination, due to the superior competence of moveable wealth, the base of commerce and modern industry. The wealth of nations is no longer exclusively linked to land or property; rather, a grand part of it consists of capital . . . destined for the production of larger profits."[31]

Liberals' redefinition of wealth represented Mexico as economically weak, for it suggested that a comparative disadvantage in natural resources and geography was not the only problem that Mexico faced. Mexico was also deficient in capital, technology, and labor. These weaknesses were deemed especially significant, for they were defined as essential to the generation of national wealth.

Foreigners' Discordant Economic Role in Mexico

Despite liberals' overriding concern with foreign economic domination, they were profoundly ambivalent about the role foreigners should play in Mexico's struggle for survival. As noted, foreign economic interests posed the central threat to sovereignty, but, contradictorily, liberals also represented foreign influence as essential to Mexico's progress and very existence.

Sierra developed a detailed theory about why foreign influence was imperative to national survival and progress. Citing Auguste Comte and Maximilien Paul Émile Littré, he based his formulation in positivist doctrine and described the nation as a "living being." First, Sierra theorized why contact with foreign nations was an important factor in national progress: "Society is a living being, so it grows, develops, and transforms. This perpetual transformation is more intense when the interior energy of the social organism reacts with exterior elements, assimilating and utilizing them to progress." According to Sierra, receiving external influence was particularly important for less "evolved" human groups. Indeed, Sierra's Darwinian imagery made foreign influence essential to national existence. He described a world order in which certain human groups were more evolved than others. He maintained that the less evolved groups had two options. The first was to be "unconditionally subordinated to the principal [groups] and lose their self-awareness and personality." The second possibility: "Take advantage of the exterior forces to consolidate personal equalization and as a result put their [the less evolved group's] evolution on the march, if not to the level of the groups on the vanguard of human movement, at least at the level of their basic needs of self-preservation and well-being." In other words, contact with superior groups was crucial to existence, for without it less evolved nations were doomed to "unconditional subordination." By absorbing and assimilating elements from evolved peoples, "self-preservation" was ensured.[32]

Sierra maintained that Mexico was a case in point. He contended that assimilating foreign economic elements was essential: "Colonization, workers and capital to exploit our wealth, and a transportation system to enable it to circulate, such was the social desideratum." He directly linked Mexico's economic progress to national sovereignty, contending that "the solution to economic problems precedes, conditions, and consolidates the realization of the supreme ideals: liberty and the nation."[33] He concluded his work by stating that Mexico had evolved—albeit it had been an "incipient evolution"—because it had successfully integrated foreign elements: "Our progress, made up of foreign elements, reveals, on analysis, a reaction of our social body with those elements to assimilate and utilize them to develop and intensify our life. In this way, our national personality has been strengthened by contact with the world."[34]

Sierra's argument had significant implications for national identity. It defined Mexico as a mestizo nation in which foreign and national elements blended together. Thus, Sierra was a precursor to José Vasconcelos, for the latter's notion of a "cosmic race" was built upon the foundations set by Sierra.[35] In Sierra's mestizo nation, foreigners were superior. Evolved foreign elements were needed to propel the backward Mexican nation forward.

Despite the fact that Sierra's analysis depicted foreigners assimilating into Mexican society, there was an extreme ambivalence toward foreigners embedded within it. On the one hand, incorporating foreign elements into the "social organism" was essential to national survival. On the other hand, inviting foreigners in opened the possibility of foreign domination. Thus, Sierra's relationship to foreigners could be likened to a vaccine, which injected dangerous microbes into the bloodstream to make the organism stronger. Ideally, the medicine would cure the patient, but there was always the possibility that it would kill the invalid. His was not an isolated voice.[36]

This paradoxical depiction of the relationship between foreigners and Mexico had very different implications for national identity. Rather than a harmonious fusion of the two elements, there was a highly contradictory position vis-à-vis foreigners, for they simultaneously strengthened and weakened sovereignty. Thus, liberals were both xenophiles and xenophobes. This made for a paradoxical national identity, for it was intensely nationalist but also denigrated the national population and held foreigners in reverence. It was this model of national identity, as opposed to Sierra's notion of assimilation, that was dominant in liberals' discourse.

Since liberals stressed Mexico's comparative disadvantage in resources and maintained that capital investment was central to the creation of wealth, it is not surprising that the area of the economy in which they called for the greatest foreign participation was in the field of investment. They maintained that large doses of foreign capital were essential to constructing a modern transportation network, modernizing agriculture, exploiting mineral resources, and creating industry. Consequently, the issue of attracting foreign capital was discussed extensively in many contexts. Mining legislation reforms during the 1880s and 1890s had strengthened private property rights.[37] They were justified by maintaining that they would attract increased foreign investment.[38] Calls by the Ministry of Development to promote smallholdings and strengthen property rights were advocated, in part, as a means to attract increased investment. Similarly, the 1905 monetary reform was hailed because it would result in elevated levels of foreign investment.[39] Indeed, in a 1906 presidential message Díaz announced that the reform had "given powerful stimulus to the investment of foreign capital in the country."[40] A financial journal maintained that one of Limantour's "principal objectives" in advocating the reform was to court foreign investment.[41] Attracting foreign investment was deemed so important that Díaz engineered major public relations and propaganda campaigns that defined Mexico as a peaceful nation that was safe to invest in to realize this end.[42] He was largely successful: in all of Latin America, only Brazil and Argentina attracted greater amounts of foreign investment than Mexico.[43]

But liberals did not look at their country's ability to attract foreign capital as solely positive. They feared that the influx of capital would result not in national prosperity but in foreign domination. After the turn of the century, U.S. capital eclipsed French, British, and German capital, and liberals became especially concerned about U.S. power.[44] This fear motivated Díaz's strategy of favoring European capital as a means of countering U.S. dominance.[45]

The title of an article in *El Progreso Latino* clearly articulated the contradictory position over foreign and especially U.S. capital: "North American Capital in Mexico: A Civilizing Instrument . . . The Vanguard of Absorption." The body of the article repeated this position, maintaining that U.S. "capital . . . can give life and death."[46] According to the journal, Mexico was between a rock and a hard place.

By the turn of the century, the nationalist elements in liberals' discourse had become more prominent. They stressed the dangers posed by foreign and especially U.S. capital. This is not surprising. American capital was entering Mexico at unprecedented levels. Furthermore, this was the age of monopoly capitalism: U.S. trusts were making their way into Mexico and were demonized by liberals more than any other form of foreign capital.

Científicos spearheaded the antitrust crusade, which began in 1900. The nature of their attack on trusts had very much to do with Mexico's place in the world economy. Their assault would probably have been quite similar to Theodore Roosevelt's class diatribe had they resided in the United States.[47] Indeed, *El Imparcial* lauded Roosevelt's antitrust campaign.[48] Owing to Mexico's dependent position in the world economy, científicos represented trusts not as a financial-industrial class dominating other classes but as foreigners challenging the authority of the Mexican nation. Científicos' adherence to a positivist notion of an organic society as opposed to a class-divided society also facilitated their nationalist attack on foreign trusts.

Part of the científicos' attack on foreign trusts manifested itself in a challenge to social Darwinist theories about the efficacy of trusts, which were articulated by the U.S. business class. *El Economista Mexicano*, for example, explicitly rejected protrust social Darwinist arguments.[49] The journal was not alone in this position.[50] In fact, científicos viewed foreign trusts both in social Darwinist terms and as an extremely negative phenomenon. Limantour's point of view concerning railroad trusts is a case in point. Railroad trusts were not a marginal concern. To the contrary, the threat of a railroad merger between two powerful U.S.–owned lines was advertised in official documents and the press repeatedly during the first decade of the twentieth century. Moreover, the fact that the Mexican government nationalized the U.S.–owned railroads in a piecemeal fashion also generated extensive coverage of the issue.

In the railroad trust discourse, Limantour stood social Darwinist protrust arguments on their head. Trusts, rather than an improvement upon the market, turned it into a war zone in which the powerful absorbed the weak. Foreign railroad trusts threatened to overcome or absorb the Mexican nation. Limantour used subtle social Darwinist terminology in his discourse. He described the process by which one railroad line took control over another as "absorption" and defined this general phenomenon as a "battle." To explain government involvement in the issue he announced that the state needed to "intervene in the fight." The immediate issue at stake in this Darwinian struggle was control over the market, for command over the railroad lines would translate into market domination. In this scenario, Limantour warned, a foreign trust would have effective power over Mexico's national and international commerce.[51] *El Economista Mexicano* echoed Limantour's assertion, maintaining that the trust "threatened to strangle the national traffic, not only in the interior of the republic, but also lines to the exterior."[52] The central issue was not commerce but sovereignty. Limantour maintained that a trust would exploit Mexican territory like a vanquished nation.[53] He warned that the railroad trust would wield tremendous political power, exerting pressure on "public questions."[54]

In the nationalist climate that characterized the last decade of the Porfiriato, it is not surprising that científico Olegario Molina (1843–1925), a Yucatecan politician and entrepreneur who became minister of development during the last years of Díaz's reign, echoed Limantour's nationalist argument when proposing mining legislation in 1908. Also in keeping with the topic of the railroad trust, mining legislation received extensive attention in the press.[55] The most controversial part of the legislation was article 144, which prohibited foreigners from owning mining enterprises. This was a legislative turnaround in the sense that legislative reforms in the 1880s and 1890s had strengthened private property rights and foreign investors' power vis-à-vis the state. Molina justified the article on the same grounds Limantour had rationalized railroad nationalization. Molina argued that foreign capital could be employed to create a trust against which the Mexican nation would be powerless. Thus he portrayed restricting foreign ownership as a means to protect sovereignty. He explained that with the "restrictive" legislation "it would be difficult for the national mining businesses to fall into the hands of powerful foreign trusts, over which neither our government nor our laws can exercise any authority."[56]

In 1907 Peust penned an overarching theoretical analysis of the effects of foreign capital that was in keeping with the contentions of Limantour and Molina, for it depicted foreign economic power as a threat to sovereignty. He argued that there was an "immense" difference between foreign and national control over key industries and cited Venezuelan railroads and Cuban sugar as two examples. He maintained that foreign economic power translated into foreign political domination, for key economic policy questions would be decided not by the host country but by the governments representing foreign entrepreneurs. He defined this as "imperialism" and claimed it was a worldwide phenomenon: "From the extreme Orient to South Africa to the states of Latin America one encounters imperialism more and more, that is to say, the aspirations of the grand powers to obtain any form of political hegemony over countries in which they have invested their immense capital."[57] In this age of economic nationalism Peust's analysis was not unique in Mexico or the Western world, for Western contemporaries developed economic theories of imperialism during this era.[58] Even though Peust's analysis of the impact of foreign capital was in keeping with the position of his Mexican contemporaries, his language was distinct. Unlike Peust, liberals rarely used the term *imperialism* in their accounts of foreign economic power and domination.

Liberals' position on foreign workers paralleled that on foreign capital. They deemed foreign blood simultaneously as safeguarding sovereignty and posing a threat to national authority. The nationalist backlash in the case of labor was highly visible but perhaps not as prominent as in the case of foreign investment, for Mexico had not been very successful in attracting foreign immigrants. In fact, the Díaz regime rejected government-sponsored immigration in the 1890s, claiming that it had not been successful.

Raigosa stressed the significance of the labor force in the international struggle for existence. He claimed that it was the central factor that determined the international pecking order. He based his assertion on the labor theory of value: "Because labor is the source of value, the nation where labor is utilized and managed most effectively will necessarily be the richest, the most prosperous, occupying the highest level of human welfare, and be called to preside over the civilization of the world."[59] Raigosa's contention that the nation with the strongest labor force "presided" over world civilization implied a struggle with winners and losers.

The technical journal *El Consultor*, edited by Manuel Francisco Álvarez (1842–1926), the president of Mexico's leading technical school, the Escuela Nacional de Artes y Oficios, sustained a similar argument, claiming that Mexico was engaged in a "struggle for life" but "without arms." The main threat was Mexico's "industrial fight with superior races." The journal argued that the way Mexico fared in the war hinged upon the quality of the labor force.[60]

Given this discourse about a Darwinian battle for survival, it is not surprising that the debate about foreign immigration examined not only the theme of wealth (as outlined in the previous chapter) but also the theme of sovereignty. Bulnes, for example, contended that "the immigration problem for Mexico, as for Chile, Argentina and Brazil, is a question of life or death; to forget it is to resign oneself to perish." Making this same point on another occasion, he equated immigration with "salvation" and contended it was essential to "conserve nationality."[61] Bulnes's position was paradoxical, for he saw national sovereignty as standing upon foreign foundations. Yet his argument is comprehensible when one considers that he denigrated Mexico's indigenous population.

Sierra also contended that attracting foreign workers was essential to national survival, but, unlike Bulnes, he envisioned miscegenation as the means to improve the workforce: "We still need to attract European immigrants, whose blood is the only one that should be crossed with the indigenous race if we don't want to descend to an inferior level, which would result in regression, not evolution." Sierra linked foreigners to sovereignty, for he warned that if Mexico was not able to attract immigrants, "death" would be the result.[62] Sierra's and Bulnes's assertions resembled Raigosa's thesis about the relationship between the labor force and national power. Political sovereignty depended—at least in part—upon the quality of the labor force. Since Sierra claimed that European immigration was essential to national existence, his analysis had overtones of European racial justifications for imperialism. Nevertheless, by stressing the positive effects of miscegenation he explicitly countered Gustave Le Bon, a leading European racial theorist who contended that miscegenation had negative consequences.[63]

A growing concern in late Porfirian Mexico that U.S. infiltration jeopardized sovereignty also countered imperialist discourses. Indeed, liberals' ambivalence about the consequences of "superior" races on the nation separated them from European racial imperialists, who stressed the positive impact of superior races. The liberals' contradictory position also divided them from European anti-imperialists, who tended to reject the notion that superior races had any beneficial effect. A final distinction can be made. The liberals focused on what scholars term *informal imperialism*, while most of the European racially based pro- and anti-imperialist discussions were about formal colonialism.[64]

Sierra's theory of assimilation is essential to understanding the liberal diatribe against foreigners. As noted above, Sierra contended that foreigners would strengthen the national organism by assimilating into it. The problem was, according to some analysts, that foreigners—and, again, particularly U.S. workers and entrepreneurs—were not assimilating. In this context, foreigners became, so to speak, a nation within a nation. In this alienated state they became a powerful foreign force that threatened to overpower, even absorb, the national organism.

Raigosa penned a frightening version of this scenario. He defined the population as the leading national problem in a study he published in 1900.[65] The dilemma, which he demonstrated with a statistical analysis, was that Americans held all the important and powerful jobs in Mexico, especially those related to commerce and production. In contrast, the vast majority of Mexicans were economically inactive or held menial jobs such as household servants and peons. And even the better employed Mexicans did not penetrate the industrial sector, for they held literary and bureaucratic positions. Raigosa, employing biological metaphors, asserted that foreign workers did not assimilate into Mexican society: "[There is a] growing infiltration in all the tissues of the national organism due to the continued affluence, crossing the vast and porous diaphragm of our border, of a profound penetrating current that does not mix with anything existing, that does not have close affinities, or remote ones, with our habits, tendencies, or language." He argued that rather than strengthening the national organism, unassimilated U.S. nationals weakened it. He explained that Americans were "relegating the Mexican more and more to the simple life of a day laborer, closing the horizons of the race and accentuating the features of its regressive evolution."

Raigosa contended that U.S. workers placed Mexican sovereignty in jeopardy: "They [Americans] are better armed for the 'battle for existence' thanks to an education that is superior in every way. Their industrial and practical education, applied to science, has given them the most powerful instrument of their own elevation." Raigosa's depiction of the Mexican masses emphasized Mexico's subordinate position in the conflict. He explained that, given "the present conditions of individual inferiority of the large masses, [they are unable] to compete successfully in the workforce."[66]

Luis Mendez, president of the Academia Central Mexicana de Legislación y Jurisprudencia (Mexican Academy of Legislation and Jurisprudence), echoed Raigosa's position. Stressing foreigners' lack of integration, he described them as a "nation within a nation." Developing this contention, he asserted that by "custom, tendencies, language, and interests they maintain links to . . . [their] nationality of origin." In keeping with Raigosa, Mendez maintained that "the entire future of the country we inherited from our fathers depends upon finding a proper solution [to the problem of foreign domination]."[67]

In the context of this nationalist discourse, even conflicts between capital and labor were couched in nationalist rhetoric. *El Progreso Latino* repeatedly depicted the conflict between capital and labor in Mexico as a consequence of the fact that foreigners were paid more than Mexicans.[68] Mexican workers also articulated a nationalist labor ideology. Native mine, railroad, and oil workers protested against the fact that foreigners received higher pay and superior living quarters. A popular saying of the age, "Mexico for Mexicans," expressed such nationalist sentiment.[69] A Mexican railroad journal, *El Ferrocarrilero*, depicted this popular movement in nationalist social Darwinist language that echoed Raigosa and Mendez. The journal claimed that foreign workers' domination of the railroad industry was a form of "peaceful conquest."[70] By highlighting the conflict between native and foreign workers, the journal deflected attention from the problem of capital-labor strife, a conflict that was severe by 1906.[71] (Liberals also minimized the problem by asserting that capital-labor conflict was only a problem in the more industrialized nations.)[72]

Consistent with their opinions about foreign capital and labor, liberals articulated a contradictory nationalist treatise about international commerce. Once again, they did not fear all international commerce but particularly U.S. commercial interests, since both Mexican imports and exports were heavily concentrated with the United States.[73] *El Economista Mexicano* maintained that commercial relations with the United States were essential to national development. The journal described this commercial interchange, in which Mexico imported capital goods and exported raw materials, as "reciprocal." It argued that importing U.S. capital goods was essential to Mexico's industrialization. Since Mexico lacked the heavy industry and technology needed to industrialize, importation was essential: "Mexico will need—every day in greater quantities—materials and elements to construct industry." Furthermore, the journal depicted Mexico's concentration of exports to the United States as positive and natural, since the two nations were neighbors.[74] Others reiterated this position. Thus, commercial relations with the United States strengthened Mexico economically.

But liberals also contended that international commerce placed Mexican sovereignty in jeopardy. This position turned the theory of comparative advantage, which suggested that the international commercial order was harmonious and reciprocal, on its head by maintaining that the international commodity market was ruled by brute force. Overproduction made exporting a necessity for the industrialized nations.[75] (Interestingly, there was also discussion of a Mexican "overproduction" problem.)[76] In fact, some analysts maintained that modern colonial wars were inspired by industrialized nations' need to secure consumer markets in an age of global protectionism.[77] Sierra contended that modern imperialism in Africa and Asia was caused by economic factors.[78]

Liberals did not portray commercially inspired formal colonialism as a threat in Mexico, however. Formal economic imperialism did not make sense, since the United States already dominated the Mexican market. Indeed, *El Progreso Latino* maintained that strong economic ties between the United States and Mexico were a deterrent to American military intervention.[79] Rather than formal imperialism, liberals portrayed U.S. commercial hegemony as a form of informal control.[80] Their concern was mainly about Mexican exports, not American imports.[81] In fact, their main complaint was that the United States possessed a form of monopoly control over Mexican exports that prohibited Mexico from exporting to other nations. From this perspective, U.S. political power exerted a neomercantilist form of control over Mexican exports.

Some depicted U.S. commercial hegemony as a threat to sovereignty. Limantour asserted that the United States had sought to dominate Mexico commercially through special trade treaties. He noted that a component of the U.S. strategy was to "destroy our commerce with Europe" in order to transform Mexico into an "economic and intellectual dependency of that powerful entity [the United States]."[82] *El Progreso Latino*, too, maintained that U.S. attempts to block Mexico's trade with Europe placed sovereignty in jeopardy: "There is no doubt that North

American commercial control in Mexico, which is precisely what is obstructing our trade with England and France, . . . can be deadly for the country, like all great entrapments."[83]

U.S. reexports of Mexican goods were identified as a component of the former's commercial and political hegemony. *El Progreso Latino* explained the problem: the United States "is not only our largest consumer, in the proper sense of the word, but also our largest buyer, because . . . it is our distributor, the secondhand seller of our products to third parties who are largely unknown to us."[84] Economist Alberto Carreño even implied that reexports were a form of slavery. After discussing the gravity of the problem, he maintained that establishing direct trade between Mexico and other nations would "free [Mexican exporters] of the yoke imposed by North American consumers."[85]

The State's Role in the Economy

According to liberals, then, the infiltration of American capital, workers, and commerce posed serious threats to Mexico's sovereignty. Liberals rejected a laissez-faire solution to this conflict. Raigosa explicitly condemned a laissez-faire solution to resolve the struggle between Mexican and foreign workers; rather, he advocated that the "national brain" (i.e., the state) intervene to protect Mexican sovereignty.[86] Similarly, *El Progreso Latino* rejected a laissez-faire solution to the trust problem: "The laissez-faire, laissez-passer of the old economists can no longer be practiced, because it leaves society in the hands of the greedy exploiters."[87]

This marked a serious breach with Spencer's brand of social Darwinism, for he had argued forcefully against state intervention in the struggle for survival; market forces should determine the outcome.[88] Writing from Britain, the imperial center, it is hardly surprising that Spencer took a laissez-faire stance. Neither is it astonishing that liberals rejected Spencer's argument, given Mexico's subordinate position in the world economy. In the age of monopoly capitalism and economic imperialism, liberals maintained that state intervention was necessary to protect sovereignty. *El Economista Mexicano* reported that state intervention was on the rise in part because of the emergence of powerful monopolies. As a result, Spencer's assertion that individuals had to be protected from the state overlooked the central issue: "Who would protect the individual from the individual?"[89] For the Mexican case a more apt question would be, Who would protect Mexico from foreign economic domination?

Despite the fact that liberals attacked foreign domination and championed state intervention in the economy, they did not articulate an anticapitalist discourse. Instead, they championed capitalism but from the perspective of an undeveloped nation. Sierra best articulated this position. He contended that the state was an indispensable tool to promote progress in "nations that had formed late and with much difficulty." Invoking the threat of "our neighbors," Sierra suggested that the central issue was not progress but sovereignty. For Sierra, then, because of the limited development of the "social organism," state tutelage was essential to safeguard national existence.[90] In keeping with Sierra's position, *El Economista Mexicano* and *El Imparcial* claimed that, owing to the weakness of civil society, only a more developed Mexican state had the power to protect the country from powerful foreign trusts. This perspective was entirely compatible with liberals' negative views of Mexico's indigenous population. Revealing this pessimistic outlook, *El Imparcial* contended that U.S. citizens could effectively combat trusts but that in Mexico the state was obliged to assume this task.[91]

These assumptions about the state and foreigners clearly influenced the solutions proposed by Limantour and Molina to foreign control over the railroads and mines. Limantour strongly suggested that the foreign railroad trusts were an unstoppable force, for he contended that the only absolute protection against them was nationalization.[92] *El Economista Mexicano* agreed, contending that national sovereignty was at stake: "If the state does not exercise control over the railroads, the railroads will exercise control over the state."[93] It appears that there was widespread consensus on this, for even the liberal opposition press lauded the Mexicanization of the railroads.[94] For Molina, too, powerful mining trusts could not be controlled. They had to be abolished. Liberals' position, then, was that railroad nationalization should not be mistaken for a command economy or socialism. In fact, they protested against this depiction of nationalization. Rather, nationalization was a defensive act.[95] During the age of empire, Mexico, a little-evolved nation, had to protect itself against foreign hegemony.

Liberals' solution to foreign domination of the labor force, too, championed state intervention. Rather than let market forces determine the outcome of the conflict between Mexican and foreign workers, they advocated public compulsory education for the indigenous population. State education would strengthen Mexican workers' position vis-à-vis foreign workers. Liberals did not envision education as a force to emancipate Indians from ignorance or to turn them into citizens but rather to make them productive workers. Indeed, some stressed forging a workforce to such an extent that they criticized a project to turn Indians into smallholders that had been forwarded by liberals during the Reforma on the grounds that it would shrink the size of the labor pool.[96]

This focus on forging a workforce was reflected in the importance given to technical education.[97] In the last chapter I noted that liberals championed technical education as a means to create a labor force. But there was a strong nationalist flavor to the discourse surrounding technical education. *El Progreso Latino*, for example, contended that educated Mexican workers could not be "conquered" foreign forces.[98] Technical education also played a significant role in liberals' plan to Mexicanize the railroad workers. Educated Mexicans would replace foreign workers. This same nationalist strain was prominent in Sierra's calls for compulsory national education. He based his appeals on concern with sovereignty, not knowledge or civilization. He also maintained that increased contact with U.S. citizens posed a grave danger to Mexico. They could dominate Mexicans to such an extent that the "character" of the latter would disappear: "The distinctive national features, although vague and indecisive, will be recast in stronger races and will disappear in the period of economic battle that began . . . the moment an American locomotive crossed the Bravo [Rio Grande]."[99] Yet there was a way to protect sovereignty and identity: state education. Education would strengthen the indigenous population and thus, Sierra argued, better prepare the nation for the struggle for survival with superior races. "The transformation of the indigenous class into a progressive class . . . [is] a condition sine qua non to the conservation of our social personality in America."[100]

El Consultor reprinted Sierra's nationalist rhetoric, highlighting a passage that warned that without education the Mexican nation could be absorbed by superior races: "We run the risk of not appearing fundamentally civilized and thus only apt to form an inferior group destined to be absorbed by a superior group with which we have intimate contact if the education of the popular masses . . . is not realized."[101] *El Consultor* likewise maintained that without technical education Mexico would be vanquished by "superior races." The journal explained that foreigners dominated Mexicans because of their "mental and physical superiority" and maintained that, consequently, foreigners would defeat Mexicans: "It is a natural law that the weak will always be vanquished when they are obligated to do battle with the strong." The paper employed a medical metaphor to show that education would fortify the Mexicans and thus better prepare them for the battle. The journal explained that the "doctor" needed to "inject" the "dying patient" (i.e., Mexico) with "technical-industrial schools" to "prolong life."[102]

This educational discourse reveals that nationalist rhetoric should not be equated with a "back to the roots" ideology of *indigenismo*, or nativism. Despite the fact that liberals' discourse was nationalist, it failed to embrace or valorize the indigenous population. On the contrary, Indians, in their present state, were useless. Only Indians that could be transformed into workers by an activist state were worthwhile.

Liberals depicted the labor market as a war zone not only from a nationalist perspective but also along gender lines, albeit much less frequently. But in the latter struggle they took an entirely different position, advocating that the market dictate the outcome. Andrés Molina Enríquez articulated a position that agreed with the liberal analysis. He argued that there was competition between Mexican men and women in the labor market and explicitly claimed that women could not survive, contending that they "lack[ed] aptitude to maintain themselves in the unequal battle of work with men."[103] He did not advocate government intervention to aid women, for he asserted that women were not fit for the workplace but only for child rearing. He was aware of feminist currents that promoted equality between the sexes but dismissed them, asserting that "feminism is a true absurdity." He claimed that the movement to create working women would fail because women were "inevitably defeated in the battles of work." He took an extreme position on the issue, asserting that even women in financial need should not work, for this need demonstrated that men were doing an inadequate job in their role of provider; hence, the solution to the problem was obligating men to fulfill their duty.[104]

Similarly, Sierra did not champion education to fortify women and thus strengthen their position in the labor market, as he had with Mexican men in their battle with foreigners. Rather, he promoted the education of women to be better homemakers. For Sierra, who explicitly countered a feminist position by warning women not to "bring your feminism to the point where you want to convert yourself into men," education was not intended to introduce women to the market but to make them successful in the domestic sphere. Explaining the compatibility between these two ends, he claimed that those who saw a conflict had it all wrong: "All to the contrary, the educated and instructed woman will be truly fitted for the home." Reinforcing this position, Sierra outlined the complementary roles played by men and women. The former's responsibility lay in the public sphere and the latter's in the private realm: "While they [males] take responsibility for the material part, to acquire sustenance, your [females'] responsibility is for the order, tranquility, and well-being of the home and, above all, to contribute with a superior food to form souls, to form spirits." Sierra's assertion that "politics" and "law" be left to men, too, made it clear that women's moral role did not expand into the public sphere.[105] His prescriptions were in accordance with the dominant discourse on women's education, which stressed domestic education.[106] More generally, Sierra's and Molina Enríquez's positions on women were in keeping with the separate spheres ideology that was popular during the era.[107]

Thus, there was an inconsistency in Sierra's and Molina Enríquez's rhetoric about male and female Mexican workers. In the case of the former, state intervention was called for to aid Mexican men in their battle with foreign workers. In the case of the latter, in keeping with Spencer's position, they advocated following the dictates of the market. This inconsistency was also apparent in liberals' adherence to biological determinism. In the case of women, biological determinism was invoked to support the idea that women's principal function was reproductive.[108] On the other hand, liberals rejected the proimperialist idea that the white race was biologically superior and thus should rule other nations. For liberals, women's economic subordination to men was positive and even appropriate, but Mexicans workers' inferiority to foreign workers was unacceptable.

Similarly, liberals protested against foreign commercial domination. The overarching idea behind liberals' proposals for trade reform was to weaken America's commercial stranglehold over Mexico by diversifying trade partners. This concern for diversification became greater in the final two or three years of the Porfiriato, but it was not a laissez-faire discourse. On the contrary, it depicted international commerce as guided and controlled by imperial powers as opposed to market forces. Mexico needed to use interventionist strategies to break free of U.S. commercial domination.

Europe played a particularly significant role in this strategy, which envisaged commercial ties with Europe as a counterweight to U.S. commercial domination.[109] This echoed Díaz's strategy of weakening the power of American capital by favoring European capital. Liberals also discussed increasing trade with Latin America, and especially Central America, quite extensively.[110] The principal strategies they promoted to diversify trade were improving Mexico's infrastructure and merchant marine, placing Mexican trade agents in foreign countries to familiarize foreigners with Mexican goods, and creating trade treaties that would facilitate diversification.[111]

Scholars generally treat discussions about the economy as pertaining solely to issues related to "development." This chapter, in contrast, has shown that a significant strain in liberals' discourse about the international economy was political. For them, the central issue was not economic growth but national sovereignty. In fact, they represented the international market, particularly U.S. expansion into Mexico, as jeopardizing sovereignty to such an extent that the threat of foreign militaries and hostile foreign diplomacy became insignificant. Geography, material conditions, and ideological trends inspired the attack on U.S. economic expansion. Not only did U.S. economic interests expand, they also concentrated into a powerful form of monopoly capitalism. The ideological influences of positivism, social Darwinism, and economic and racial determinism interacted with these material and geographic factors to engender a nationalist critique of U.S. economic power. The influence of positivism, with its organic conception of society, facilitated a nationalist application of social Darwinism. Economic determinism suggested that the market was the battlefield upon which the struggle for existence was waged. Given liberals' assumptions that Mexico was racially and economically weak, it is unsurprising that they feared U.S. economic hegemony.

The liberal discourse about the international economy established national priorities. By defining sovereignty as the central concern, issues such as political democracy and the distribution of wealth within Mexico took a back seat. The stress on national production to safeguard sovereignty underscored Mexicans' role as workers as opposed to consumers, which also served to deemphasize the issue of the way the economic pie was divided. Focusing on the international menace also minimized the problems of class and racial tensions within Mexico. The liberal position also affected policy, for liberals invoked the threat of U.S. expansion to explain and justify policies on immigration, education, commerce, finance, and the regulation and nationalization of foreign enterprises.

Liberals had a paradoxical impact on national identity. Despite powerful nationalist strains, their writings erected the Mexican nation on foreign foundations. While Bulnes's model was perhaps extreme in that it totally rejected a national element in Mexican identity, even Sierra's assimilationist model defined foreigners as superior. Liberals' worship of foreigners stemmed from their adherence to racial determinism, evolutionary thought, and social Darwinism: the atavistic Mexican organism/nation had to be fortified with foreign blood and capital if it was to survive and evolve. Foreigners, particularly northern Europeans, were not mere window dressing. Sovereignty, paradoxically, was dependent upon them. This made for a contradictory national identity, for it was intensely nationalist but also denigrated the national population and held foreigners in esteem. Even the statist discourse that called for the regulation and nationalization of foreign interests did not reject foreign models. By eschewing foreigners and embracing the national state, it just chose a new tool to effect Mexico's modernization.

4 "Egotistical Capitalism"

The Evils of the Market in Trinidad Sánchez Santos's Rhetoric

Social Catholicism, a movement that originated in nineteenth-century Europe, became influential in Mexico during the late Porfiriato. This chapter analyzes the market discourse of social Catholicism's leading publicist in Porfirian Mexico, Trinidad Sánchez Santos. For him, the market was an almighty but extremely negative force. It was the principal cause of the "social problem," that is, poverty, a widening class divide, capital-labor strife, radicalism, and the dissolution of the family. Thus, the market defined his crusade, for he portrayed it as the main social villain. It also shaped his reform platform. He represented it as a demon to be exorcized and constructed the moral economic order he championed to replace it as the antithesis of the hellish market.

Conceived broadly, Sánchez Santos's rhetoric paralleled developmentalist liberalism. Stressing economics and deemphasizing politics, he presented the market as the dominant symbol in his editorials. Discussing commerce, workers, and material progress, he focused on some of the same issues as liberals. Market rhetoric also played a decisive role in the formation of his identity and platform. Despite these general similarities, his market discourse was distinct. In contrast to liberals' ambivalence regarding the market's strength and effects, for Sánchez Santos it was consistently a powerful and destructive force. His Christian concept of genesis and rejection of an evolutionary concept of creation directed him to downplay the issue of race. Since Sánchez Santos conceptualized the world from an international Catholic perspective, he minimized nationalism. In contrast to liberals' racialist-nationalist discourse, he highlighted the family and class relations. Also departing from liberals, his social critique and reform program were more ideological than structural. He defined the ideology of "liberal political economy" as opposed to liberal economic structures (such as private property) as the principal problem.[1] Consistent with this critique, the thrust of his reform agenda was adopting a different economic philosophy. He advocated replacing liberal political economy with Christian political economy, an economic vision, he maintained, that rejected the liberal tenets of materialism and individualism by using morality and collectivism as its philosophical building blocks.

Trinidad Sánchez Santos and Developmentalist Liberalism

Even though Sánchez Santos focused his attack on ideology, developmentalist liberalism, the dominant ideology in Mexico, was not his target. In contrast to developmentalist liberalism, which stressed order, the collective, and the generation of wealth, Sánchez Santos critiqued an individualist and egalitarian brand of economic liberalism. One might characterize the form of liberalism he attacked as a blend of laissez-faire economic doctrine and egalitarian strands of political liberalism. The model of liberalism he critiqued stressed the individual as opposed to the collective. Further departing from developmentalist liberalism, the form of liberalism he attacked emphasized freedom, emancipation, and equality, not order and social control. Materialism was the only theme that was common to both variants of liberalism, that of the brand Sánchez Santos critiqued and that of the developmentalist liberals.

Why didn't Sánchez Santos attack the positivist variant of liberalism that was dominant in Mexico? The influence of European social Catholicism was a major factor. A strand in European social Catholicism that attacked economic liberalism and laissez-faire became more pronounced in the latter part of the nineteenth century.[2] The works of Pope Leo XIII and Wilhelm Emmanuel von Ketteler, two giants of the movement, clearly illustrate this trend. Wilhelm von Ketteler's pioneering 1864 work, *The Labor Problem and Christianity*, harshly condemned economic liberalism, particularly the commodification of labor and free and unrestricted trade, as the principal cause of the workers' plight.[3] Pope Leo XIII's 1891 encyclical, *Rerum Novarum*, was another key document in social Catholicism.[4] The encyclical forcefully rejected an individualist brand of liberalism. In its stead the encyclical championed a Thomist corporate social order in which not the market but moral and religious principles would regulate economic processes. This corporate-religious system, in which social "justice" was the divine regulator, would relieve workers from the plight they faced under capitalism.[5] Sánchez Santos, who cited both Bishop Ketteler and (especially) Leo XIII, was strongly influenced by this corporatist and anti-laissez-faire trend in social Catholic thought.

Sánchez Santos also cited radical and liberal critics of capitalism such as Henry George and John Kells Ingram in his antimarket diatribe. Whether he was actually influenced by these thinkers or just cited them to gain greater support for his assertions is unclear. Whatever the case may be, the important point is that this radical and liberal critique from which he borrowed also attacked a laissez-faire brand of liberalism, as we will see below. This international anticapitalist discourse, which Sánchez Santos integrated into his social critique, did not focus on the specific variant of liberalism that reigned in Mexico.

Perhaps there were also rhetorical reasons why Sánchez Santos did not critique the dominant form of liberalism in Mexico. In an age marked by economic inequality, economic imperialism, intense capital-labor strife, and the concentration of wealth in the form of mergers and trusts, he constantly pointed out the contradictions in liberalism's emancipatory egalitarian doctrine. During this age of monopoly capitalism, the emancipatory brand of liberalism that Sánchez Santos attacked was an excellent straw man.

His association between monopoly capitalism and feudalism is a case in point. Pointing to an irony in liberalism, Sánchez Santos contended that features of feudalism and monarchy that liberalism had supposedly dissolved actually had reemerged, albeit in new forms. Tyranny, the political force associated with absolute rule that supposedly had been destroyed by liberalism, for instance, endured. More importantly, a new nobility had emerged under liberalism, namely, the kings of capital. He labeled the new nobility the "aristocrats" of oil and railroads and maintained that even though they did not have royal titles they were even mightier than conquistadores and feudal lords: "No feudal lord had the power of Rothschild, no monarch ruled more than Hanna, no conquistador was more terrible than Cecil Rhodes." Special privileges, or *fueros*, aristocratic entitlements that were supposedly destroyed by the leveling force of the market, also survived intact under market society in Sánchez Santos's analysis. He cited usury and speculation as modern privileges.[6] According to Sánchez Santos, the market was directly responsible for the formation of the economic aristocrats, for the "liberty of association and commerce" had facilitated their creation.[7] This contention stood classic liberal dogma on its head, but it fit well with Catholic dogma: individual materialist freedom was a license that led to sin. Thus, Sánchez Santos portrayed liberalism's emancipatory doctrine as an illusion, for while liberalism "proclaimed equality," it really "invented methods to make the rich richer and the poor poorer."[8]

Morality, Materialism, and Markets

The cornerstone of Sánchez Santos's attack on market society focused on materialism and individualism. According to him, these two components of market ideology were intertwined. Indeed, the main social evil he associated with materialism was promoting individual interests over the common good. Thus, materialism and individualism reinforced each other. Sánchez Santos claimed that there were dire consequences to excessive materialism and unchecked individualism. In fact, he attributed what might be described as a laundry list of negative repercussions to unrestrained individualism: "It [unchecked individualism] explains the growing lack of discipline and corruption in youths worldwide, the favorable reputation of divorce, the increase in illegitimate births, privileges that support speculation, monopolies, immense wealth of a few and the bitter poverty of workers, economic disequilibrium, anarchism in towns and the imperialism of governments, in a word, the destruction of order . . . that is the triumph of barbarism."[9] In keeping with this critique, Sánchez Santos lamented that liberal economic ideology had stripped morality from the economic sphere. He expanded upon this critique when he discussed political economists' notions of human nature. He chastised them for conceiving of humans as material beings and claimed that economists had "complete ignorance of true notions of the human personality."[10] He offered a corrective: "Man is necessarily a *moral* being."[11]

Sánchez Santos offered an alternative to the liberal political economy that was consistent with his conception of human nature. Indeed, the central platform of his economic program was reinserting morality into the economic realm. Sánchez Santos, quoting a work on economic doctrines written by the Irish economist John Kells Ingram, invoked the authority of political economy to promote infusing economics with morality. He cited a section of Ingram's work that criticized Adam Smith for overlooking man's moral side and, echoing Ingram's critique, reprimanded liberal political economy for its "materialist current." Further countering the materialist focus of liberal political economy, he championed "Christian political economy," which, in contrast, did "not find it necessary to divorce the moral truths and religious principles, nor was it influenced by materialism."[12]

Sánchez Santos, in essence, protested against the intellectual developments that had occurred in the field of economics during the eighteenth and nineteenth centuries. During this period economics had emerged as an individual discipline divorced from politics and morality. By arguing that self-interested economic actors unwittingly served the greater good, Bernard de Mandeville and Adam Smith had liberated economics from morality.[13] Sánchez Santos's assertions underscored the conceptual development of the emancipation of economics, for he maintained it was the source of social ills. He articulated a theory about the social order that supported his contention that morality needed to be reinserted into the economic realm. According to him, social harmony was created by striking a proper balance between individual desires and societal obligations:

> What is the "condition" of the existence of human society, knowing that its object is the happiness of the individual and society? Well, this condition cannot be anything but securing an order that provides each individual his proper sphere of action . . . [and is] limited by the rights of others. True liberty is nothing but an order in which, like the physical order, balance is obtained by two opposing forces, which are the centrifugal force of individual impulses and the centripetal force of society.

Liberal ideology, however, had upset this harmonious order. "Modern ideas," which Sánchez Santos associated with the "Anglo-Saxon race," had "destroy[ed] the balance between the two powerful social forces, developing . . . individual impulses at the expense of . . . society."[14] Sánchez Santos, then, countered a Smithian formulation in which unrestrained individualism unintentionally resulted in the greater good. To the contrary, a healthy social body could only be realized if individual desires were restrained.

Despite this fundamental difference, there was a similarity between Sánchez Santos's political economy and classical political economy. Both doctrines called for limited state intervention in the economic system, albeit for different reasons. Sánchez Santos, while not confronting the issue directly, implicitly rejected a significant role for the state in the economic system by arguing that countering the reigning ideology of materialism with a strong dose of moralism would largely solve the problems caused by the market. While it would be inaccurate to claim he never supported intervention, he clearly placed less emphasis on it than the *Rerum Novarum* did.[15]

Sánchez Santos's critique of individualism was not totally at odds with the analyses made by liberals and the Partido Liberal Mexicano (PLM). Even if these groups did not frequently attack individualism, their ideologies stressed the collective. On the other hand, Sánchez Santos's position on materialism was in conflict with other Mexican ideologies. As illustrated in chapter 2, liberals embraced materialism, maintaining that evolved groups had a materialist ethos. Not surprisingly, the liberals' position on materialism was at odds with that of Sánchez Santos. Their social critique, which focused on Indians, contended that there was not too much materialism but rather too little. Inculcating Indians with a materialist ethic was one of the liberals' major concerns. There were also significant differences between Sánchez Santos and the liberal and radical opposition. But the bone of contention was not materialism; rather, it was the Church's role in society. Sánchez Santos's moral solution required a greater role for Christian values in civil society. Liberal and radical opponents, in contrast, made a major issue out of reducing the Church's societal role.

The Market and the Labor Force

In keeping with European social Catholicism, the most prominent theme in Sánchez Santos's discourse was the plight of workers under capitalism. Social Catholics and Sánchez Santos were not alone in this focus, for the PLM, too, highlighted labor exploitation. In 1906 labor conditions became a major theme in the national discourse because of increased tensions between capital and labor and highly publicized strong-arm tactics used by the government to break labor. Sánchez Santos's labor discourse employed a similar rhetorical strategy as his feudal treatise. He explicitly challenged a liberal tale that associated a capitalist labor market with workers' emancipation.

Sánchez Santos utilized a variety of rhetorical strategies to counter a liberal narrative. One tactic was to represent the driving force in the creation of the proletariat as coercion: "Machines absorb small workshops everywhere, workers are regrouped in factories, the independent artisan of earlier days is abased and proletarianized." In this passage, proletarianization was the antithesis of freedom. Artisans were forced into the market by the transformation in the process of production. Moreover, by describing artisans as "independent," the passage suggests that the factory signified dependence. Sánchez Santos's rhetorical questions emphasized the negative impact of proletarianization: "Is the worker happier? Is the work more worthwhile? Is the cost of living cheaper and easier?"[16]

Further contesting the association between the market and worker emancipation, Sánchez Santos inverted the meaning of the liberal phrase "freedom to work." He showed that, in reality, labor was controlled by capital. Powerful magnates called the tune by "raising or lowering wages and opening or closing avenues of work."[17] In Sánchez Santos's analysis, capital had the upper hand. He quoted a Spanish Catholic journal that made this same point. The journal argued that labor was not paid for all it produced and maintained that this unequal distribution of wealth was "protected by the same principles of the classical economy." Hence the journal implied that while liberal market rhetoric spoke the language of equality and fairness, it really resulted in worker exploitation.[18] *El Tiempo*, quoting a European social Catholic source, also maintained that the free market did not bring liberty but rather exploitation: "We are not among those that see true progress in the free play of economic forces." These conditions put "workers under the dependence of owners." The paper offered a solution: "Put a brake on the power of capital."[19]

Completely undermining the association between the market and freedom, Sánchez Santos claimed that the conditions of the modern wage worker were akin to those of slaves. He quoted an author that boldly made this claim: "It can be clearly seen that the condition of the modern worker is similar to the old slave, for both of them are obligated, in order to live, to serve machines that produce wealth for the boss without obtaining the elements necessary for meeting their needs."[20] Sánchez Santos pointed to the irony in this similarity between slavery and liberalism, for the latter "proclaimed equality of man and rights for all."[21]

Sánchez Santos made yet another charge against the market: it stripped the humanity from the relationship between workers and owners. The implied villain in this critique was capital's overriding desire for profits. Sánchez Santos, invoking the authority of political economy by citing John Kells Ingram, contended that owners viewed labor not "as humans but as machines."[22] This critique had similarities to Pope Leo XIII's analysis, which criticized capital for conceptualizing labor as a "thing."[23] According to social Catholic doctrine, then, the market divested humanity from the relationship between workers and owners, for capital, guided by materialist desires, viewed workers exclusively as a source of profit or, in other words, as a commodity.

The market also generated heated conflict between capital and labor. Mexican social Catholics did not argue this point forcefully until 1906, when the "worker question"—a phrase that referred to heightened tensions between capital and labor—became a national issue. Sánchez Santos applied his materialism-run-amok thesis to explain the conflict: "Egoism from above [that is, capital] has ignited egoism from below [that is, workers], and the fight between these two forms of egoism is inevitable, like the collision of two locomotives that come at each other from opposite direction on the same track and have no brakes."[24]

El Tiempo had a similar analysis. The paper represented materialism as the reigning ideology for both the working class and capital. The paper maintained that these groups were driven by a thirst for "gold." The dominance of a materialist ethic made conflict inevitable: "From this arises the owner's desire to pay little and gain much and the worker's desire to work little and gain much, and from here the war that is insensible to reason between the worker and owner."[25] Thus, materialist ideology inevitably resulted in capital-labor conflict.

At the same time as capital-labor conflict became an issue of national debate, a related topic, radicalism, also received extensive attention in the press. In the context of increased conflict between capital and labor and the rise of the PLM, the emergence of radical worker movements became a popular topic of discussion. In Sánchez Santos's rhetoric on the causes of radicalism, the market was the principal villain. In an editorial entitled "El anarquismo y sus factores económicos" (Anarchism and its economic factors), Sánchez Santos explained that anarchism followed from a "feeling of desperation in the masses of the proletariat caused by the poverty that results from a system of distribution of wealth under which riches are accumulated in the hands of a few . . . while the majority remain unable to provide for . . . their necessities."[26] He contended that poverty radicalized workers. The poor came to hate the rich and falsely believe that their salvation lay not in God but in socialism. The dominance of the materialist ideology also made Mexicans susceptible to radical doctrines. Sánchez Santos quoted a passage from Victor Hugo to make this point. It stated that when humans' sole purpose was to satisfy material needs, they became desperate, for they lacked religious faith, which revealed that suffering was a "law of God." He interpreted Hugo, contending that people needed to have faith in something more than "material well-being."[27] By portraying radicalism as a consequence of economic liberalism, Sánchez Santos was following an argument made in the *Rerum Novarum*. In contrast, the Díaz regime blamed radicalism on foreign agitators.

In keeping with Sánchez Santos's central thesis, infusing Mexicans with proper moral values was the main solution he offered to resolve the conflict between capital and labor. He voiced this moral solution in a critique of *El Imparcial*. He claimed that the financial solution that *El Imparcial* advocated to resolve the conflict between capital and labor was unworkable.[28] He contended that "[t]he primary [answer to the conflict] is the restoration of Christian customs, for without them all solutions are illusions."[29] Inculcating Mexicans with a moral ethic, it appears, would resolve tensions by encouraging capital and labor to focus on their responsibilities to society as opposed to their individual desires.

Sánchez Santos's representation of the social order made his solution to the worker problem appear reasonable. He depicted humans, and, in particular, capital and labor, not as individuals but as a part of a corporate order. He was following Pope Leo XIII, who cited St. Thomas to support his claim that workers and owners were not individuals but part of "the same thing," or a corporate whole.[30]

This social body was not egalitarian and horizontal but rather hierarchical and vertical. A complete social leveling was not only impossible but against God's plan. Despite inequalities, capital and labor were not antagonistic but complementary. As Pope Leo XIII explained, they were interdependent. One could not exist without the other. If each group knew its proper station and fulfilled its social obligations, then harmony could be achieved.

Even after the conflict between capital and labor emerged as a national problem in 1906, pro-Porfirian ideologues attempted to downplay the issue, contending that capital-labor relations were harmonious. They contrasted Mexico with Europe, arguing that conditions in the latter that had resulted in labor strife were absent in Mexico. Despite this attempt to sweep this issue under the rug, Sánchez Santos and the social Catholics were not the only ones who discussed the exploitation of workers. The PLM, too, stressed this issue. The two were not in agreement about the ways to improve conditions for workers, however. *Regeneración*, the PLM's periodical, disagreed with social Catholics' solution, which stressed capital-labor harmony: "How can you reconcile these two interests [those of capital and labor] diametrically opposed? In no way." The paper charged that social Catholics' policy of reconciliation weakened the labor movement: "Friars . . . want to divert the tendencies of the Mexican workers movement."[31]

Market, Family, and Society

Sánchez Santos discussed the ways in which the market economy hurt not only workers but also families. The family was a central theme for him, for rather than individuals, Sánchez Santos posited an organic society composed of families. Stressing the immense significance of the integrity of the family unit, Sánchez Santos claimed that it was the foundation of civil society. He stressed the family much more than liberals and radicals. The former emphasized a larger collective identity, the social organism, and the latter highlighted the working class.

Sánchez Santos attacked the market in his discourse about the family. He argued that market workers' meager earnings were insufficient to support a family. It should be noted, however, that the prominence of the market in his dialogue about the destruction of the family varied. Sometimes the market was an explicit villain, but more often it was implicit, for low wages were not always directly linked to market capitalism. In fact, on one occasion Sánchez Santos even subscribed to a liberal explanation for low wages: limited productivity.[32]

Sánchez Santos's writings on the family were based upon his gendered conceptions of the public and private spheres. He represented the public realm of the market as male and the domestic domain as female. He explained that women reigned in the "home."[33] Sánchez Santos's position followed the *Rerum Novarum*, which asserted that women were "born for domestic affairs."[34] In this analysis, women were responsible for reproduction and the moral education of the family. Women's moral influence extended over their husbands as well as their children. Men, on the other hand, were the breadwinners.

There was a dynamic relationship between the public and private spheres. Women's moral domestic role, Sánchez Santos contended, had a profound influence on the public sphere. Stressing this influence, he explained workers' unacceptable behavior by pointing to deficiencies in the domestic sphere: unmarried workers were promiscuous and transient laborers, shifting from job to job in search of new lovers. He complained that "the family does not exist." To right this situation he proposed that workers "needed to be civilized," a task he delegated to the domestic sphere, asserting that "civil society begins in the home." The private sphere, then, had a profound impact on the public realm. Not only did it restrain males' sexuality, but it created a stable workforce. Conversely, the existence of the domestic sphere was dependent upon the male worker, for only if men provided for the family's economic needs could women perform their domestic duties.[35]

The market, however, was breaking down this proper division between the public and private spheres. Sánchez Santos quoted an author who explained the way this disintegration was occurring in Europe: "The conditions of the market and the law of capital do not always permit the worker, with only his salary, to satisfy the needs of his [family]." Consequently, mothers and children were forced into the workforce. The result was the dissolution of the family: "The moment this [the wife is forced to work] happens, the family is seriously threatened. The worker only sees his [family] for brief moments. The woman is obligated to give the care of her children and the domestic work to strange hands, almost always hired. Who can be surprised that in these conditions the working family has disappeared from some industrial regions of Germany and will disappear from other regions of Europe?" Sánchez Santos clearly thought the German example had relevance for his Mexican readers. He asserted that "these reflections by a celebrated author have suggested very important ideas that we will explain further another day."[36]

The insufficient wages received by men, particularly "Indian" males, also forced children into the labor force, according to Sánchez Santos. He maintained that under the current wage levels there were no alternatives to child labor. He made this point forcefully in a debate about the education of Indian children. Sánchez Santos claimed that low wages made child labor a necessity to the survival of the Indian family. Thus, education was useless, since Indians could not afford to attend school. He argued that once the economic problem was solved, Indians would not have to be compelled to attend school but would go on their own initiative.[37] Children, then, faced the same problem that women, particularly mothers, confronted. They were forced into the market by economic necessity and thus were unable to engage in appropriate activities.

In contrast to liberals, Sánchez Santos's analysis suggested that the root of the "Indian" problem was economic as opposed to racial. Perhaps Catholic doctrine steered Sánchez Santos away from racial explanations. After all, the most radical forms of racial determinism were grounded in the notion of polygenism, a concept that was totally at odds with the Christian notion of creation.[38] True, polygenism had been rejected by the second half of the nineteenth century. However, theories of racial hierarchy that replaced it were based in a Darwinian notion of evolution, a concept that also countered a Christian view.[39]

Sánchez Santos argued that low wages threatened the very existence of the family. Male workers elected not to marry and raise families because they did not have the financial means to support a wife and children. The problem was not that men wanted lives of luxury for their families; rather, they were not able to provide the basic necessities of food, clothing, shelter, and education. Sánchez Santos stressed the gravity of the problem, claiming that the very basis of human society, that is, reproduction of the population, was seriously threatened.[40] To counter the problem of low salaries Sánchez Santos championed the family wage. Stressing the immense significance of the issue as well as the importance of the family unit to social stability, he stated: "It is necessary to incessantly repeat it: the question of salaries is intimately linked to the whole social order."[41]

His discourse on wages countered that of *El Imparcial*, for the semiofficial periodical contended that wages were determined by the "laws of supply and demand."[42] Sánchez Santos's position was in keeping with Pope Leo XIII, who explicitly attacked the notion that the market should be the divine arbiter by contending that the "unchecked greed of competition" was one of the forces that caused the deterioration of workers' existence.[43] The pope argued that not the market but rather workers' needs should dictate wages. He maintained that wages "should be sufficient for the sustenance of a frugal worker."[44] Sánchez Santos, reprinting an article from a Catholic journal from Madrid, echoed the pope's position, contending that workers were not "goods" and that wages should not be determined by the laws of supply and demand; rather, wages, considered as compensation for human work, should be sufficient to meet "the necessities for the conservation of the worker's existence."[45] Following the pope's encyclical, Sánchez

Santos advocated a combination of "indirect" state intervention, employer initiative, and workers unions to increase wages. He contended that relying on charity alone was insufficient.[46]

Not only the worker and the family but also society were negatively affected by the market, according to Sánchez Santos. His societal analysis condemned the capitalist distribution system, for he maintained that under it Mexicans did not have access to basic necessities. While his analysis of the problem was unique, Mexicans of all political views were concerned about the issue. Rising prices placed basic goods out of the economic reach of many Mexicans during the last years of the Porfiriato.[47]

Neo-Thomist thought informed Sánchez Santos's analysis. He conceived of society as a hierarchical corporate body. Social equilibrium was realized when all parts of the corporate body functioned properly. Disequilibrium occurred when one of the parts malfunctioned.[48] Based on this theoretical edifice, Sánchez Santos defined Mexicans' inability to gain access to basic goods (food, shelter, clothing, education) as an "economic disequilibrium." From Sánchez Santos's corporate worldview, the disequilibrium had a negative impact on the entire society. No wonder he spilled much ink on the problem.[49]

Economic disequilibrium was a grave problem, for Sánchez Santos equated exchange (that is, equilibrium) with not only social well-being but also national existence: "The prime necessity, the supreme condition of social life, is commerce in its fullest expression. Only by exchange of products, services, and ideas between men can there be a society and nation, and they will be more prosperous and stronger when this exchange—commerce—is more active."[50] In another passage, which he based on the ideas of St. Paul and St. Thomas, he made a similar claim: "It [society] cannot exist but for the mutual exchange of services between its members, and it is more perfect when the services given from one to another are more varied and facile."[51] Sánchez Santos was clearly not referring to capitalist commodity exchange; rather, exchange was a form of organic reciprocity, for it expressed the mutual interdependence of all members of society.

Sánchez Santos represented the absence of exchange (i.e., economic disequilibrium) as the antithesis of a healthy society. Indeed, he claimed that the inability to exchange resulted in social "dissolution."[52] Supporting this claim, he repeatedly listed a number of social ills that were generated by economic disequilibrium: health problems such as epidemics; increased infant mortality; and population decline, since Mexican men were electing not to marry because they could not afford to support a family.[53]

Sánchez Santos cited "bestial egoism" as the cause of economic disequilibrium, contending that it existed because "egotistical" Mexicans did not fulfill their obligations to society.[54] He applied the concept of unbridled materialism to explain the problem. Unrestrained materialism in the form of "speculation" resulted in overpriced goods that were out of the economic reach of the masses. Charges of speculation are usually part of a liberal discourse, but this was not the case. Speculation was a consequence of the market as opposed to an aberration from it, for it was a result of too much freedom. Indeed, Sánchez Santos linked speculation to an "'abused freedom of commerce.'"[55] By putting the phrase in quotation marks, it is clear that he was contesting the liberal concept as opposed to reinforcing it. "Free" meant, it appears, a free hand to exploit. On another occasion he made the same claim but singled out railroad companies, charging that they jacked up prices because they had too much "liberty."[56]

Sánchez Santos's rhetoric implied that a commercial system guided by morality as opposed to self-interest would go a long way toward solving distribution problems. A commercial system guided by avarice caused disequilibrium and scarcity, but one governed by morality reaped balance and abundance. For Sánchez Santos, a commercial order guided by morality meant placing societal needs before individual desires: "Before the interest of the merchant . . . is the life of society; before the interests of . . . unchecked speculation are the health and development of the population and the . . . nation." He quoted economist John Kells Ingram to make this same point. Ingram criticized political economy's concept of commerce precisely because it placed too much stress on profits and not enough on morality. Avarice is "the doctrine that has legitimated in large part the commercial and economic movement of modern times, hailing profits the supreme criteria for commercial life, until the point that it seems they have forgotten the moral precepts that guide the commercial order."[57] Morality, that is, societal as opposed to individual interests, should regulate distribution.[58] *La Voz de México*, on one occasion, made a similar point. The paper complained that wealthy Mexicans spent their money on luxury and vice as opposed to the community even though there was a dire need for hospitals and schools. The publication argued that substituting moralism for materialism would solve the problem: "If the rich were the true administrators of the goods God has placed in our hands, how much misery would be remedied! But for the majority of the wealthy egoism reigns."[59]

Social Catholics' distributive system was predicated on the existence of haves and have-nots. As Pope Leo XIII put it, "It is not possible to overcome social inequality."[60] Accordingly, the pope gave a key role to the state, the Church, and the wealthy in the distribution process. Guided by Jesus' proverb "It is better to give than to receive," the powerful were expected to redistribute their wealth to the poor. Charity, pious social works, and morality, then, played a key role in the pope's program of distributive justice.[61] Sánchez Santos's discourse on distribution, which stressed morality, was in keeping with the pope's position.

Liberals and the PLM attacked social Catholics' theories of distribution. Científico Francisco Bulnes contended that the Church's practice of hoarding all the wealth and then ("supposedly," according to Bulnes) redistributing it to the poor led to economic "ruin." He invoked the laws of "political economy" to support his criticism.[62] *Regeneración,* asserting that the Catholic Church amassed immense wealth too, implicitly critiqued Sánchez Santos's ideas about redistribution.[63]

This chapter has demonstrated that the discourses of liberals and Sánchez Santos were similar since they both underscored the power of the economic sphere as opposed to the political realm. Also in accordance with developmentalist liberalism, Sánchez Santos constructed his identity around the symbol of the market, for it was the principal theme in his discourse. Despite the fact that both liberals and Sánchez Santos spoke the language of the market, they were engaged in distinct conversations. Whereas developmentalist liberalism was a brand of liberalism that was heavily influenced by positivism, social Darwinism, and racialist thought, Sánchez Santos's discourse was shaped by neo-Thomist Christian philosophy. Thus, the representations of the market that the two articulated differed significantly. While liberals' discourse stressed the state, racial hierarchy, and the nation, Sánchez Santos's market rhetoric critiqued an egalitarian brand of laissez-faire economic doctrine. He debunked a liberal tale that associated the market with an egalitarian and harmonious social body. Countering this version, he maintained that the market resulted in social malaise and inequality. The hegemony of materialism, individualism, and freedom, that is, the ideological tenets of economic liberalism, were the main culprit. The ideology of freedom resulted in economic concentration in the form of trusts and monopoly capitalism. Powerful capitalists, armed with a materialist-individualist ideology, exploited workers, causing the impoverishment of the laboring classes. A grave effect of workers' poverty was the dissolution of the family. Not only was misery so great that adults rejected the idea of raising families for lack of economic means, but poverty also drove mothers into the wage economy, forcing them to abandon their crucial domestic roles as teachers of morality. Tensions between capital and labor also stemmed from the market. Sánchez Santos warned that these strains were a seedbed for an even greater problem, the widespread appeal of radicalism. The market was an unmitigated social evil.

But Sánchez Santos used the symbol of the market to define not only what he stood against but also what he stood for. The Christian political economy that he championed was the antithesis of liberal political economy. Rejecting a horizontal social body associated with market society, he embraced a vertical social organization. A corporate order in which people knew their proper social station would result in social harmony if individualism and materialism, the mainstays of liberal ideology, were eschewed. Placing society's needs in front of individual desires and stressing moralism as opposed to materialism would go a long way toward ameliorating social ills. Protesting against the liberal intellectual movement of the eighteenth and nineteenth centuries that divorced morality from the market, Sánchez Santos sought to reinsert Christian ethics into the economy. Thus, his reformist doctrine called for increasing the Church's influence in civil society.

Since Sánchez Santos championed expanding the Church's role in civil society, his writings challenged the status quo. If he contested the existing order in some ways, he reinforced it in others. By emphasizing the significance of adopting a new worldview to ameliorate social ills, he downplayed structural issues such as the need for land reform and an expanded social role for the state, platforms that a fraction of the liberal opposition that emerged during the late Porfiriato embraced.

5 From "Tyranny" to "Slavery"

Shifting Symbols in the Mexican Liberal Party's Market Discourse

Scholars disagree about the PLM's significance during the Mexican Revolution. This chapter provides a distinct point of entry into this controversy by analyzing the symbols in the PLM's rhetoric within a larger ideological context. I divide the PLM's symbolism into two phases, an early one (1900–1906) and a late one (1907–11). Despite continuities (such as anticlericalism), this division makes sense because the PLM's market symbolism changed. Even if there was no specific moment when this shift occurred, it can be broadly asserted that the early phase was marked by liberal symbolism and the late by radical imagery.

During the early phase, the PLM identified itself with Mexican liberalism, nationalism, and indigenismo. As the PLM's platform radicalized during the late phase, however, it eschewed these familiar national symbols and adopted an anarchist discourse that highlighted the international brotherhood of workers.[1] Given the power of nationalism during the late Porfiriato, the PLM's internationalism had to fight an uphill ideological battle. This is not to say that the PLM did not have an impact on the Mexican Revolution. However, as the party's market rhetoric radicalized, its identity became less associated with dominant symbols in Mexican national discourse. Ironically, the PLM's radicalism initially led scholars to assume that the party played a significant role in the revolution, but the group's liberal rhetoric probably resonated more with the dominant symbols of the late Porfiriato and the revolutionary era.

Considering the separate issue of market rhetoric's impact on the PLM's own identity and platform, radical market discourse was clearly more influential. Since the PLM's liberal rhetoric represented the market as a relatively weak and ambiguous agent, it is unsurprising that this discourse did not significantly direct policy or forge identity. During the radical period the market transformed into the principal social demon and thus strongly shaped the party's strategy and identity.

Even during the early (liberal) phase, the PLM's market imagery differed from that of developmentalist liberals. True, the PLM articulated a nationalist critique of the market that echoed liberals' analysis, but nationalism was not the PLM's main theme; rather, expressing a social liberal position, the PLM critiqued the market from class and ethnic perspectives and called upon the state not to protect Mexico from external threats but to defend workers and Indians from internal enemies. The PLM's liberal arguments, however, had much in common with Sánchez Santos's discourse, for both attacked the market from a class perspective. Ironically, during the PLM's late phase there were even more commonalities between the two, for the party's radical writings minimized the issues of race and nationalism. Despite the fact that both stressed the issue of class, the solutions that the PLM and Sánchez Santos proposed were distinct. Eschewing Sánchez Santos's philosophical remedies, the PLM championed structural change.

The PLM's Early Phase, 1900–1906

Even though an antimarket strain existed during the early period, the market was a relatively weak and ambiguous symbol, for aspects of the PLM's rhetoric diluted and subverted its critique of the market. Given that the PLM articulated a social liberal ideology, this is unsurprising, for this philosophy was ambivalent about capitalism.[2] It acknowledged that modern capitalism had negative social consequences but sought to ameliorate social ills by reforming the system rather than rejecting it altogether. The PLM's social liberal rhetoric criticized the market from both class and nationalist perspectives, claiming that capital exploited labor and that foreign capital threatened sovereignty. Modern monopoly capitalism, even if the PLM did not detail its features, appears to have been the agent of exploitation in this discussion. Since the PLM represented reform as an effective method to ameliorate the distress caused by monopoly capitalism, the market was not an all-powerful force. Further, the market was not the only source of social ills, for the PLM also advertised problems generated by "feudalism" and politics. Finally, the market was a contradictory symbol. While it caused problems, it also solved them.

The PLM stressed not only economic "misery" but also political "tyranny."[3] In fact, when *Regeneración* first appeared in 1900 it placed more stress on political problems than on economic ones. This focus on politics would diminish over time to the point where the PLM would claim that all problems had economic causes. Yet this form of economic determinism was not present during the early phase. The PLM focused on the themes of freedom of the press, political democracy, and the separation of Church and state.[4] Not surprisingly, it found much to criticize about the Díaz government, for not only did the regime adhere to an authoritarian and antidemocratic brand of liberalism, but it also failed to strictly enforce the reform laws that restricted the Church's power. The PLM linked the party closely to Benito Juárez, the Reforma, and the 1857 Constitution. This was key to the political identity of the *magonistas* (followers of Ricardo Flores Magón), for the party portrayed itself as the true apostle of the liberal project initiated by Juárez and other liberals during the Reforma. The magonistas condemned the Porfirian government as betraying and even blocking the liberal project initiated during the Reforma.[5]

The PLM's stress on the political sphere was largely in keeping with the critique articulated by the liberal opposition to Díaz, which focused mostly on political problems and especially Díaz's long tenure in office. Unlike some members of the liberal opposition, however, the PLM also heavily stressed economic problems.[6] The PLM explicitly stated that solving political problems was not enough, for the economic realm also had to be addressed. An early draft of the PLM's 1906 manifesto, a document that outlined the PLM's program in a detailed fashion, put it this way:

> Our political collaborators realize that we give great importance to the conquests we want to achieve in the economic terrain. We cannot deny that political liberty is indispensable to the progress of the people, but we also have the firm conviction that only political liberty does not aid the immense majority of the inhabitants of a nation if the unchecked tyranny of the capitalist weighs upon them. It is necessary, due to this, to control capitalism... so the working and intellectual classes in our society can breathe easier.[7]

Thus, in addition to political liberalism, the PLM also articulated a social liberal ideology that stressed the harm caused by "capitalists." This social liberal discourse focused on the plight of urban workers, rural workers, and the landless.

Despite this critique of "capitalism," the market was a paradoxical symbol, since the PLM portrayed it as both an oppressive power and a liberating force. This contradictory depiction of the market stemmed from social liberal philosophy, which both embraced and critiqued capitalism. The PLM's criticism of Mexican "feudalism" also weakened the party's antimarket discourse, for it suggested that precapitalist as opposed to capitalist forces caused social ills.

The PLM's arguments about labor clearly illustrate its ambiguous rhetoric. For example, the PLM depicted capitalism as a force that oppressed labor. The party stated that "the sovereign capitalist imposes labor conditions . . . that are always disastrous for the worker."[8] This antimarket diatribe was also a discourse of opposition, for it portrayed the Díaz regime as an agent of capital. The party stated that the "bayonets of the dictatorship" were employed to repress labor unrest.[9] Capital's exploitation of labor reaped dire social consequences. The PLM maintained that workers were so impoverished by capital that they could not afford to buy basic necessities.[10] The PLM's 1906 manifesto dedicated space to the problem of widespread underconsumption, contending that the internal market was extremely small due to the limited purchasing power of the majority.[11] *El Colmillo Público*, a magonista periodical, also stressed Mexicans' extremely limited purchasing power.[12]

Policy implications flowed from the PLM's antimarket discourse. Indeed, the PLM's analysis suggested that poverty was not a consequence of racial traits such as laziness or lack of aptitude but rather capital's systematic exploitation of labor. Emphasizing this point, the PLM dedicated the largest section of its 1906 manifesto to labor reform. For the PLM, individualist solutions were not adequate. In this age of economic concentration, powerful forces were needed to offset the strength of almighty capital. The PLM advocated labor unions, state intervention, and labor legislation to check the tyranny of capital.[13] These forms of intervention, which would strengthen the position of labor vis-à-vis capital, would ameliorate workers' suffering. Thus, while monopoly capitalism was highly oppressive, it could be regulated in such a way as to provide an adequate existence to the wage worker.

The PLM painted an even grimmer picture of labor conditions among rural workers, but it did not explicitly identify capitalism as the source of worker exploitation; rather, it suggested that workers' ills stemmed from precapitalist conditions. This analysis was in keeping with the PLM's depiction of the rural economic system, which the party portrayed as a hybrid institution that contained both capitalist and feudal elements. Fittingly, the PLM labeled hacendados "modern feudal" lords.[14] In contrast to Sánchez Santos, who explicitly associated feudalism with monopoly capitalism by labeling Cecil Rhodes and other capitalists "feudal lords," the PLM's analysis suggested that Mexican "feudalism" was precapitalist.

The PLM's attack on this hybrid economic system implied that the market was not a negative force, for the party did not explicitly link labor exploitation to capitalism. To the contrary, by attacking feudal elements it suggested, albeit weakly, that the market was a positive force. Indeed, much of the PLM's attack on "feudalism" insinuated that wage labor was a form of emancipation for workers. More often than not, the PLM's attacks on coercive agrarian labor systems read like a liberal attack on feudalism. The PLM, for example, labeled debt peonage, under which "ever-increasing" debts were passed on from father to son, "slavery."[15] Similarly, *El Colmillo Público* referred to Yucatecan hacendados who utilized debt peonage as "slave owners who have feudal rights like those of the Middle Ages."[16] The PLM also attacked another form of labor coercion, the practice of shipping labor to Yucatán and other areas to work.[17] *Regeneración* condemned forced labor in Yucatán from a liberal perspective and predicted that labor coercion would lead to "rebellion" and "anarchy." The paper blamed worker exploitation on "arbitrary and despotic" political leaders and advocated replacing them with leaders who were "liberal and progressive."[18] By constructing a critique of coercive labor systems within the framework of liberalism, the PLM implied that market-controlled labor was liberating. The limitations of language make this association difficult to avoid. Associating debt peonage and physical coercion with "slavery," "feudalism," "anarchy," and "rebellion" implied that wage labor was free. Of course, one could make an analysis of Yucatán labor conditions that vilified capitalism. After all, Yucatán was firmly integrated into the international market. Nevertheless, the PLM's arguments did not emphasize this and thus can be read as an attack on a noncapitalist system.

If the PLM's writings about labor relations only explicitly critiqued capitalism in the case of urban workers, the party's analysis of property relations was an even weaker attack of the market. The PLM emphasized the problems of land concentration and a landless peasantry. Magonistas especially reprimanded the Porfirian regime for taking Yaquis' land, but they also discussed the Mayas as well as other Indians who were referred to with the overarching term of "Indian tribes."[19] The link that the party made between land concentration and market forces was very weak and ambiguous, however. In fact, its analysis suggested that political forces more than economic ones resulted in land concentration.

In one rare article magonistas directly implicated the market. The column maintained that market forces were behind the expropriation of Yaqui Indians from their land in Sonora. The article asserted that "ambitious and egotistical capital" had prolonged the government's war. The cost was high, for the war resulted in the destruction of "property" and worsening conditions for "many indigenous peoples."[20] This type of explicit attack on the market was uncommon, however.

More than market forces, it appears that the PLM attributed expropriations to political power. In the 1906 manifesto the PLM maintained that the "dictatorship" appropriated lands in order to "distribute them among its favorites."[21] An early draft of the 1906 manifesto made the same argument.[22] Further departing from the notion that the market was behind expropriations, the PLM complained that the huge landholdings created during the Porfiriato were not cultivated. Clearly, this was not a discourse that demonized economic modernization and the dynamism of capitalism. Rather, the PLM depicted the Porfirian land expropriations as a form of neofeudal takeovers. The regime employed political leverage to confiscate land and then never cultivated it.[23] The party portrayed land concentration as a consequence of this practice of neofeudalism on other occasions.[24] Further countering the idea that land concentration was a consequence of capitalism, the PLM claimed that land was still concentrated in the hands of the Catholic Church.[25] And, in keeping with its pro-Porfirian liberal counterparts, the PLM represented the Church as economically backward.

The PLM criticized the market to a greater degree in its solution to the land concentration problem. Nowhere in its solutions, for example, did the party celebrate the free market. Not the market but social justice guided its land redistribution program. The party called for the land to be divided equally to ensure that everyone had access. (It is unclear if this included women, for they were never directly referred to.) Further countering a reliance on market forces, the party maintained that the state should redistribute land.[26]

This statist solution to the land concentration problem had similarities to the PLM's resolution to the capital-labor conflict in the case of urban workers. In both instances the market was conceived not as a place of freedom but of exploitation. Indeed, the PLM's statist solution was a defensive act to "avoid the possibility of capitalists monopolizing the land again."[27] This was the age of monopoly capitalism, not yeoman farmers. The state had to protect the people against the tyranny of capital. This language underscores the ambiguous nature of the symbol of the market. In contrast to some magonista analyses that did not portray capitalism as the cause of concentration, this one did.

In accordance with the PLM's discourse on workers, the party did not attack capitalism to such an extent that it condemned private property; rather, consistent with social liberalism, the PLM called for state intervention not to do away with the market but to minimize its oppressive tendencies. The PLM envisioned state intervention as a force to create a nation of smallholders. This was not a communal vision but a yeoman farmer dream. While one can read a weak petite bourgeoisie strain into it, for it mentioned increased production, the discourse stressed emancipation. Having access to land would enable Mexicans to produce their own food and thus be emancipated from hunger and "misery." Transforming the landless into individual owners would also liberate them from the "overseer."[28] This had similarities to the agrarian vision of some of the liberals from the Reforma era.

The PLM differed significantly from Reforma liberals when it came to the question of the Indians, however. Unlike Reforma liberals, who championed the privatization of the *ejido*, the PLM called for Indians' communal lands to be re-turned.[29] For the PLM, the destruction of Indian lands and the creation of private property did not symbolize progress and civilization but rather robbery and social malaise. Hence magonistas aligned their movement with Mexico's Indian heritage. In fact, the PLM explicitly tied its movement to Mexico's pre-Columbian past by representing the "noble blood of Cuauhtémoc" as a precursor to its movement.[30]

While one can credit magonistas with a degree of cultural relativism, it would be an exaggeration to claim that the PLM articulated an "Indianist" discourse in the sense of embracing, promoting, and representing pre-Columbian cultures as a model for Mexico. Countering "Indianism," the PLM maintained that Indians needed to be "educated" to "contribute . . . to the strengthening of our nationality."[31] On this count the PLM was in accordance with developmentalist liberals. Both groups advocated that Indians be remade via education.

The international market was a less prominent theme in the PLM's analysis, but it received coverage nonetheless. The party depicted Mexico as a homogeneous unit pitted against an external threat. Since this image had strong nationalist overtones, it undermined the PLM's class analysis. Charging that Porfirian elites were selling the nation to foreigners (particularly in the forms of territory and loans) for their own personal gain, the PLM's nationalist rhetoric discredited the Porfirian regime.[32]

Unlike developmentalist liberals, who focused on the problems generated by informal economic imperialism (which was also articulated in popular discourse as fear of a "peaceful conquest"), the PLM stressed the dangers of formal imperialism. And in contrast to contemporary analyses that stressed the economic basis of imperialism, the party highlighted the power of the military. Indeed, the PLM's principal attack on the international market harked back to the French

Intervention. *El Colmillo Público* repeatedly contended that eventually Mexico would be unable to pay its foreign loans, which would result in a repeat performance of the French Intervention.[33] The PLM's 1906 manifesto, which called for an end to foreign loans, also explicitly conjured the scenario of foreign occupation.[34] It is worth noting that the issue of loans was a very visible one, for during the late Porfiriato Mexico contracted large foreign loans after decades of being denied foreign credit.[35] By attacking foreign loans the PLM implicitly identified itself with Juárez and the liberal nationalist movement to repel the French. Conversely, the PLM's rhetoric associated Díaz with unpatriotic conservatives.

The PLM also articulated a nationalist discourse about land, though it too was little developed. In contrast to its position on loans, the PLM did not contend that foreign ownership of land would result in armed invasion; rather, it vaguely stated that foreign ownership threatened "national integrity." To counter this peril the PLM's 1906 manifesto made it mandatory for foreign landowners to become Mexican citizens.[36]

Although it did so even less frequently, the PLM also attacked foreign labor. In 1901 *Regeneración* published two reviews that praised Genaro Raigosa's study of the Mexican population.[37] Raigosa's study, as noted in chapter 3, underscored the Mexicans' low level of training vis-à-vis foreign immigrant workers and argued that foreign laborers posed a serious threat to Mexican sovereignty. *Regeneración* echoed Raigosa's social Darwinist formulation, claiming that the low level of the Mexican workforce would not bode well in the "grand international battle for life."[38] The market did not cause inequality between classes but between nations. The PLM's 1906 manifesto, which called for an end to Chinese immigration, also articulated a nationalist labor platform.[39] Even when U.S. troops entered Mexico to repress a strike at the Cananea mine in 1906, the PLM, highlighting threats to sovereignty, criticized the action from a nationalist as opposed to a class perspective.[40]

The PLM's Radical Phase, 1907–1911

The PLM began to radicalize after party members were forced to flee to the United States in 1904.[41] Radicalization of the party was, in part, a consequence of a power struggle between the radical and liberal factions represented by Ricardo Flores Magón and Camilo Arriaga, respectively.[42] While the latter espoused a liberal ideology, the former was influenced by anarchism as well as liberalism. Flores Magón won the power struggle, and Arriaga was forced out of the movement.[43] The influence of anarchists in the United States also served to radicalize the PLM. By 1907 Flores Magón had begun to express his anarchist leanings more openly. Flores Magón and other leaders of the movement were caught and jailed in the United States from 1907 to 1910. In August 1910, shortly before the outbreak of the Mexican Revolution, Flores Magón was released from jail, and he began publishing *Regeneración* again. His anarchist philosophy was even more visible at this point, leading some PLM followers to abandon the movement.[44] In the PLM's famous manifesto of September 23, 1911, Flores Magón explicitly expressed his anarchist principles.[45]

The radicalization of the PLM significantly altered its market rhetoric. The influence of anarchism transformed the market into an unambiguous symbol of oppression. Furthermore, unlike the early period, when the market was one of several sources that generated social ills, during the anarchist phase it was the sole cause of Mexico's problems, and it was such a powerful force that the state could not check its destruction. The beast could not be tamed. It had to be destroyed.

There were some continuities with the early period, however. In keeping with its early writings, the PLM's antimarket position did not valorize traditional society as would, for example, Zapatistas.[46] Rather than constructing a traditional society as a force to liberate Mexicans from the oppressive social order generated by the market, the PLM's antidote to the social ills caused by the market lay in a modern communal order that was to be forged by civilized workers with a high level of class consciousness.

During the late period, all traces of magonistas' earlier arguments that implied that "reform capitalism" had some redeeming features vanished. Magonistas' positions on labor were a case in point. The PLM subverted the association between the market and freedom by consistently labeling wage workers as "slaves." The term *slave* had a connotation different from the one used in the PLM's earlier analysis. In the early era, slavery had been invoked to attack forms of coercion such as debt peonage, but during the late period the PLM raised the issue of slavery to criticize wage labor. In this new context, wage labor, something the PLM had been ambivalent about earlier, was a form of slavery.[47] In fact, the PLM argued that wage labor was even worse than slavery, for the paternalistic qualities that, to a degree, could alleviate slaves' suffering were absent under capitalism.[48]

There were, according to the PLM, dire social consequences to the oppressive conditions that workers faced under capitalism. Impoverished by exploitative capital, workers had no alternative but to steal and even become assassins in order to obtain sufficient money to support their families. Working-class women, facing the same economic hardships, were forced to become prostitutes.[49] Thus, in keeping with Sánchez Santos's analysis, the market symbolized lawlessness and immorality rather than a civilizing force.

Similarly, the PLM countered earlier magonista rhetoric that depicted the creation of rural smallholders as a form of emancipation from an oppressive capitalist-feudal order. The party clearly stated its new position in a critique of land reform proposals that emerged at the outset of the revolution. The PLM contended that a proposal to break up the haciendas and redistribute them to smallholders (even with long-term credit) would simply create a "rural bourgeoisie."[50] It would just be a matter of time before even greater inequalities were generated. The group criticized the idea of family plots on similar grounds.[51]

The PLM disavowed its earlier reformist stance in part because the party reconceptualized the relationship between politics and economics. No longer did the PLM adhere to the position that politics could shape the economic sphere and thereby ameliorate the problems generated by monopoly capitalism. Indeed, the PLM attacked the bourgeois liberal notion that rule by law was a means to emancipate individuals from the chains of tradition, hierarchy, and inequality and therefore an effective tool to realize and protect freedoms. For the PLM, bourgeois law created new chains that enslaved the proletariat. Articulating this position, Flores Magón contended that law did not bring justice or protect workers because it was written by the capitalist class and represented their distinct class interests. Based on the same argument, he asserted that citizenship, too, did not bring true freedom but rather was an illusion of liberty. In support of this radical formulation, Flores Magón reversed the signifiers attached to the liberal construct of "rights" by asserting that under capitalism Mexicans "did not have rights to anything but to die from hunger." He explicitly rejected political solutions to social ills: "We have the conviction that political liberty by itself is impotent to bring happiness to the people, and it is because of this that we work with firmness to make the people understand that their true interest is to work for economic liberty, the solid cement upon which the grand structure of human emancipation can be built."[52] Ironically, both Flores Magón and Bulnes were economic determinists.

The PLM's discourse about the state provides yet another example of the immense power that the party attributed to the economic sphere and capitalism. During the late era, the PLM forcefully rejected statist political solutions to counter the misery and inequality generated by the market. Magonistas represented the state as the ally of capital and hence labor's enemy. *Regeneración* explained that the forces of state repression were necessary for the "maintenance of the political and social inequality" generated by capitalism.[53] The state, then, was an ally of the bourgeoisie in their war with the proletariat. But the state was clearly the junior partner in this relationship. The PLM contended that "governments are representatives of capital, hence they need to oppress the proletariat." Whether states chose to or not, they were forced to play this supportive role. Magonistas maintained that even the best-intentioned state that sought to aid workers would fail in this task because capital, at base, ruled.[54]

Capitalism became not only a more powerful force but also a more focused one in the sense that it had fewer adversaries. Rejecting its earlier nationalist strain, during the late period the PLM depicted workers as the only casualty of capitalism. Adopting an internationalist position was key to magonistas' renunciation of the PLM's nationalist thesis. During the PLM's later phase, the war between capital and labor knew no national boundaries.[55] The PLM represented capital-labor battles of national scope as part of international workers' war against global capitalism. The PLM conceptualized the Mexican Revolution in this international framework: "This formidable battle between the two social classes in Mexico is the first act in the great universal tragedy that will quickly cover the entire planet."[56] From this internationalist position, nationalism became a negative force because it divided the international labor movement.

Creating international labor solidarity was no easy task, however. The PLM discussed the dynamics of the Mexican case, claiming that a high level of foreign involvement in the country, and specifically the nationalist sentiment it generated, weakened and divided the labor movement. The PLM claimed that the foreign entrepreneurial class—with the cooperation of the Mexican state—utilized a divide-and-conquer strategy to weaken the solidarity of the Mexican labor movement. Key to this strategy was pitting foreign and indigenous workers against each other. Capitalists, the PLM contended, paid foreign workers higher wages to break the solidarity of native and foreign labor. The PLM lamented this division between Mexican and foreign workers, noting it impeded the emergence of a strong labor movement in Mexico.[57] Expressing this internationalist position on another occasion, the PLM criticized a strong nationalist sentiment in the Mexican press, claiming it overlooked the true enemy, namely, "capital."[58] Unsurprisingly, the PLM urged international solidarity between Mexican workers and laborers from other nations.[59]

The PLM's critique was insightful. As illustrated in chapter 3, much of the Mexican labor force adhered to a nationalist ideology. Their demands for better conditions vis-à-vis capital were often expressed in nationalist as opposed to class rhetoric. The Porfirian government's rhetoric responded to and thus perpetuated this nationalist worker discourse, as ideological governmental initiatives such as the Mexicanization of the labor force in the railroad industry reveals.

Given the PLM's position that the capitalist class controlled the state and the legal system, it is unsurprising that the group rejected a gradualist socialist approach that represented the legal system as a vehicle to dismantle capitalist society. From the PLM's perspective, this type of solution was doomed to failure.[60] The PLM developed its argument to a logical end. If laborers were enslaved under capitalism and the state could not ameliorate workers' suffering, then the only avenue for their emancipation was the complete destruction of capitalist society. Hence the party's portrayal of capitalist market society was fundamental to its call for violent revolution.[61]

The PLM repeatedly asserted that workers were the key ingredient in the revolutionary movement: "The emancipation of the workers should be the job of the workers themselves."[62] This claim was more specific than it appears. "Worker" was a gendered concept associated with males. This points to a similarity between all the groups examined in this study: they adhered to a separate spheres ideology that restricted women to the domestic realm. Women's role in the revolution, according to Flores Magón, was to support men. He explained, "Your [women's] responsibility is to help a man, to be with him when he vacillates, to animate him, to be at his side when he suffers, to lessen his pain, and to laugh and sing with him when triumph smiles." Flores Magón implored women to play this role, despite the fact that they did not "understand" the world of "politics."[63]

Práxedis Guerrero, a key member of the PLM during the late era, articulated a similar position (though he was not specifically discussing the revolution).[64] Guerrero criticized a tendency in the feminist movement that erased the differences between women and men and cited women police officers as an example of feminism gone astray. To counter this trend he advocated that women take on responsibilities that were in accordance with their "sweet sex."[65] In this same vein, on another occasion Guerrero portrayed women as "sweet" and "tender" and explained they needed a "dignified man" to "appreciate," "conserve," and "defend" them.[66] In the PLM's analysis, then, labor, the force that would play the main part in the revolutionary movement and rule the earth after it was successfully accomplished, was dominated by males. Despite the fact that the PLM preached equality between the sexes and even asserted that both men and women had equal right to the land, in magonista revolutionary discourse men had more power than women.

In the PLM's rhetoric, Indians were also insignificant revolutionary actors. In sharp contrast to their high visibility during the magonistas' early phase, Indians almost entirely vanished in the PLM's late era. Topics that were stressed during the early period such as Indians' lands, culture, and labor were largely absent in the late period. This was not just a question of oversight. During the late epoch Flores Magón predominantly identified Mexicans not by language, ethnicity, culture, race, region, occupation, or generation but by class. He conceived of Mexicans as members of either the capitalist or the working class. The PLM's focus on class made Indians much less visible. Thus, highlighting class resulted in the disappearance not only of nationalism from the PLM's discourse but also of indigenismo.

The PLM's ideal revolutionary worker had a collective spirit. Not only was solidarity essential to revolution, but it was workers' true nature too. Challenging the social Darwinist assumption that humans were cutthroat by nature, magonistas asserted that not competition but rather its antithesis, solidarity, represented workers' true interests. Similarly, the party attacked social Darwinist rhetoric that portrayed national workers as competing races and also countered Hobbes's portrayal of men as "wolves."[67]

Guerrero invoked "nature" to support collectivism. He asserted that "nature had established [solidarity] between members of the species" and labeled avarice a "false interest." He supported this position by arguing that human society was an interdependent collective and not unconnected individuals. Seeking to fulfill individual interests instead of collective ones was detrimental not only to the collective but also to the individual. Guerrero explicitly made this point: "Robbing bread from another is to put in certain danger one's own sustenance. To snatch happiness from others is to place oneself in chains. . . . To aspire to achieve one's own happiness through the misery and pain of others is equal to desiring to strengthen a building by destroying its foundation."[68]

Flores Magón's representation of solidarity as an evolved trait was yet another factor that made Indians insignificant symbols in his revolutionary discourse. Flores Magón associated a collective spirit not with pre-Columbian cultures but with modern civilization. He maintained that the human traits of "domination" and "superiority" were at the forefront when "society was in its infancy." In the brutal world that he described these competitive traits were deemed "necessary for man not to perish." As society advanced, however, "civilization refined." Consequently, the trait of "solidarity" strengthened, and these primitive attributes, which Flores Magón defined as solidarity's "antithesis," "lessened."[69] Hence Flores Magón did not locate the roots of the collectivism he revered in pre-Columbian Mexico. Flores Magón disagreed with Peter Kropotkin, the Russian anarchist who heavily influenced the PLM, on this issue. Kropotkin stressed the fact that the roots of contemporary communalism went back to "primitive" societies.[70]

In keeping with this evolutionary perspective, Flores Magón's ideal revolutionary actor was a product of modern capitalist culture. He had a high level of class consciousness, for his bonds with his fellow workers made even national boundaries insignificant. The revolutionary actor was a sophisticated and cosmopolitan character. Flores Magón described the revolutionary man as a "cultured" and "superior species" who understood laborers' common plight.[71] Hence Flores Magón's revolutionary actor had some similarities to Marx's, for both revolutionaries represented him as a product of modern capitalism and stressed the importance of class consciousness.[72] So capitalism did not create immoral people, as social Catholics believed, but more generous united ones.

In contrast to developmentalist liberals, who championed education as a tool to instill a materialist ethic, the PLM stressed the importance of education to achieve class consciousness. This departed significantly from the junta's earlier educational discourse, in which the principal problem was not a market ethos but a Catholic worldview. The remedy, too, differed. Whereas secularizing education had been the goal in the early period, antibourgeois education was the focus of the late era.[73] The PLM asserted that liberal education was a factor that impeded the emergence of a collectivist mentality in workers. Using the United States as a case in point, the group noted that the U.S. educational system taught Americans to revere capitalism: "It teaches children to admire the skill with which some men know how to take advantage of the sweat and fatigue of their fellow men, to convert themselves into the kings of steel, oil, and other things."[74]

Countering bourgeois education, Guerrero advocated an educational system based on the ideas of the radical Spanish educator Francisco Ferrer.[75] Magonistas hailed education as a tool that would break the ideological hold that bourgeois society and schooling had on Mexicans, for it would teach them to eschew materialism and individualism and express their collective nature. Stressing the importance of education to solidarity and a collective spirit, the PLM repeatedly advocated reduced work hours and higher wages. While one might suspect this was a gradualist approach, it was really revolutionary, for decreased work hours and improved material conditions would free up workers' time so they could become educated. Education was crucial to a successful revolution, for it would only be successful if workers understood their collective plight.[76]

By locating the emergence of the revolutionary class in modern capitalist society, magonistas were unable to link their movement to the pre-Columbian roots of Mexican culture. To the contrary, the PLM represented the Mexican Revolution as one part of an international revolution that depended upon civilized workers who had a revolutionary consciousness. Indians did later come to have a role in the PLM's rhetoric about revolution, but not until revolutionary activity increased in 1911.[77]

The PLM's antimarket discourse did more than just support the group's radical program of overthrowing capitalism via a workers' revolution. Market rhetoric was also key to the construction of the PLM's communal order. The PLM constructed its communal paradise by making it the antithesis of the oppressive market. The former was natural, egalitarian, plentiful, emancipating, and harmonious; the latter was artificial, hierarchical, impoverished, enslaving, and discordant. There were rhetorical similarities between the PLM's (anarchist) and social Catholics' (Catholic political economy) alternatives to market society. In both cases the market was the contrast against which alternatives were constructed.

Establishing communal land was the keystone of the PLM's collective paradise. Private land was represented as the linchpin of the exploitative capitalist system. In contrast, according to the PLM, communal land would have a very positive effect on the social order. It would liberate Mexicans from hunger and free workers from the yoke of capital. No wonder, then, that the PLM adopted the anarchist slogan "land and liberty" in 1910. Unsurprisingly, the PLM repeatedly contended that the first and most decisive step in the revolution was expropriating the capitalists from the land and establishing communal property.[78]

The PLM invoked nature to support its contention that land was not private but communal. Indeed, the party cited "natural law" and "natural rights" to sustain its claim that the land belonged to "everyone," a group, the PLM repeatedly asserted, that included men and women.[79] Hence, the PLM turned the tables: private property was illegal, and communal land was in accordance with natural law.[80] In keeping with the PLM's position on human nature, magonistas did not legitimate communal land by pointing to its pre-Columbian roots in Mexico.

For the PLM, communal land symbolized equality and autonomy. Replacing private land with communal holdings would result in a social leveling, for it would break the hierarchical capitalist class system. Owners, the group that dominated labor, would no longer exist after communal land was established. A related consequence was worker autonomy. With the abolition of owners, workers would no longer be dependent upon *amos* (masters) for wages. In the PLM's symbolism, capitalism was associated with a social hierarchy and dependence and communalism with a horizontal egalitarian order and independence.[81]

Wealth was another of communal land's laudable properties. For the PLM, transforming privately owned land into communal holding was a rags-to-riches story. Indeed, the PLM contended that this transformation would end all misery, for the needy would "cease to be poor." Rather than their miserable lot under capitalism, the masses would live in a state of "well-being." Hence communal lands were a symbol of abundance. According to the PLM's analysis, this rags-to-riches story was not fantastic at all. The PLM contended repeatedly that land was the basis of wealth or, as Flores Magón put it on one occasion, the "ancient fountain of wealth." The reason for scarcity lay not in insufficient production of wealth, as the científicos argued, but rather in unequal distribution of riches. Under capitalism profits went to the owners of the means of production, not the workers. Hence, the PLM's analysis implied that once land was communally controlled and distribution was more equitable, scarcity would cease to be a problem. As chapter 3 illustrated, this association between land and wealth was quite at odds with liberals' discourse, which maintained that significant capital investment was needed to make land produce abundance, a position that was, ironically, in keeping with the ideas of Kropotkin.[82]

Despite the fact that the exchange of goods was very rarely discussed, the PLM's arguments about it paralleled the party's position on land. The group associated abolishing the market and establishing communal control with liberation in this realm, too. The PLM advocated abandoning production and exchange based on market principles and adopting production and distribution based on social need. The PLM associated the latter with abundance, claiming that by working communally laborers would "work less and produce more."[83]

This chapter has argued that the strength that the PLM attributed to the market to shape the political and social spheres increased over time. While the market clearly influenced political and social developments in the party's early discourse, it nevertheless became much more powerful in the PLM's late dialogue. Unlike the early phase, when the market was just one of several "enemies," during the late period the market became the main villain in the PLM's discourse. This shift can be explained by the evolution of the PLM's ideology, which changed from social liberalism to a variant of anarchism marked by economic determinism. Thus, during the PLM's anarchist phase, the party held not only that the market was a destructive force but also that the economic sphere shaped the social and political realms. No wonder, then, that the PLM represented the market as an all-powerful demon.

Since the PLM's vilification of the market increased over time, the party's market rhetoric had more significant implications for political strategy during the late period. During the early phase, the PLM contended that the negative consequences of monopoly capitalism—labor exploitation, land concentration, expropriations, and the impoverishment of the masses—could be ameliorated by political reform, which the PLM vigorously championed. In contrast, during the late era, the PLM articulated a powerful form of economic determinism, contending that economic forces were so powerful that even the state could do nothing to counter them. In fact, economic forces shaped political developments. From this perspective, political reform was insufficient to alleviate the social ills generated by the market. Thus, revolution was the only way to emancipate the masses from the market. As the main demon in magonista discourse, the PLM invoked the market to explain and justify its revolutionary movement to overthrow the capitalist order. Market imagery, too, was crucial to the PLM's representation of the revolutionary communal order, for it was a modern paradise that was constructed as the antithesis of the harsh market.

As the PLM's market rhetoric radicalized, it employed symbols that were less familiar in the Mexican context. During the late era, as Flores Magón reconceptualized human nature, community, the state, and the nation and how they all related to the market, he moved away from a symbolization that employed conventional Mexican characters. Indeed, even though the PLM still championed workers' rights and land reform, the symbols it employed changed. By representing the Mexican Revolution as part of an internationalist movement that pitted global capital against worldwide labor, the PLM broke its earlier identification with Mexican nationalism. The PLM's rejection of indigenismo also reflected this departure from nationalism. Rather than referring to specific groups (i.e., Indians), the PLM represented a homogeneous working class confronting a homogeneous capitalist class. The PLM's evolutionary perspective, too, was critical to this negation of Indian symbols, for the PLM's emancipatory doctrine was forward-looking. The PLM's ideal communal order was not rooted in earlier traditions but in the creation of "postcapitalist" man. The PLM's battle, then, was not a nationalist and ethnic struggle for Mexican workers and Indians but a universal war between international capital and transnational labor. As the PLM's market symbolization radicalized, then, magonista identity became more removed from familiar national emblems. In contrast, salient themes in the PLM's early discourse—indigenism, statism, and nationalism (in regard to labor)—proved to be dominant topics in the debates of the revolutionary period.

6 Conclusion

Symbols in Porfirian Market Discourse

There is a central irony in Adam Smith's classic work *A Wealth of Nations*. The book has been associated with the birth of modern political economy, a fundamental component of which is the separation of economics from politics, ethics, and society. Paradoxically, if we treat classical political economy as a social discourse as opposed to a science we come to the opposite conclusion: politics, ethics, and society are integral themes in classic economic liberalism. Political intervention by the state is not necessary, for the "invisible hand" regulates. The market's ability to autonomously govern the social order is uncanny, almost magical. From this vantage point, the market is transformed into a kind of secular religion to be worshiped. The insight gained from this irony—that politics, ethics, and society are fundamental components of market discourse—is the central premise of this study. It follows a little-developed trend in scholarship about the market's symbolic significance that was pioneered by Albert Hirschman, who analyzes discussions about the market as a form of sociopolitical discourse. While Hirschman's work was influential, the only study I am aware of that explicitly follows his model is an article by Ricardo Salvatore that tests Hirschman's conclusions about Europe in the case of Latin America.

The central question of my study is based upon Hirschman's approach: what social, cultural, and political powers did Porfirian elites ascribe to the market? I have also modified and expanded his methodology. First, I have emphasized the relationship between market discourse and the construction of identity, a topic Hirschman did not examine. Salvatore cogently raises this issue but does not fully explore it in his article. Second, I stress race, gender, class, and nationalism, themes related to identity that Hirschman neglected to highlight. Third, I have not defined the term *market* precisely the way he did. Hirschman's first work mostly conceived of the market as a synonym for commerce and his second as a synonym for capitalism. Following the variegated contours of Porfirian discourse and the theoretical insights of James Carrier, I reject universalism by asserting that there were a number of market models. I conceive of discussions about land, labor, capital, and commerce as discrete market discourses, and I make distinctions between national and international markets. More broadly, I also interpret dialogues about material progress and capitalism as particular market discourses.

I have argued that late Porfirian Mexico is a fruitful case to which to apply this methodology, for the market became a dominant symbol in national discourse at that time. Indeed, during the Porfiriato, the political topic of state building that had prevailed during the nineteenth century was eclipsed by economic themes. A number of factors explain this shift. On the political and material planes, the Porfiriato was an era of unprecedented stability and economic progress, developments that resulted in increased attention to the economy. On an ideological level, it was an epoch marked by the ascendance of economics and the decline of politics, for during this age of "order and progress" the government became obsessed with material progress. From a different ideological vantage point about economic modernization, it was an era when the "labor" and "social" questions gained national notoriety. In the international economic arena, it was a period of unparalleled expansion. In an age marked by racialist ideology, economic determinism, and social Darwinism, this development gained widespread attention, but Mexicans were highly ambivalent, conceiving of foreign economic culture as both a savior and an executioner. As these distinct but related themes suggest, not only were there numerous conceptions of the market, there were also different discourses about its effects. Despite the fact that the market was an inconstant signifier, there was a commonality: it was in relation to markets, represented as a force that shaped the social and political spheres, that liberals, conservatives, and radicals constructed their identities and planned their courses of action.

I have placed my greatest attention on the group I have labeled developmentalist liberals, that is, those who voiced government and business interests. I have devoted a chapter to the central issue that preoccupied Hirschman's first work: the power of the market to shape the behavior of individuals. Tailoring this theme to the specific concerns of the Porfirian age, I explore the market's ability to shape political and economic behavior. I have argued that the ways that liberals conceived humans and human nature had a decisive impact on their discourse. A nineteenth-century rejection of the Enlightenment's universalist project, a component of which was an assault against the notion of a universal human nature, influenced liberals. A particular of this attack, the assertion that there were distinct racial types, manifested itself in liberals' representations of the market. Rejecting the notion of homogeneous economic man and adhering to Darwinian evolutionary thought, liberals maintained that some races and social groups were higher on the evolutionary scale than others. Conceiving the professional and wealthy classes as Ricardo's "economic man," whose central desire was economic gain, a fraction of the liberals maintained that material progress, which would translate into increased economic opportunities and economic satisfaction, would forge political peace. This contention fit nicely with the Porfirian regime's design of stressing economics over politics. Conversely, material progress would not turn Indians into workers or hacendados into entrepreneurs, for these groups, according to liberals, were low on the evolutionary scale and were thus the very antithesis of Ricardo's economic man. Since economic incentives were lost on them, forms of social engineering (immigration and education) and coercion were deemed necessary. In addition to shaping policy, this discourse affected identity by praising foreigners (especially northern Europeans) and criticizing the dominant racial heritages of Mexico, the indigenous and the Spanish.

I pose another large question that is the topic of the subsequent chapter: what impact did the international market (defined as the international flow of capital, workers, and goods) have on Mexican politics and society, according to liberals? Hirschman does not feature this theme, but, given Porfirian Mexico's high level of integration into the world economy, it should not be overlooked. The issue of race, in keeping with the previous chapter, looms large in this issue, for foreign elements were deemed racially and economically superior. In contrast to the inconsistent power that liberals ascribed to material progress to shape character, they depicted the international market, especially in the forms of capital and labor, as an invariably almighty force. But liberals were intensely ambivalent about the international market, particularly the U.S. economy. On the one hand, adhering to evolutionary social Darwinist thought and economic determinism, Sierra and others maintained that national evolution and even survival depended upon foreign capital, technology, and immigrants propelling the atavistic Mexican nation to a more advanced stage. Although more broadly conceived and dependent upon the integration of foreign components, this national regeneration program was not unlike the cultural project to manufacture workers and entrepreneurs that was examined in the previous chapter. On the other hand, liberals warned that foreign economic elements would overpower the nation. Emphasizing the immense power of the market, liberals maintained that the threats posed by foreign militaries and diplomacy paled in comparison to the economic danger. Invoking the foreign threat justified the regulation and nationalization of foreign industries. Liberals described another economic battle for survival, but it did not involve foreigners, for it was a struggle between Mexican men and women. Adhering to a separate spheres ideology, Sierra maintained that women belonged in the home, and thus, in contrast to his position about Mexico and foreigners, he rejected state intervention to bolster females' economic power. Since much ink was spilled over liberals' ambivalent preoccupation with foreigners, it influenced their identity. Paradoxically, liberals worshiped Europeans and Americans, denigrated Mexicans, and were intensely nationalist.

I have also examined the market discourses of social Catholics and the Mexican Liberal Party, two significant opposition groups that emerged during the late Porfiriato. My study of social Catholicism has been limited to an analysis of the writings of Trinidad Sánchez Santos, the movement's leading publicist who was strongly influenced by European social Catholicism and particularly Pope Leo XIII. Embracing the notion of a moral being, conceptions of human nature, too, influenced Sánchez Santos's rhetoric. He contested not only liberals' valorization of materialism but also their emphasis on race and nation, for he adhered to a Catholic universalism and thus rejected social Darwinist evolutionary thought. Given this divergence, it is unsurprising that his stress on the worker, family, and community departed from liberals' rhetoric. The question I have posed in his case is not as pointed as the previous ones: how did the market figure in his discourse of opposition? Despite Díaz's interminable reign, Sánchez Santos focused on economics, not politics. His principal target was not economic structures but rather economic culture as he railed against the social evils wrought by the influence of liberal economic ideology on social values. He maintained that the dominance of individualism and materialism—the philosophical foundations of liberal political economy—explained the "social problem," that is, the inequitable distribution of wealth and power, the conflict between capital and labor, and the dissolution of the family, a component of which was mothers' involuntary entry into the job market owing to inadequate wages paid to their husbands. He largely championed a cultural solution, the reinsertion of religious ethics into the economy, in the form of "Christian political economy." By constructing liberal political economy as the principal social demon, his rhetoric about the market strongly shaped his identity and political agenda.

In contrast to the limited scholarly attention to social Catholicism, the Mexican Liberal Party has been examined extensively. My aim has been to provide a different vantage point on the group by studying its imagery within the broader setting of national symbols. By evaluating the "strength" attributed to the market in the party's discourse, I essentially pose the same question that I raised for Sánchez Santos. The PLM is the only group that I have studied chronologically. I have, somewhat artificially, divided my study of the party into an early phase (1900–1906) and a late era (1907–11). I have maintained that during the early phase the PLM's economic and social philosophy was characterized by a blend of social liberalism and laissez-faire, with the former being far more influential. During the late era, an anarchist strand came to dominate. In contrast to the other groups, during the early period the PLM placed as much emphasis on politics as economics. Further weakening the symbol of the market at that time, the party depicted it as an ambiguous force. The market was clearly the villain in the PLM's platform, which attacked industrial capitalism from a class perspective, maintaining that capitalists, who wielded immense power, exploited workers. Similarly, a nationalist strain—albeit a weak one—echoed developmentalist liberals' attack on foreign labor. But an ethnic theme that lamented exploitative working conditions and expropriations endured by Indians did not clearly attack the market, for it was an imprecise analysis that vaguely suggested that not economic forces but rather political powers were the source of Indians' misery. Whatever the cause of social ills, the PLM partly built its identity around the themes of the nation, Indians, and workers. The PLM also associated itself with a reformist state, for the party championed state intervention to redistribute land, protect workers, and safeguard the nation.

During the late era, the PLM redefined societal problems, attributed far more power to economic forces, and unambiguously attacked the market. Nationalist and ethnic themes receded as the PLM conceived the international order as a battle between worldwide capital and global labor. Conflict between capital and labor in Mexico, according to the PLM, was just one battlefield in this global war. Asserting that the only way to break the strength of all-powerful capital was via violent worker revolution, market rhetoric shaped the party's identity and strategy. In contrast to Sánchez Santos, who lamented capitalism's cultural impact, the PLM hailed the market's effects on values, claiming it helped forge a collective consciousness. But the party also championed education to manufacture the postcapitalist man who knew neither "race, color, nor nation." Celebrating universal "brotherhood" represented the new order as male dominated, for females were assigned a subordinate revolutionary role, a separate spheres ideology that was in keeping with the gender symbolism of social Catholics and liberals. By eschewing statism, nationalism, and indigenism, the PLM rejected themes in its early discourse that would later prove to be prominent in revolutionary rhetoric.

Broader conclusions about the symbols in economic discourse in Porfirian Mexico can also be explored. Despite the fact that a number of studies have shown that Porfirian policy departed from laissez-faire, conventional wisdom still assumes that laissez-faire philosophy reigned. (This is not to imply that deeds and rhetoric need to be consistent.) My study has countered this assumption. The image of the free market was practically invisible in the economic symbolism I examined. Only the discourse of Trinidad Sánchez Santos invoked the free market, but it conjured it for the rhetorical purpose of erecting a straw man to be toppled. True, Ricardo Flores Magón's rhetoric had liberal elements during the early era (1900–1906), but they were characterized more by social liberalism, which championed state intervention, than a celebration of free markets. And even if it cannot be denied that the philosophy espoused by developmentalist liberals was broadly liberal (for it supported private property and private initiative), it was nevertheless a far cry from classic liberalism.

To delve further into this, it will be helpful to consider some specific aspects of classic economic liberalism. First and foremost, its concept of society was based in individualism. Sánchez Santos, in contrast, embraced a corporate and hierarchical order. Flores Magón stressed class, the collective, and, to a lesser degree, ethnicity as opposed to the individual. Liberals eschewed individualism by favoring the collectivist social organism. In classic economic liberalism, the individual was of a distinct and homogeneous type: the economically rational man. Sánchez Santos consciously countered this materialist depiction of human nature by insisting that humans were moral beings. Magonistas' early discourse did not directly confront this topic, but their late rhetoric explicitly attacked the very concept of self-interest by asserting that the foundations of society were collective. Liberals undermined Ricardo's universalism by conceiving society as racial groups that were at different evolutionary levels. While the most advanced were imbued with the traits of economic man, the atavistic lacked a materialist ethos. Classic economic liberalism also rested upon the notion of a competitive market comprised of atomistic individuals. Sánchez Santos challenged this conception by stressing the monopolistic nature of modern capitalism and by championing a distributive system grounded in morality as opposed to materialism, a position that the PLM's "late" rhetoric also voiced, albeit from a different philosophical vantage point. By emphasizing the immense power of foreign trusts in Mexico and the control that foreign commercial interests had over Mexican exports, liberals represented a social order governed by monopoly capitalism, not competitive markets. Finally, classic liberalism sought to scale back the state's economic role. Sánchez Santos's social order, based in morality, albeit for distinct reasons, also minimized the state, as did the PLM's "late" discourse. But the party's early discourse and, to a much greater degree, liberals' rhetoric emphasized the state. In liberals' evolutionary, economic determinist, and social Darwinist thought, Mexico was represented as an atavistic nation in a hostile world that needed to be protected and bolstered by the state if it was to survive.

A composite picture of the economic imagery of the Porfirian age does not feature the atomistic economic man operating in a competitive market. A varied assortment of symbols, namely, social organism, community, collective, social classes, evolved races, atavistic groups, and moral beings, all eclipsed the portrait of individualistic *Homo economicus*. And a collection of images, too, contradicted the free market: monopolies, an overproduction crisis, commercial entrapment, peaceful conquest, foreign trusts, state regulation, and nationalization.

Notes

Chapter 1. Market as Symbol in Porfirian Mexico

1. There is a growing literature that examines the development of Porfirian markets. On market legislation, see Armstrong, *Law and Market Society;* Carmagnani, *Estado y mercado;* and Coatsworth, *Los orígenes del atraso.* On capital markets, see Haber, *Industry and Underdevelopment;* Haber, "Industrial Concentration and Capital Markets"; Marichal, "Obstacles"; and Rosensweig, "Moneda y bancos." On commodity markets, see Kuntz Ficker, *Empresa extranjera;* and Cerutti, *Burguesía, capitales e industria.* On labor markets, see Anderson, *Outcasts;* Gamboa, "La comunidad obrera de León"; Gamboa, "Mercado de bolsa de trabajo." On land markets, see González Navarro, *Historia moderna;* Hernández Chávez, *La tradición republicana del buen gobierno;* Holden, *Mexico and the Survey of Public Lands.* On the relationship between market expansion and the Mexican Revolution, see Knight, *The Mexican Revolution;* Tutino, *From Insurrection;* Hart, *Revolutionary Mexico;* and Joseph and Wells, *Summer of Discontent.*

2. The major works of intellectual history of the era focus on political themes. See Zea, *El positivismo en México;* Hale, *The Transformation of Liberalism;* Raat, *El positivismo durante el porfiriato.* Jesús Reyes Heroles's massive three-volume work on the nineteenth century (*El liberalismo mexicano*) examines economics as well as political and social themes; however, it does not cover the Porfirian period. For two works that provide a cursory introduction to Mexican economic thought during the national period and briefly discuss the Porfiriato, see Silva Herzog, *El pensamiento económico;* and López Rosado's four-volume work, *Historia y pensamiento económico de México.* Similarly, works on Latin American economic thought are rare, but there are isolated fine works on the topic. See, for example, Love, *Crafting the Third World.*

3. Hale, *The Transformation of Liberalism,* ix.

4. Despite the fact that works on economic policy reveal that the Porfirian regime departed from laissez-faire, conventional wisdom holds that Porfiristas, in keeping with other Latin American elites, subscribed to laissez-faire ideology. See, for example, the popular textbook by Skidmore and Smith, *Modern Latin America,* 43. One of the ironies in this portrayal is that it assumes Mexicans were aping European laissez-faire doctrine. However, Europeans critiqued laissez-faire at this time, and these critiques were not lost on Mexicans. See n. 47 below.

5. There are works that examine the impact of social Darwinism, positivism, and racism on Porfirian thought, but they focus on social and political ideas, not economics. See Hale, *The Transformation of Liberalism;* and Guerra, *México: Del antiguo régimen a la revolución.* For an excellent overview of the influence of social Darwinism, positivism, and racialist ideas on Latin America, see Hale, "Political and Social Ideas."

6. See, for example, Haber, ed., *How Latin America Fell Behind;* and Coatsworth and Taylor, eds., *Latin America and the World Economy.*

7. There are exceptions, however, for some works examine the symbolic significance of economic discourse. See Platt, "Divine Protection and Liberal Damnation"; Greenfield, "The Great Drought"; Salvatore, "Market Oriented Reforms"; Rojas de Ferro, "The 'Will to Civilize'"; and Gootenberg, *Imagining Development.*

8. For a work that treats economics as rhetoric, ideology, and discourse and thus explores the main currents in this scholarship, see Samuels, ed., *Economics as Discourse.* For a rhetorical approach, see McCloskey, *The Rhetoric of Economics;* Backhouse and Dudley-Evans, eds., *Economics as Language;* and Klamer, McCloskey, and Solow, eds., *The Consequences of Economic Rhetoric.* For works that apply discourse analysis to economics, see Foucault, *The Order of Things;* Amariglio, "The Body, Economic Discourse, and Power"; and Tribe, *Land, Labour, and Economic Discourse.*

9. One historian of economic thought explains this positivist approach this way: "The history of economic theory is a history of progressive, scientific-theoretical investigations and discoveries, or work producing an ever-growing and improving body of real knowledge and understanding of its subject matter" (Taylor, *A History of Economic Thought,* xi). In Schumpeter's imposing work, this positivist methodological approach was labeled "economic analysis" (*History of Economic Analysis,* 38–41).

10. See Dilley, ed., *Contesting Markets;* Carrier, ed., *Meanings of the Market;* Haskell and Teichgraeber, eds., *The Culture of the Market;* and Mandel and Humphrey, eds., *Markets and Moralities.*

11. A different approach examines market representations in literature. See Kaufman, *The Business of Common Life;* Teichgraeber, *Sublime Thoughts/Penny Wisdom;* Trotter, *Circulation.* Another trend focuses on market culture. See Salvatore, "The Normalization of Economic Life"; Sellers, *The Market Revolution;* Agnew, *Worlds Apart;* and Haskell and Teichgraeber, eds., *The Culture of the Market.*

12. Salvatore, "The Strength of Markets," 23.

13. Hirschman, *The Passions and the Interests.*

14. Hirschman, *Rival Views of Market Society,* 105–41. In addition to Salvatore's article, Forget's "Disequilibrium Trade as a Metaphor" also takes an approach similar to that of Hirschman.

15. Kropotkin was a leading theorist of anarchism; see his influential work *Mutual Aid*. For a socialist utopian response to capitalism, see Bellamy, *Looking Backward*. For secondary works on radical responses to the market, see Thompson, *The Market and Its Critics;* and McNally, *Against the Market*. For key documents in social Catholicism, see Ketteler, *The Social Teachings;* and León XIII, *Encíclicas: Rerum Novarum*. For secondary works on social Catholicism, see Misner, *Social Catholicism;* Charlton, Mallison, and Oakeshott, *The Christian Response;* and Moody, ed., *Church and Society*.

16. The well-known economist John Kells Ingram, for example, launched an attack on laissez-faire in the 1870s; see his *A History of Political Economy*. For a secondary study of this liberal challenge to laissez-faire, see Boylan and Foley, *Political Economy and Colonial Ireland*, 116–60. The German historical school also critiqued classical political economy during the nineteenth century. For a contemporary account of their critique, see Ely, *The Past and Present*. Also see Kahn, "Towards a History of the Critique of Economism." More generally, the liberal response to industrialism was a form of reform liberalism labeled "social liberalism." On social liberalism, see Hall, "Variants of Liberalism."

17. David Ricardo's theory of comparative advantage played a significant role in liberalizing Britain's trade during the nineteenth century; see his *Principles of Political Economy;* see also Polanyi, *The Great Transformation*, 135–40. Conventional wisdom assumes that Adam Smith's *A Wealth of Nations* was central to this liberal economic project, but the significance of his text to establishing a laissez-faire order, at least during the early nineteenth century, was quite ambiguous. On Smith, see Tribe, *Land, Labour, and Economic Discourse*, 110–21; and McNally, *Against the Market*, 42–61.

18. Holy, "Culture."

19. To cite two conspicuous examples, anti-NAFTA rhetoric was prominent in the Zapatistas' 1994 uprising, and the protesters against the World Trade Organization meeting in Seattle demonized globalization. But lamenting the social ills generated by the market has not been limited to radicals and so-called marginal groups. The liberal scholar and journalist Walter Russell Mead, for example, strongly argues that instability in the global market threatens to result in political disaster. See his newspaper opinion articles: "Markets Pose the Biggest Threat" and "A Real Crisis Looms." Members of the financial class make similar claims. See Altman, "Global Markets' Massive Extraterritorial Power." Some conservatives, too, demonize globalization. See Buchanan, *The Great Betrayal;* Gray, *False Dawn;* and Soros, *The Crisis of Global Capitalism*.

20. Jameson, *Postmodernism*, 263.

21. For a theoretical discussion of competing discourses, see Terdiman, *Discourse/ Counterdiscourse*.

22. Stubbs, *Discourse Analysis*, 1.

23. For a contemporary discussion of the press, see *Directorio profesional, industrial y de comercio*, 77–84. For an interesting contemporary account of the government's press subsidy policy, see López-Portillo y Rojas, *Elevación y caída*, 341. There have been a number of scholarly studies of the Porfirian press. See Camarillo Carbajal, *El sindicato de periodistas;* Bringas and Mascareño, *Esbozo histórico de la prensa obrera;* Bravo Ugarte, *Periodistas y periódicos mexicanos;* Novo, ed., *El periodismo en México;* and Cosío Villegas, *Historia moderna de México (segunda parte)*, 9: 525–95. For a study of *El Imparcial*, see Aguilar Plata, "El Imparcial."

24. Agnew, *Worlds Apart*, 17.

25. Carrier, ed., *Meanings of the Market*, 20–22.

26. Haskell and Teichgraeber, eds., *The Culture of the Market*, 3–16.

27. This imprecise definition, which makes the market a synonym for capitalism, has been recognized by scholars. See Carrier, ed., *Meanings of the Market*, 6. Haskell and Teichgraeber, too, note that the market and capitalism have been treated as "closely affiliated words" (Haskell and Teichgraeber, eds., *The Culture of the Market*, 3). Hirschman applies a similar definition in his work *Rival Views of Market Society*, even if he does not explicitly define the term market. In contrast, his work *The Passions and the Interests* emphasizes commerce.

28. On Díaz's reconciliation policy, see Schmitt, "Catholic Adjustment to the Secular State" and "The Díaz Conciliation Policy." For Díaz's strategy for consolidating power during the early Porfiriato, see Perry, *Juárez and Díaz*; Bertola, Carmagnani, and Riguzzi, "Federación y estados."

29. Cockcroft, *Intellectual Precursors*.

30. On the PLM's role in the revolts, see Albro, *Always a Rebel*, chaps. 4 and 6.

31. On social Catholicism in Porfirian Mexico, see Ceballos Ramírez, *El catolicismo social*; Adame Goddard, *El pensamiento político*; González Navarro, *Historia moderna*.

32. On European social Catholicism, see Misner, *Social Catholicism*; and Charlton, Mallison, and Oakeshott, *The Christian Response*.

33. There were a number of currents in the crusade that differed over issues such as the degree of state intervention, the role of Christian trade unions, and the extent to which the liberal order should be challenged. See Misner, *Social Catholicism*.

34. León XIII, *Encíclicas: Rerum Novarum*.

35. Ceballos Ramírez, *El catolicismo social*, chap. 1.

36. Ibid., 175–252; Adame Goddard, *El pensamiento político*, 189–94; González Navarro, *Historia moderna*, 365–66.

37. Ceballos Ramírez, *El catolicismo social*, 272–78.

38. Ibid., 268–71; Adame Goddard, *El pensamiento político*, 189–94.

39. Ceballos Ramírez, *El catolicismo social*, 256–67.

40. On the Protestant opposition to Díaz's policy of reconciliation, see Bastian, "Las sociedades protestantes."

41. Ceballos Ramírez, *El catolicismo social*, 144.

42. Ibid., 152.

43. Ibid., 420–21.

44. Hale, *Mexican Liberalism*, chap. 8.

45. Covo, *Las ideas*, chap. 7.

46. See Carreño, *Temas económicos*, 305.

47. Enrique Martínez Sobral, "Los fisiócratas-socialistas," *Economista Mexicano*, 6 November 1909, 158. See Gide, *Curso de economía política*. On Gide's economic ideology, see James, *Historia del pensamiento económico*, 33.

48. Bernecker, "Foreign Interests"; Potash, *Mexican Government*, 12–38; Thompson, "Protectionism."

49. On the bank, see Potash, *Mexican Government*, 39–125.

50. Covo, *Las ideas*, 408–51.

51. Duncan, "For the Good of the Country," chaps. 3 and 5.

52. Bernstein, *The Mexican Mining Industry.*

53. Beatty, *Institutions and Investment,* chap. 4.

54. For works on Porfirian policy that show a departure from laissez-faire, see Topik, "La revolución" and "The Economic Role." Also see Beatty, "Commercial Policy." For a reinterpretation of the state's role in the economy during the age of export-led growth in all of Latin America, see Love and Jacobsen, eds., *Guiding the Invisible Hand.*

55. Beatty, *Institutions and Investment,* chaps. 3 and 6.

56. On Porfirian railroad nationalization, see Parlee, "Porfirio Díaz, Railroads, and Development"; Calderón, "Los ferrocarriles"; and Kuntz Ficker, *Empresa extranjera.*

57. Salvatore, "The Strength of Markets"; Knight, "El liberalismo mexicano." Thompson, discussing the Reforma, maintains that "debate about economic policy receded in importance" ("Protectionism," 137).

58. Hale, *Mexican Liberalism,* 74; Reyes Heroles, *El liberalismo mexicano,* 1: 40.

59. Sinkin, *The Mexican Reform,* chaps. 4, 5, and 6.

60. Even though Lerdo himself stressed the economic significance of Ley Lerdo, some contemporaries emphasized its significance to nation building. See ibid., 125. For an in-depth discussion of commentary on Ley Lerdo, see Covo, *Las ideas,* 408–30.

61. Potash, *Mexican Government,* 42; Bernecker, "Foreign Interests," 78.

62. Hale, *Mexican Liberalism,* 284–85.

63. On nationalism, see Sinkin, *The Mexican Reform,* chap. 9.

64. For a historical discussion of political and economic imperialism, see Mommsen, *Theories of Imperialism.*

65. Sinkin, *The Mexican Reform,* 97.

66. Hale, *Mexican Liberalism,* 227.

67. Ibid., 215–16.

68. Covo, *Las ideas,* 399–400.

69. Duncan, "For the Good of the Country," 136–40.

70. Covo, *Las ideas,* 301–5; Duncan, "For the Good of the Country," chap. 3; González Navarro, *Los extranjeros en México.*

71. Bernecker, "Foreign Interests," 73–74.

72. Ibid., 78; and Potash, *Mexican Government,* 43. In contrast, doctrinaire liberals charged that an increased state role would deprive Mexicans of their "liberties." See Potash, *Mexican Government,* 49–50. For an extended discussion on debates over protectionism, see Reyes Heroles, *El liberalismo mexicano,* 1: 165–212, 3: 419–529.

73. María del Refugio González maintains that the Mexican press focused on social and political themes at midcentury, but during the Porfiriato a large number of commercial publications appeared ("Comercio y comerciante," 140).

74. For an excellent summary of the significance of external factors to Latin America's export boom, see Weaver, *Latin America,* chap. 3.

75. On the American colony, see Schell Jr., *Integral Outsiders.*

76. Not surprisingly, the Porfirian paper criticized the Congress's economic proposals: "The financiers of the monetary conference in Puebla have clearly understood the grand forces that move humanity in the twentieth century [i.e., economics], but they have forgotten their

complete incapacity to move those forces" ("La conferencia monetaria clerical de Puebla: El proyecto de un banco," *El Imparcial,* 7 March 1903, 1).

77. Social Catholics' theories on banking attracted critical attention from *El Economista Mexicano,* a financial weekly ("La economía política y sus detractores," *El Economista Mexicano,* 24 April 1909, 67–68).

78. For a liberal opposition paper that stressed economics and articulated a form of social liberalism, see *El Paladín.*

79. On the way market discourses are conditioned or shaped by the dominant discourse, see Carrier, ed., *Meanings of the Market,* 47–54.

80. "Regeneración," *Regeneración,* 7 August 1901, 1–4.

81. On the ideological controversy over material progress, see Weiner, "Challenges." For radical critiques of the Porfirian concept of material progress, see, for example, "El progreso material," *El Colmillo Público,* 11 February 1906, 79; "Como se nos denigra," *El Colmillo Público,* 11 July 1906, 398–99.

82. Two central periodicals in the debate were the financial weekly *Semana Mercantil* and the Catholic daily *El País.* "El fiasco de la prosperidad," *El País,* 7 January 1908, 1; "Prosperidad," *El País,* 8 January 1908, 1; "La prosperidad nacional," *Semana Mercantil,* 13 January 1908, 15–17; "La agricultura en relación de la prosperidad nacional," *Semana Mercantil,* 27 January 1908, 44–45; "La prosperidad nacional," *Semana Mercantil,* 17 February 1908, 88–89; "El progreso de México," *Semana Mercantil,* 1 March 1909, 113–15; "El progreso de México," *Semana Mercantil,* 8 March 1909, 128–29.

83. Kahn, "Demons."

84. On industrial policy, see Beatty, *Institutions and Investment.*

85. On the labor movement, see Anderson, *Outcasts.*

86. "Otro cáncer de la industria," *El País,* 15 March 1901, 1.

87. For a popular contemporary account that stressed the exploitative labor conditions in Yucatán, see Turner, *Barbarous Mexico.*

88. On the social crisis during the late Porfiriato, see Hart, *Revolutionary Mexico.*

89. Carreño, *Temas económicos,* 305.

90. On the other hand, some members of the científicos camarilla labeled themselves "científicos." See Bulnes, *El porvenir,* 370.

91. Hale, *The Transformation of Liberalism,* 123–24. For other discussions about who belonged to the científico camarilla, see Cosío Villegas, *Historia moderna de México (segunda parte),* 9: 858; Raat, "Positivism in Díaz Mexico," 293–301; and Rice, "The Porfirian Political Elite," 11–16.

92. Madero maintained that the force of the world economy, not governmental initiatives, accounted for Mexico's material progress (*La sucesión presidencial,* 211–31). On the ideologies of competing Porfirian factions, see Guerra, *México: Del antiguo régimen a la revolución,* 2: 79–143; Knight, *The Mexican Revolution,* 1: 47–77.

93. There were differences not only within the government but also inside specific branches. Clifton Kroeber, for example, identifies competing policy agendas within the Ministry of Development (*Man, Land, and Water*).

94. Knight, "El liberalismo mexicano." For another account of Mexican liberalism that spans the nineteenth century, see Hale, "José María Luis Mora."

95. Hale, *The Transformation of Liberalism,* chap. 4.

96. Ibid., 257.

97. For works on the liberal and radical opposition, see Cockcroft, *Intellectual Precursors;* Guerra, *México: Del antiguo régimen a la revolución;* Knight, *The Mexican Revolution.* On the liberal agrarianist Andrés Molina Enríquez, see Shadle, *Andrés Molina Enríquez.*

98. As Jean Meyer has shown, the revolutionary state attacked the Church because it was a powerful adversary (*The Cristero Rebellion;* see also Quirk, *The Mexican Revolution*). For a revisionist study that argues that the Church retained a significant amount of power even after the Cristero Rebellion, see Reich, *Mexico's Hidden Revolution.*

99. Ceballos Ramírez, *El catolicismo social.*

100. During the 1910s an antimarket theme was still present in social Catholic ideology. See *El resurgimiento mexicano,* 19; Ceballos Dosamantes, *Jesuitas y pseudo-científicos.* A number of the themes in Porfirian social Catholic thought were stressed by Mexico's semifascist Catholic integralist movement of the 1930s and 1940s, which labeled itself the Unión Nacional Sinarquista. Both movements attacked liberalism, socialism, and materialism and condemned class conflict. Both movements embraced the family, religion, social hierarchy, and private property.

101. On the leading role of Trinidad Sánchez Santos and *El País* in social Catholicism, see Ceballos Ramírez, *El catolicismo social,* 142–53; González Navarro, *Historia moderna,* 364–65; Cosío Villegas, *Historia moderna de México (segunda parte),* 9: 574.

102. For biographical works on Trinidad Sánchez Santos, see Islas García, "Biografía"; Márquez, "Sánchez Santos, periodista."

103. Ceballos Ramírez, *El catolicismo social,* 195–96.

104. Ibid., 146.

105. Cosío Villegas, *Historia moderna de México (segunda parte),* 9: 574, 583–84.

106. Márquez, "Sánchez Santos, periodista," 45–47.

107. Ibid. For an example of the regional distribution of the paper, see González, *San José de Gracia.*

108. Quirk, *The Mexican Revolution,* 30.

109. Márquez, "Sánchez Santos, periodista," 51.

110. For some works specifically on the radical opposition, see Hart, *Anarchism;* Albro, *Always a Rebel;* Albro, *To Die on Your Feet;* Blanquel, *Ricardo Flores Magón;* MacLachlan, *Anarchism.*

111. Cockcroft's influential interpretation maintained that the PLM strongly influenced revolutionary ideology (*Intellectual Precursors*). For revisionist accounts that minimize the PLM's influence, see Knight, *The Mexican Revolution,* 1: 44–47; Anderson, *Outcasts,* 314–18.

Chapter 2. "Material and Political Movements Depend on Character"

1. There are many forms of market rhetoric that emphasize freedom as opposed to discipline. For one variant, see Love Brown, "The Free Market," 99–128. For a different analysis but one that also views the market as a form of emancipation from an oppressive state, see Holy, "Culture," 231–43. For another variant that emphasizes the ways the market frees individuals from traditional cultural restraints, see Wiener, "Market Culture," 136–60.

2. Liberals also critiqued the economic practices of the middle class but not nearly as extensively as they attacked Indians and hacendados. They complained that professionals enriched themselves through their connections to the state as opposed to those in the realm of production. This was a form of "parasitism." On the middle class, see Bulnes, *El porvenir,* 321–52; Díaz Dufoo, "Industrial Evolution," 107.

3. Paul Vanderwood examines the Díaz regime's public relations efforts. He contrasts the regime's public image with reality and argues that while a degree of political stability had been established, the "paz Porfiriana" was perhaps more rhetorical than real (*Disorder and Progress,* esp. chaps. 8 and 11). On Mexico's participation in the World's Fair, see Tenorio-Trillo, *Mexico at the World's Fair.* For a broad summary of Díaz's image-building campaign, see Cott, "Porfirian Investment Policies," 72–76.

4. Furthermore, even accounts about the way political stability was achieved during the early Porfiriato did not stress the market's role in the process. To the contrary, Rafael de Zayas Enríquez (1848–1932), a prominent Porfirian writer who was noted for his journalism, novels, and historical works, stated the opposite: Porfirian material progress was a consequence of political stability. In a study of the Porfirian era, he contended that peace was the "first and indispensable element of the material progress of nations" (Zayas Enríquez, *Los Estados Unidos Mexicanos,* 1). Díaz made this same assertion in presidential messages. See Cámara de Diputados, *Los presidentes de México,* 435, 526, 539.

5. Chevalier, "Prefacio," 15.

6. Sierra, *México social y político,* 29.

7. On Sierra's role in *La Libertad,* see Hale, *The Transformation of Liberalism,* chap. 2.

8. González Ramírez, ed., "Manifiesto de los oaxaqueños," 14–18.

9. "La conferencia monetaria clerical de Puebla: El proyecto de un banco," *El Imparcial,* 7 March 1903, 1.

10. In the 1880s, before becoming involved in *El Imparcial,* Reyes Spíndola published the Mexico City daily *El Universal.* Manuel Flores, who was a member of the Chamber of Deputies, and Tomás Braniff, an investor who was a member of the Mexican Monetary Commission, were also significant figures in *El Imparcial.* On the paper's distribution, see Cosío Villegas, *Historia moderna de México (segunda parte),* 9: 525–31. Also see Moisés González Navarro, who states that by mid-1907 its circulation reached 125,000 (*Historia moderna,* 677–81).

11. Bulnes, *El porvenir,* 339–40. For a brief biography of Bulnes, see Silva Herzog, *El pensamiento económico,* chap. 16.

12. Bulnes, *El porvenir,* 370.

13. On the division of the economic sphere from the realms of morality, religion, and politics, see Dumont, *From Mandeville to Marx;* and Minowitz, *Profits, Priests, and Princes.*

14. Ricardo, *Principles of Political Economy;* Oakley, *Classical Economic Man,* 123–41; Minowitz, *Profits, Priests, and Princes,* 63–93.

15. Hirschman, *The Passions and the Interests,* 100–113.

16. Bulnes, *El porvenir,* 105.

17. Ibid., 370.

18. Some of Bulnes's contemporaries in Ireland made the same argument. As scholars Thomas Boylan and Timothy Foley explain, Irish political economists contended that "political economy was non-political. Politics was the place of turmoil, division and passion, whereas

political economy was an oasis of calm rationality, a place of harmony rather than conflict, and, in a frequently used metaphor an uncontested 'common ground'" (*Political Economy and Colonial Ireland*, 132). Similar ideas have emerged in Latin America today; see, for example, Valdés, "Changing Paradigms," 127–38; Constable and Valenzuela, *A Nation of Enemies*, 199–221.

19. Despite the fact that Justo Sierra was also an economic determinist and believed Mexico needed to focus on the economy for the time being, he hoped that in the future the political realm could also evolve. Thus his position was not identical to that of Bulnes (Sierra, *Evolución política*, 364).

20. Bulnes, *El porvenir*, 361.

21. Ibid., 370. *Semana Mercantil* also made a link between material satisfaction and political peace, yet it differed from Bulnes's position in that it included a reformist element, claiming that radical worker movements only surfaced in areas where there was a "unequal distribution of wealth" ("1906–revista anual," *Semana Mercantil*, 31 December 1906, 631–34).

22. Bulnes, *The Whole Truth*, 22–24. Even though he was probably unaware of Bulnes's analysis, scholar Friedrich Katz's explanation of the source of Porfirian peace makes the same argument ("Mexico," 61).

23. Bulnes, *El porvenir*, 353.

24. Ibid., 369.

25. Ibid., 370–71.

26. Díaz Dufoo, "La evolución industrial," 158. Díaz Dufoo quoted from Bulnes, *El porvenir.*

27. Díaz Dufoo, "La evolución industrial," 158.

28. González Ramírez, ed., "Manifiesto de la Convención," 4.

29. Ibid., 4–5, my emphasis.

30. González Ramírez, ed., "Manifiesto de los oaxaqueños," 15.

31. *El Imparcial*, countering the assertion that progress caused delinquency, directly challenged the notion that material progress had negative consequences ("El aumento de la delincuencia y la civilización," *El Imparcial*, 11 January 1901, 1).

32. On the alcabala, see Carmagnani, "El liberalismo," 471–98; and Peralta Zamora, "La hacienda pública," 904–17.

33. Limantour, *Breves apuntes*, 3.

34. José Yves Limantour, "Iniciativas de reformas constitucionales para la abolición de las alcabalas," in *Memoria que presentó el Secretario de Hacienda* (1895), 543.

35. During the 1870s Macedo was a coeditor of *El Foro*, a periodical of jurisprudence that Sierra and Limantour also edited. In the 1880s with his brother Miguel he established *Anuario de Legislación y Jurisprudencia*. He contributed three articles ("La evolución mercantil," "Comunicaciones y obras públicas," and "La hacienda pública") to Sierra, ed., *México, su evolución social*. For a discussion of Macedo's economic ideas, see Silva Herzog, *El pensamiento económico*, 296–302.

36. Macedo, *La evolución mercantil*, 113.

37. Ibid., 111.

38. Díaz Dufoo had been involved in the periodicals *Revista Azul* and *El Imparcial* during the 1890s. He wrote various texts on economics, for example, a biography of Limantour *(Limantour)*, a work on foreign investment *(Los capitales extranjeros)*, and an article on Mexican

industry ("La evolución industrial") in Sierra, ed., *México, su evolución social*. For a short biography of Carlos Díaz Dufoo, see Silva Herzog, *El pensamiento económico*, 325–33.

39. Díaz Dufoo was a close friend of Limantour, the minister of finance. The fact that *El Economista Mexicano* was published on a government press established yet another link between the journal and the government.

40. Díaz Dufoo, *Limantour*, 56.

41. Macedo, *La evolución mercantil*, 120.

42. The commission's report was reproduced in *El Progreso Latino*, 1 February 1906, 118. Over a decade earlier, científicos had articulated a similar position in their famous 1892 manifesto that called for Díaz's reelection. Rather than focus directly on commerce, it spoke of the political merits of a more general but clearly related phenomenon, communications, contending that the "development of communications" over the past "three decades" had resulted in social cohesion: "[Communications] put us in contact with ourselves and with the world [and] have centuplicated our national cohesion" (González Ramírez, ed., "Manifiesto de la Convención," 5).

43. Argentine elites articulated a concept of workers that had similarities to the Mexican case. See Rojas de Ferro, "The 'Will to Civilize,'" 150–73. The German school was a nineteenth-century academic movement that explicitly challenged the concept of economic man. For a contemporary account of the school, see Ely, *The Past and Present*. For an excellent secondary account, see Kahn, "Towards a History of the Critique of Economism."

44. Ricardo's disregard of the issue of race was not unique but rather a dominant trend in economists' works. On this issue, see Schumpeter, *History of Economic Analysis*, 791–92.

45. Ricardo, *Principles of Political Economy*.

46. Pimentel, "Memoria," 173; Hale, *Mexican Liberalism*, 240–41.

47. For discussions on the impact of liberalism and individualism in Latin America during the age of independence, see Guerra, "El soberano"; Rodríguez, *The Independence*.

48. Hale, *Mexican Liberalism*, 217–19.

49. For ideas about the transformative power of private property during the early republic, see Hale, *Mexican Liberalism*, chap. 7. For the 1860s, see Pimentel, "Memoria," 166–68; Pimentel, "La economía política," 226–27, 240.

50. On treatment of the indigenous population, see Powell, *El liberalismo*.

51. Urías Horcasitas, "El pensamiento económico," 265–74.

52. Hale maintains that pre-Reforma liberals discussed Indians very little (*Mexican Liberalism*, 215–18). Beatríz Urías Horcasitas also claims that liberals largely ignored Indians, preferring to focus on the entrepreneurial class ("El pensamiento económico," 265–74).

53. Banton, *Racial Theories*, 1–64; Gould, *The Mismeasure of Man*. Hale examines this transition in Latin America ("Political and Social Ideas," 367–441).

54. On the negative impact of Mexico's climate, for example, see Romero, *Mexico and the United States*, 522. On diet, see Bulnes, *El porvenir*, 9–42. On the colonial heritage, see Carreño, *Problemas indígenas*, 149–223.

55. For the revisionist scholarship, see Stabb, "Indigenism and Racism"; González Navarro, "Las ideas raciales"; Raat, "Los intelectuales"; Powell, "Mexican Intellectuals," 19–36.

56. It appears that the unstable conditions earlier in the nineteenth century were not conducive to an emphasis on labor productivity, for during the period many fortunes were

made not in the realm of production but by exploiting and controlling the state's wealth. Historian David Walker argues that political favoritism, not greater productivity, brought profits. Financing the state debt was a major source of profits (Walker, *Business, Kinship and Politics*). Barbara Tenenbaum, in *The Politics of Penury*, her study of *agiotistas* (moneylenders), makes the same basic point. On the profitability of money lending and financing the state debt, see also Marichal, "Obstacles."

57. On this shift, see the following: *La crisis monetaria*, 9; "La depreciación de la plata," *Semana Mercantil*, 4 July 1893, 319; "La agricultura nacional y la depreciación de la plata," *El Economista Mexicano*, 4 September 1897, 49; "Horizonte mexicano: Presente y porvenir," *El Progreso Latino*, 21 July 1906, 65; "Horizonte mexicano: Presente y porvenir," *El Progreso Latino*, 28 July 1906, 97–98; "La plata," *Boletín de la Sociedad Agrícola Mexicana*, 31 May 1897, 315; "Nuestra agricultura. Su importancia como base de la riqueza pública. Oro es lo que oro vale," *Boletín de la Sociedad Agrícola Mexicana*, 8 October 1897, 584–85; "Nuevas opiniones," *Boletín de la Sociedad Agrícola Mexicana*, 16 December 1897, 727; R. López y Parra, "Agricultura y minería," *Boletín de la Sociedad Agrícola Mexicana*, 17 February 1900, 124–27; Leroy Beaulieu, "La depreciación de la plata," trans. Emilio Pardo, reprinted in a series of issues of *Boletín de la Sociedad Agrícola Mexicana*, August 1886–June 1887.

58. This argument was in keeping with developments in early-nineteenth-century classical political economy, which rejected Physiocrats' theories about landed wealth and embraced the labor theory of value. On this shift, see Foucault, *The Order of Things*, 254; Tribe, *Land, Labour and Economic Discourse*; and Polanyi, *The Great Transformation*.

59. Científicos in particular challenged the idea that nature was the basis of wealth that had been popularized in Mexico since the colonial era. See Macedo, *La evolución mercantil*, 175–78; Zayas Enríquez, *Los Estados Unidos Mexicanos*, 176–77; García, *Nociones de economía política*, 13; Díaz Dufoo, "La evolución industrial," 101–4; Cora, "Reseña histórica," 8. For a secondary work on this issue, see González Navarro, *Historia moderna*, 138–42.

60. There were exceptions to this position, for some Porfirian elites embraced racial determinism but put the Indian race on a pedestal. See Tenorio-Trillo, *Mexico at the World's Fair*, 89–94.

61. Castellanos, *Algunos problemas*, 93.

62. Quoted from Powell, "Mexican Intellectuals," 27.

63. While this was the dominant position, there was a weak voice that called for minimal protection for Indians' communal existence. Congress passed a law in 1900 calling for increased protection of ejidos. On the law, see Cámara de Diputados, *Diario de los debates*, 1: 562–65. For commentary on the law, see Cora, "Reseña histórica," 102. Wistano Luis Orozco, the famous critic of Porfirian land policy, celebrated the law as a means to protect indigenous communities (*Los ejidos de los pueblos*, 193). For a brief but valuable study of the Díaz government's attempts to protect Indians' communal lands, see Stevens, "Agrarian Policy."

64. "Las necesidades de nuestra agricultura," *Boletín de la Sociedad Agrícola Mexicana*, 1 June 1901, 404–13.

65. Raigosa, "La evolución agrícola," 38. Some of Raigosa's governmental economic functions included negotiating a commercial treaty with Germany, serving as a Mexican delegate on the 1899 congress on international commerce, and serving as a financial agent in England. He was a member of the Mexican Academy of Jurisprudence and Legislation.

66. "La falta de brazos en la República," *Semana Mercantil,* 26 February 1906, 98–99.

67. Unfortunately, my attempts to locate biographical information on Hegewisch proved totally fruitless. By championing increased state support for the chamber of commerce, the establishment of commercial agents in foreign nations to stimulate Mexican exports, and protective tariffs to aid domestic manufacturing, the journal advocated government support for business. The analyses and general outlooks of *Semana Mercantil* and *El Economista Mexicano* were similar in many respects, but there were distinctions. My sense is that *Semana Mercantil,* representing business interests, had greater autonomy from the government than *El Economista Mexicano* did. While the two financial journals generally did not engage in debate, they did on occasion. In 1908 they engaged in a series of debates over the issue of protectionism. Alberto Carreño, publishing in *El Economista Mexicano,* championed free trade, countering *Semana Mercantil*'s protectionist position. For a reprint of Carreño's *El Economista Mexicano* articles, see Carreño, *Temas económicos. Primera parte,* 167–217.

68. Bernal Díaz, one of the conquistadores, for example, was amazed at the size, order, and diversity of goods in the Aztecs' market. He maintained it was larger than anything he had ever seen (Díaz, *The Conquest of New Spain,* 231–34). Some Porfirian intellectuals depicted pre-Columbian Indians in a favorable light. See Sierra, *Evolución política,* 9–46.

69. There were rare exceptions, however. Enrique Martínez Sobral (1875–1950), an economist who worked in the Ministry of Development and published several works on economics, wrote a series in *El Economista Mexicano* in 1904 entitled "The Indigenous Race." He maintained that just a few decades earlier the task of modernizing the Indian seemed impossible. However, he contended, the last few decades had surprisingly and unexpectedly brought an answer. Progress, in the form of railroads, telegraphs, and industry, had transformed the Indian. The emergence of the market had broken down cultural barriers and integrated Indians into modern Mexican society (E. Martínez Sobral, "La raza indígena: Breves reflexiones, VI," *El Economista Mexicano,* 17 December 1904, 222–24). For an account of Martínez Sobral's economic ideas, see Silva Herzog, *El pensamiento económico,* 333–41.

70. Carreño, *Problemas indígenas,* 53.

71. Ibid., 307–19.

72. Quoted in González Navarro, "Las ideas raciales," 579.

73. For biographical information on Peust, see Bartra, "Los indios."

74. Peust, "Situación económica."

75. Peust, *Estadista agrícola,* 259. He made a similar claim on another occasion (Peust, "Situación económica"). For similar racialist assertions about Indian labor, see Peust, *México y el problema obrero rural.*

76. Peust, *Estadista agrícola,* 259.

77. Ibid., 260. On an earlier date, Peust implicitly backed his claim that increased wages would not entice Indians to work by asserting that agrarian workers' wages were relatively good. But there was an inconsistency in his argument, for he went on to acknowledge that rural labor was being attracted to urban areas because wages were higher (Peust, "Situación económica").

78. "Los jornaleros agrícolas," *Semana Mercantil,* 12 February 1906, 73–74; González Navarro, *Historia moderna,* 152. One might assume that the discourse about increasing wages

in Mexico in order to stop immigration to the United States countered Peust's position, but it did not, for this discourse did not target "Indian" workers. See Escobar, "La emigración," 28–41; "Los trabajadores mexicanos en los EU: Interesante a los hacendados," *Boletín de la Secretaría de Fomento* (January–June 1906–7): 234–35. See also "Why Peons Leave Mexico," *Boletín de la Asociación Financiera Internacional* (January 1907): 26–27.

79. True, labor did respond to market forces, but only in specific regions. On labor markets, see Cerutti, *Burguesía, capitales e industria;* Gamboa, "Mercado de bolsa de trabajo."

80. There were exceptions, however. Alberto Carreño explicitly attacked coercive methods of obtaining and retaining workers. He called peonage a form of slavery and also noted the coercive aspects of the company store. To liberate workers he advocated abolishing loans to workers, increasing wages, and outlawing payment with tokens (Carreño, *Problemas indígenas,* 263–66). For another contemporary critique, see Molina Enríquez, *Los grandes problemas nacionales,* 170–71. For a classic contemporary account of Porfirian labor coercion, see Turner, *Barbarous Mexico.* See also Katz, *La servidumbre agraria.*

81. For attacks on different forms of labor coercion, see the following articles in *El Paladín:* "Un negrero en una hacienda: Peón brutalmente golpeado," 29 December 1901; "El tráfico de carne humana," 4 August 1904, 1; "Infelices enganchados," 7 August 1904, 1; "Reglamento de enganchadores: El triunfo de *El Paladín,*" 11 August 1904, 1; "Los trabajadores en las fincas rurales," 29 August 1907, 1. See also Anakreon (pseudonym), "¡Faltan brazos!" *El Colmillo Público,* 21 January 1906, 33; Anakreon, "La tiranía científica," *El Colmillo Público,* 31 December 1905, 829–30; "Negreros," *El Hijo del Ahuizote,* 20 April 1902, 1250; "Las negrerías de Yucatán," *El Hijo del Ahuizote,* 4 May 1902, 1278; "La situación en Sonora," *El Nigromante,* 5 March 1906, 2; "La esclavitud en Yucatán," *Regeneración,* 31 January 1901, 4.

82. On vagrancy, see "¿Faltan trabajadores o sobran vagos?" *El Progreso Latino,* 28 February 1906, 193–94. On vagrancy laws, see Knight, *The Mexican Revolution,* 1: 94. On forced consumption, see Castellanos, *Algunos problemas,* 105–10. On enganche, see the following articles in *El Economista Mexicano:* "No faltan brazos en la República," 17 August 1895, 27; "La cuestión bracero en México," 14 September 1895, 75–76; "La cuestión de brazos y la inmigración," 14 December 1895, 230–31. The journal did not depict labor contractors as coercive. To the contrary, it argued that they were necessary because of the limited development of Mexico's transportation network.

83. On the debate over Indian education, see Stabb, "Indigenism and Racism." For the increased call for educating Indians in the late Porfiriato, see Bazant, *Historia de la educación.* On the high hopes liberals placed on education to integrate Indians into the nation, see Bazant, "Prólogo."

84. The term *Indianist,* which indicates a valorization of pre-Columbian culture and a rejection of Westernization, is taken from Knight, "Racism, Revolution, and Indigenismo." Scholars have noted that Porfiristas' modernizing schemes did not validate Indian traditions. See Villoro, *Los grandes momentos,* 175–86.

85. In 1901 Sierra, for example, contended that "we still need to completely change the mentality of the indigenous population by educating them in school" (*Evolución política,* 398).

86. Bulnes, *El porvenir,* 107.

87. Ibid., 100. Sierra, citing former president Juárez, made a similar point, though he

advocated Protestantism as opposed to education to discourage Indian economic donations to the Catholic Church. Sierra viewed this as a means to promote a "bourgeois" society (*Evolución política*, 369).

88. See Castellanos, *Algunos problemas*, 105–10.

89. Liberals were divided over the impact smallholding would have on the size of the labor pool. See Castellanos, *Algunos problemas*, 95.

90. On adult technical education, see Carreño, *Problemas indígenas*, 51–62; Romero, *Mexico and the United States*, 518; Bazant, *Historia de la educación*, chap. 5; González Navarro, *Historia moderna*, 655–56. On technical education at the primary education level, see Correa, "La nueva ley," 47–51; Wilson, *Mexico*.

91. See, for example, "La educación comercial en los estados unidos" and "La enseñanza industrial en los estados unidos," *El Economista Mexicano*, 11 May 1901, 172–73; "La educación económica del pueblo Alemán," *El Economista Mexicano*, 6 March 1909, 494–95; "Las escuelas industriales," *Semana Mercantil*, 4 March 1907; "Las escuelas industriales," *Semana Mercantil*, 11 March 1907.

92. *Memoria presentada al Congreso* (1885), 1: 39; *Memoria presentada al Congreso* (1897), 12.

93. See, for example, Ramos Lanz, *Estudio sobre inmigración y colonización*, which advocated state-sponsored immigration.

94. See Manuel Fernández Leal, Mexico's minister of development, on this issue in *Memoria presentada al Congreso* (1897), 13; *Memoria presentada al Congreso* (1908), 14–15. See also Covarrubias, *Varios informes*, 346.

95. Sierra's thought is a perfect example of this. Within the same paragraph he championed education for Indians and contended it was crucial to inject the Mexican stock with foreign (European) blood (Sierra, *Evolución política*, 398).

96. "Año nuevo–1905," *Semana Mercantil*, 2 January 1905, 1–3.

97. Castellanos, *Algunos problemas*, 83.

98. Gayol, *Dos problemas*, 5. Northern Europeans were not the only group liberals sought, but they were the favored group. Liberals were ambivalent about Anglos, and particularly U.S. immigration, for nationalist reasons. Some liberals were opposed to Spanish immigration, a position that is not surprising, owing to their negative views about Mexico's colonial heritage. *Semana Mercantil* promoted Asian immigration on economic grounds, arguing that Europeans could not be enticed to Mexico because wages were too low. On immigration, see González Navarro, *Los extranjeros en México*, 2: 135–201, and *La colonización de México*.

99. Díaz Dufoo, "La evolución industrial," 106. For the original, see Romero, *Mexico and the United States*, 521.

100. González Navarro, *Historia moderna*, 151.

101. Hale, *Mexican Liberalism*, 180–83. For a brief account of ideological attacks on the hacienda during the nineteenth century, see González Navarro, "Las tierras ociosas."

102. On the privatization of Church lands, see Bazant, *Alienation of Church Wealth*; Knowlton, *Church Property*. On the privatization of Indians' communal lands, see González Navarro, *Historia moderna*, 187–215; Tannenbaum, *Peace by Revolution*; Friedrich, *Agrarian Revolt*; Tutino, *From Insurrection*. For a revisionist interpretation of Porfirian land policy, see Holden, *Mexico and the Survey of Public Lands*.

103. For a counterinterpretation, see Alberto Carreño, who stressed the Porfirian government's attempts to break up the hacienda (*Temas económicos*, 314–16).

104. Raigosa, "La evolución agrícola," 38.

105. Castellot served as both a deputy and senator. *Boletín de la Asociación Financiera Internacional,* the financial paper he edited during 1906 and 1907, wed his interests in journalism and finance. In his early career in Campeche he was a journalist, and later he became involved in finance. He helped establish banks in Mexico City, Hidalgo, Michoacán, and Veracruz.

106. The monthly journal had one section published in English and another in Spanish, although the sections were not identical. The English section tended to focus more on foreign investment, and the Spanish section stressed Mexican national problems. The semiofficial publication had a twenty-year charter from the Mexican government, and the government had the power to place two of the five board members. In 1907 the publication reported its circulation for the first two years of its existence (1906–7) at 85,000. See José Castellot, "Report on the Internacional Financial Association," *Boletín de la Asociación Financiera Internacional* (July 1907): 28–29.

107. "Mexican Land Owners," *Boletín de la Asociación Financiera Internacional* (July 1907): 13.

108. "La agricultura y su porvenir," *La Gaceta,* reprinted in *Semana Mercantil,* 21 September 1908, 523–24.

109. "Movimiento agrícola de México," *Boletín de la Sociedad Agrícola Mexicana,* 9 August 1900, 583–86.

110. Palacios, *El problema de la irrigación,* 18–19.

111. "El Regadío de tierras: ¿Falta de valor, rutinarismo, o indolencia?" *El Progreso Latino,* 21 January 1906, 69–70.

112. One example of the journal's concern with the plight of Mexicans with limited economic means was its regular publication of excerpts from Henry George during 1905 and 1906. In addition, the journal expressed sympathy for the position of workers after capital-labor strife increased in 1906. My search for biographical information on Roman Rodríguez Peña proved unsuccessful.

113. For a biography, see Shadle, *Andrés Molina Enríquez.* For the impact of his ideas on twentieth-century agrarian reform, see Kourí, "Interpreting."

114. To take the example of property, consistent with developmentalist liberals' evolutionism, Molina Enríquez depicted communal property as low on the evolutionary scale and private property at the top. Nomads were even lower than Indians who lived in communal villages. While he hoped that the latter could be converted to private property owners, he advocated that the former be conscripted into the army (Molina Enríquez, *Los grandes problemas nacionales,* 191–96). Similar evolutionary ideas about property were articulated by members of the Porfirian regime. See Castellanos, *Algunos problemas,* 93; Carreño, *Problemas indígenas,* 97. For an analysis of similarities between the ideas of Molina Enríquez and members of the Porfirian regime, see Córdova, "El pensamiento social," 11–68.

115. Molina Enríquez, *Los grandes problemas nacionales,* 158–59. He also likened hacendados to the French nobility before the Revolution (ibid., 199).

116. Ibid., 157. Jose L. Cosío's 1911 defense of the hacienda suggests that the assumption that it was a feudal holdover from the colonial era was fairly widespread. Though he

sought to defend the hacienda, he acknowledged that "many people have affirmed that the large property concessions given during the colonial era have kept rural property amortized and because of this there is insufficient property for towns" (Cosío, *Cómo y por quiénes*, 7).

117. Molina Enríquez, *Los grandes problemas nacionales*, 165.

118. Ibid., 120.

119. Ibid., 307.

120. For the classic work that depicted the hacienda as a feudal structure, see Chevalier, *Land and Society*. For revisionist scholarship, see Kizca, *Colonial Entrepreneurs;* Bazant, *Cinco haciendas mexicanas;* Van Young, *Hacienda and Market*.

121. See, for example, "Mexican Land Owners," *Boletín de la Asociación Financiera Internacional* (July 1907): 13; "Una ley que no se ha dada, pero que debiera darse," *Boletín de la Asociación Financiera Internacional* (December 1908): 44–45; "Tierras cultivadas y tierras incultas," *Semana Mercantil,* 10 December 1906, 592–93; "La descentralización de las grandes extensiones territoriales," *El Economista Mexicano,* 4 December 1909, 1801; "Las cuatro preguntas de *El Progreso Latino*," *El Progreso Latino,* 21 April 1906, 460; "Inversión de capitales cortos: Las pequeñas empresas agrícolas," *El Progreso Latino,* 14 April 1906, 421; "Editorial: Política sobre la repartición de las tierras," *El Heraldo Agrícola* (March 1910): 2.

122. Bulnes, *El porvenir,* 374–75.

123. For opponents of the tax, see "Una idea inaceptable," *El Economista Mexicano,* 1 December 1906, 177–78 (this article was reprinted in *Boletín de la Sociedad Agrícola Mexicana,* 25 December 1906, 945–46); "Tierras e impuestos," *El Economista Mexicano,* 22 December 1906, 246–47. For proponents of the tax, see "Editorial: Política sobre la repartición de las tierras," *El Heraldo Agrícola* (March 1910): 2; "Tierras cultivadas y tierras incultas," *Semana Mercantil,* 10 December 1906, 592–93; "La agricultura y su porvenir," *Semana Mercantil,* 21 September 1908, 523–24.

124. "Tax Unoccupied Lands to Encourage Colonization," *Mexican Herald,* 29 October 1908, 2.

125. "Un impuesto injustificado," *El Economista Mexicano,* 7 November 1908, 111–12. For a similar position, see "El impuesto sobre las tierras," *El Tiempo,* 5 November 1908, 1; "La contribución sobre terrenos," *El Tiempo,* 11 November 1908, 2.

126. For the government's position, see *Memoria presentada al Congreso* (1911), lxi–lxxx, 223–25. For governmental policies promoting redistribution in 1909, see González Navarro, *Historia moderna,* 194–95. For press commentaries on the proposed legislation, see "Iniciativa de una nueva ley de tierras: Su transcendencia económica," *El Economista Mexicano,* 11 April 1908, 21–22; "Iniciativa de una nueva ley de tierras: Su transcendencia económica," *El Economista Mexicano,* 25 April 1908, 57–58.

127. Palacios, *El problema de la irrigación,* 18–19.

128. Zayas Enríquez, *Los Estados Unidos Mexicanos,* 177.

Chapter 3. A "Battle for Existence"

1. Hobsbawm, *The Age of Empire*.

2. For the classic formulation on comparative advantage, see Ricardo, *Principles of Political Economy,* 147–67.

3. Some scholars have countered this interpretation by emphasizing Porfirian economic nationalism. See Cott, "Porfirian Investment Policies," for nationalist economic policies during the last decade of the Porfiriato. Knight argues that Porfirian economic nationalism was a precursor to the PRI's nationalism (*The Mexican Revolution*, 1: 22; Knight, *U.S.–Mexican Relations*). See also Cosío Villegas, "Séptima llamada particular," xi–xxviii.

4. Revisionist scholarship on policy has challenged conventional wisdom, which maintains that the Porfirian regime adhered to laissez-faire (see chap. 1, n. 54).

5. On the reception of Darwinism in Mexico, see Moreno, "Mexico." It appears that social Darwinism became much more prevalent in Mexico at the turn of the century, for while it was very visible in the sources I examined for the first decade of the twentieth century, Hale maintains it was less influential during the 1870s, 1880s, and even the 1890s (*The Transformation of Liberalism*, 229, 252).

6. On the different strands of social Darwinism, see Himmelfarb, *Victorian Minds*, 314–32; Peel, *Herbert Spencer*, 232–37. For the impact of social Darwinism on the discipline of economics, see Schumpeter, *History of Economic Analysis*, 788–90.

7. On the influence of positivism in Mexico, see Zea, *El positivismo en México*. Dirk Raat and Charles Hale have written revisionist scholarship on the subject. See Raat, "Los intelectuales," "Leopoldo Zea and Positivism," and *El positivismo*. See also Hale, *The Transformation of Liberalism;* and Guerra, *México*, 1: 376–93. On positivism in Latin America, see Woodward, *Positivism*.

8. Limantour, "Discurso pronunciado," 303.

9. Macedo, "La hacienda pública," 388–89.

10. Macedo, "Comunicaciones y obras públicas," 277–78. Detailed formulations like Macedo's that equated the market with life were rare. However, short phrases in which the economy was a metaphor for life were more common. Sierra, for example, claimed that the practice of money lending at exorbitant rates (*agio*) "was an invading parasite that impeded us from living" (*Evolución política*, 366).

11. "Los extranjeros residentes," *El Progreso Latino*, 14 April 1906, 417–18.

12. Ibid.

13. Sierra, *Evolución política*, 364.

14. Ibid.

15. Bulnes, *El porvenir*, 161–64. For the Mexican press's reaction to the war, see Bobadilla González, "La opinión pública."

16. Romero, *Estudio sobre la anexión*. His work also contains copies of Mexican periodicals' reactions to his work. Francisco Bulnes, too, maintained that U.S. military intervention no longer posed a threat (*El porvenir*).

17. See *El Tiempo* articles of 4 June 1899 and especially 28 June 1889, which were reprinted in Romero, *Estudio sobre la anexión*, 39–42, 62–67.

18. Pereyra, "Prólogo," iv.

19. For the liberal opposition press, see Anakreon, "La conquista pacífica: Civilicemonos a lo gringo," *El Colmillo Público*, 12 June 1904, 374–75; "El Congreso Pan-Americano (de nuestra inventiva particular)," *El Alacrán*, 2 February 1900, 3; "Los insolentes Yankees," *El Paladín*, 24 January 1901, 1; "La conquista pacífica," *El Paladín*, 9 June 1901, 1; "Lo que 'El Mundo' aplaude lo llorara más tarde la patria: El capital anglo-sajon," *El Paladín*, 23 June

1901, 1; "Unión contra despotismo," *El Ferrocarrilero,* 23 June 1904, 1; "México . . . ¡Alerta!" *El Paladín,* 13 June 1901, 1; "El peligro Yankee," *El Paladín,* 3 October 1901, 1; "Sigue la conquista pacífica: La venta de las fábricas de cigarros a un sindicato americano," *El Paladín,* 2 October 1902, 1; "Los insolentes Yankees," *El Paladín,* 24 January 1901, 1; "Un ejemplo de patriotismo," *El Paladín,* 27 January 1901, 1; "México para los extranjeros: Los mexicanos sin patria. La conquista pacífica toca a su fin. Siniestros augurios," *El Paladín,* 16 August 1906, 1; Fausto Garibay Pachuca, "Los americanos conquistarán México, no con las armas, sino con la industria y su dinero," *El Paladín,* 23 February 1908, 1; "La codicia yankee: La Baja California en peligro," *El Paladín,* 5 April 1908, 1. For the conservative press, see "La conquista pacífica y la agresión armada," *El País,* 1 June 1901, 1; "'The Mexican Herald' y la conquista pacífica," *El País,* 8 June 1901, 1; "La conquista 'espiritual' de México: Los ideales anglo-americanos de ayer y hoy," *El País,* 12 June 1901, 1; "Ave Cesar," *El País,* 20 June 1901, 1. For a secondary account of the notion of the "peaceful conquest," see González Navarro, *Los extranjeros en México,* 2: 226–43.

20. On Mexico's abundant mineral and agricultural resources, see Humboldt, *Political Essay,* esp. 2: 401–513, 3: 1–161. José María Luis Mora, Mexico's leading liberal thinker in the early republic, for example, was influenced by Humboldt. Following in Humboldt's footsteps, Mora celebrated Mexico's abundant resources (*México y sus revoluciones,* 1: 23–34). For the strong impact of Humboldt's essay in Mexico, see Alamán, *Historia de Méjico,* 1: 138; Prieto, *Economía política,* 225; Hale, *Mexican Liberalism,* 254; Cosío Villegas, *American Extremes,* 154–76.

21. On this shift, see chap. 2, n. 57.

22. Díaz Dufoo, "La evolución industrial," 103.

23. Ibid., 107.

24. Ibid., 100.

25. Macedo, *La evolución mercantil,* 175–78.

26. Zayas Enríquez, *Los Estados Unidos Mexicanos,* 176–77.

27. For an expanded discussion of this topic, see Weiner, "Rich Colony, Poor Nation."

28. Raigosa, "La evolución agrícola," 41.

29. Díaz Dufoo, "La evolución industrial," 107.

30. García, *Nociones de economía política,* 13.

31. But Cora was suspicious of capital also. He claimed that it could be "extremely dangerous because it lacked the consistency that constituted land" (Cora, "Reseña histórica," 8).

32. Sierra, *Evolución política,* 362.

33. Ibid., 363–64.

34. Ibid., 397.

35. Vasconcelos, "The Latin American Basis," 3–102.

36. *El Progreso Latino* made its ambivalence extremely explicit. The paper asked readers on repeated occasions if Americans should be feared. See, for example, "¿Temor al Yankee?" *El Progreso Latino,* 7 November 1905, 505–6; "Los problemas nacionales," *El Progreso Latino,* 7 January 1906, 8.

37. The 1884 and 1892 mining legislation overturned earlier legislation that was inherited from Spanish colonial law. Colonial law gave the state control over subsoil rights and required leasers (they were technically leasing as opposed to owners) to fulfill a variety of

obligations such as working the mine continuously and employing specific numbers of workers. The 1892 law changed this situation by making titles irrevocable (as long as taxes were paid) and by not requiring owners to exploit their property. Despite strengthening property rights, Bernstein maintains the law did not revoke the government's control over subsoil rights, as some contemporaries believed (*The Mexican Mining Industry*, 27–29; see also Nava Oteo, "La minería," 306–7).

38. On mining legislation, see *Memoria presentada al Congreso* (1897), 70–71; Vera Estañol, "Juridical Evolution," 751; Crespo y Martínez, "Evolución minera," 82; Baca, *Reseña histórica*, 73. Díaz's presidential messages also hailed the law (Cámara de Diputados, *Los presidentes*, 352, 469, 483).

39. For the Mexican government's study on monetary reform, see *Comisión monetaria México*. It is evident that the 1905 monetary reform sought to increase foreign (and especially American) investment in Mexico. American financial advisors Charles Conant and Jeremiah Jenks helped shape policy. In fact, an article about the gold standard by Jenks was translated into Spanish and published in the Mexican government's study on the monetary reform ("Problemas monetarios," 105–8). On Conant's and Jenks's roles in Mexico, see Rosenberg, "Foundations," 169–202; see also Parrini and Sklar, "New Thinking," 571–73. For a study on the monetary reform, see Borja Martínez, *La reforma monetaria*.

40. "President Díaz to Congress: The Monetary Reform," *Boletín de la Asociación Financiera Internacional* (April 1906): 2–3.

41. "The Gold Standard," *Boletín de la Asociación Financiera Internacional* (July 1907): 27.

42. On Díaz's image-building campaign, see Turner, *Barbarous Mexico*, chap. 13; and Cott, "Porfirian Investment Policies," 72–76.

43. On foreign investment in Porfirian Mexico, see Topik, "The Emergence of Finance Capital"; Cott, "Porfirian Investment Policies"; Ceceña, *México en la órbita imperial*; Katz, *The Secret War*; d'Olwer, "Las inversiones extranjeras."

44. According to Myra Wilkins's estimates, U.S. investment in Mexico doubled from 1897 to 1902, reaching half a billion dollars. It had doubled again by 1907, reaching a billion dollars. Over half of U.S. foreign investment went to Mexico (Wilkins, *The Emergence of Multinational Enterprise*, 125). On U.S. dominance over European competitors, see also d'Olwer, "Las inversiones extranjeras," 1013, 1149–67; and Topik, "The Emergence of Finance Capital."

45. See Brown, "The Structure of the Foreign-Owned Petroleum Industry" and *Domestic Politics*.

46. *El Progreso Latino*, 28 October 1907, 553.

47. On Roosevelt's antitrust position, see Sklar, *The Corporate Reconstruction*, 340–46. On populist class rhetoric against trusts, see Lustig, *Corporate Liberalism*, 39–46, 70–71.

48. "El nuevo pacto de hambre: Peligros de monopolio," *El Imparcial*, 27 January 1903, 1.

49. *El Economista Mexicano*, for example, reprinted a protrust article that was originally published in the *Mexican Journal of Commerce* but criticized it (*El Economista Mexicano*, 6 September 1902, 452–53).

50. *El Imparcial*, 16 May 1902, 1.

51. *Memoria que presentó el Secretario de Hacienda* (1909), 412–27.

52. *El Economista Mexicano*, 6 June 1903, 205–7.

53. Parlee, "Porfirio Díaz, Railroads and Development," 261.

54. Limantour, *The Railway Merger,* 2.

55. There was an extensive debate between the American and Mexican press in Mexico over article 144. For the most part, the Mexican press supported the article, and the American press opposed it. For supporters of article 144, see "La retirada del art: 144 del proyecto de ley de minería," *Semana Mercantil,* 26 October 1908, 589–90; "No hay sentimiento antiextranjero en México," *El Economista Mexicano,* 4 July 1908, 272–74; "El proyecto de la nueva ley minera," *El Economista Mexicano,* 11 July 1908, 294–95; "El proyecto de la nueva ley minera: Las compañías extranjeras," *El Economista Mexicano,* 18 July 1908, 315–16; "Se traeran capitales extranjeros para la minería," *La Clase Media,* 1 March 1909, 3; "La incapacidad de las sociedades extranjeras para adquirir minas, considerada bajo el aspecto económico," *El País,* 3 July 1908, 1; "La ley minera," *El Tiempo,* 17 June 1908, 2; "Los extranjeros y la ley minera," *El Tiempo,* 23 June 1908, 2; "Las reformas a la ley minera" and "Habló al fin," *El Tiempo* 27 June 1908, 2; "La ley minera y los extranjeros," *El Tiempo,* 3 July 1908, 2; "Habló al fin, II," *El Tiempo,* 4 July 1908, 2; "El eterno argumento," *El Tiempo,* 8 July 1908, 1. *Boletín de la Asociación Financiera Internacional* opposed the tax; see the following: "Autorizada interpretación de la nueva ley minera" (September 1908); "Mexican Mining Laws" (July 1906): 18; "Change in Mining Laws" (April 1907): 15; "Nueva ley minera de México" (August 1908): 53. See the following from the *Mexican Herald,* which also opposed it: "Anti-Foreign Mining Measure Opposed," 30 May 1908, 1; "Argument Advanced by Leading Mexican," 1 June 1908, 1; "The New Mining Law," 2 June 1908, 1; "Foreign Companies and Mines," 3 June 1908, 1; "Minister Molina on Proposed Mining Law," 7 June 1908, 1; "The Abstention of Capital," 12 June 1908, 1; "New Law Would Bar British Capital from Investment in the Mexican Republic," 4 June 1908, 1; "El Imparcial's Explanation," 21 June 1908, 1; "More about Foreign Capital," 30 June 1908, 1; "Two Distinct Issues," 2 July 1902, 1.

56. *Memoria presentada al Congreso* (1910), 189.

57. Peust, *La defensa nacional,* 5. For a direct rebuttal to Peust's attack on foreign capital, see the pamphlet written by Manuel de la Peña, editor of *Boletín de la Sociedad Agrícola Mexicana,* entitled *Algunas problemas sociales y económicos,* 13–16. Peust's pamphlet was not without supporters, however. (Nevertheless, supporters did not directly comment on the section of his text that examined foreign capital.) See "Un folleto sobre México," *El Tiempo,* 22 May 1907, 2; "El folleto sobre México de Otto Peust: La Doctrina Monroe," *El Tiempo,* 11 June 1907, 2. Even in this nationalist climate there were analysts who claimed that foreign investment had no negative effects. See "Credit and Business," *Boletín de la Asociación Financiera Internacional* (September 1905): 34; and "The Affairs of the World and Mexico," *Boletín de la Asociación Financiera Internacional* (October 1905): 1.

58. Peust's definition of imperialism as a form of informal control had similarities to Rudolph Hilferding's analysis, for he, too, discussed formal and informal imperialism (*Finance Capital,* 311–36). For other contemporary theorists on economic imperialism, see Conant, *The United States and the Orient;* Hobson, *Imperialism.*

59. Raigosa, "La evolución agrícola," 21.

60. "Enseñanza industrial," *El Consultor,* 1 September 1899, reprinted in Eguiarte Sakar, ed., *Hacer ciudadanos,* 149.

61. Bulnes, *El porvenir,* 274, 366.

62. Sierra, *Evolución política*, 398.

63. For Sierra's critique of le Bon, see *México social y político*, 8–9.

64. On racial justifications for imperialism, see Gould, *The Mismeasure of Man*, 118–19. On race and anti-imperialism, see Banton, *Racial Theories*, 58–59.

65. Raigosa, *El problema fundamental*.

66. Ibid., 51–55. In another essay Raigosa made a similar claim about Mexicans being unprepared for the struggle for existence ("La evolución agrícola," 38).

67. *Revista de Legislación y Jurisprudencia* 29 (July–December 1905): 566. Mendez's treatise was commented upon in the financial press ("Un problema interesante," *Semana Mercantil*, 12 February 1906, 122–23). Schell's recent monograph supports Mendez's contention about Americans' insular nature, for it shows that during the last decade of the Porfiriato the American colony in Mexico grew significantly and also became insular and culturally American (*Integral Outsiders*, 52).

68. "El obrero mexicano y el capital extranjero," *El Progreso Latino*, 28 July 1906, 111; "Huelga en Aguascalientes," *El Progreso Latino*, 7 August 1906, 133; "Las huelgas y las obreros mexicanos: El espíritu yankee," *El Progreso Latino*, 7 August 1907, 142–43.

69. For some contemporary commentary on this issue, see "La cuestión de los despachadores," *Semana Mercantil*, 26 July 1909, 407–8; and "Documentos de interés," *Semana Mercantil*, 16 August 1909, 450–53. On foreign workers in the oil industry, see Brown and Linder, "Oil." On the government's nationalist labor policies and ideology in the railroad industry, see González Roa, *El problema ferrocarrilero;* and Brown, "Trabajadores nativos."

70. "Unión contra despotismo," *El Ferrocarrilero*, 23 June 1904, 1.

71. On class formation, see Katz, "Mexico." On capital labor relations, see Anderson, *Outcasts;* and González Navarro, *Las huelgas.*

72. For the argument that conditions in Mexico were not ripe for major conflicts between capital and labor, see "Los fogoneros," *El Imparcial*, 15 October 1902, 1; "El socialismo en México," *El Economista Mexicano*, 13 September 1902, 468–69. Even after capital-labor conflict became an issue of national debate in 1907, *Semana Mercantil* still denied that it was an issue in Mexico. "Siguen las huelgas—hay una mala semilla," *Semana Mercantil*, 13 May 1907, 251–52.

73. Beatty, "The Impact of Foreign Trade."

74. *El Economista Mexicano*, 5 October 1907, 1–2.

75. Developmentalist liberals articulated the popular sentiment that the overproduction crisis in Europe and the United States made exporting a necessity. On this issue, see Mommsen, *Theories of Imperialism*, 4–28; and Hobsbawm, *The Age of Empire*, chaps. 2 and 3.

76. In 1902 the Mexican government sent a trade commission to South America to seek outlets for Mexican goods. The commission explained that the trip was motivated by the fact that production exceeded national demand. On the commission, see "La industria mexicana," *El Imparcial*, 27 May 1902, 1; and Martínez Sobral, *Principio de economía*, 525. Also see Haber, *Industry and Underdevelopment*. On the overproduction problem, see Domínguez, *Relaciones comerciales*, who contended that Mexico needed to export to South America owing to "excessive" production.

77. On the commercial basis of imperialism, see Bulnes, *El porvenir*, 155–57; Peust, *La defensa nacional*, 6–11.

78. Silva Herzog, *Nueve estudios mexicanos*, 295. This was in keeping with Hobson's analysis, which emphasized the creation of formal empires to create markets for consumer goods (*Imperialism*, 15–27).

79. "Comercio exterior de México: Reflexiones sobre sus cifras," *El Progreso Latino*, 21 November 1906, 633–34.

80. For a more recent academic theory of informal trade imperialism, see Robinson and Gallagher, "The Imperialism of Free Trade."

81. Interestingly, this concern differed from the desires of some U.S. expansionists who valued Mexico and Latin America as consumers of American goods. See Conant, *The United States and the Orient*, 74–79.

82. Limantour, *Apuntes sobre mi vida pública*, 196–99.

83. "Comercio exterior de México."

84. "Comercio exterior," *El Progreso Latino*, 28 April 1906, 481–82.

85. Carreño, *Temas económicos*, 40–41. *Semana Mercantil*, too, advertised the reexport problem, contending that the United States was the middleman between Mexico and Europe ("Los puertos del golfo y el tráfico europeo," *Semana Mercantil*, 15 June 1908, 323–24).

86. Raigosa, *El problema fundamental*, 55.

87. "El trigo: Previsión y monopolio," *El Progreso Latino*, 14 July 1905, 69.

88. Peel, *Herbert Spencer*, 90–96.

89. "Estatismo," *El Economista Mexicano*, 2 October 1909, 579–80.

90. Sierra, *Educación nacional*, 166–67.

91. *El Imparcial* explained: "For us, the government protects the interests of the people, and where its sphere of influence ends, there is no other power that emerges to defend public interests" ("Contra los monopolios: Lo que hace el pueblo," *El Imparcial*, 1 May 1902, 1; see also "¿Pueden combatirse los trusts mexicanos?" *El Economista Mexicano*, 12 April 1902, 24).

92. This was not his only justification for railroad nationalization, however. He also complained about the problem of parallel lines, inefficiency, and a poor geographical distribution of the railroads. Limantour first developed these arguments in his 1898 *informe*. See *Memoria que presentó el Secretario de Hacienda* (1902), 401–15.

93. *El Economista Mexicano*, 3 October 1908, 2–4.

94. The liberal opposition paper *El Paladín*, for example, supported some of the government's early nationalist initiatives ("El ferrocarril interoceánico: Previsión del gobierno mexicano," *El Paladín*, 2 October 1902, 1). At the other end of the spectrum, *Boletín de la Asociación Financiera Internacional*, a journal that generally opposed nationalist economic measures, also supported it ("The Purchase of Mexican Central," *Boletín de la Asociación Financiera Internacional* [January 1907]: 30–31; and "Mexico Buying Railroads Wholesale," *Boletín de la Asociación Financiera Internacional* [May 1907]: 19–20). There was some opposition to nationalization, however. The harshest and most prolific critic of railroad nationalization was Toribio Esquivel Obregón. For one of his critiques, see *El Tiempo*, 12 June 1908, 2. He contended that nationalization scared foreign capital and created a national as opposed to a foreign monopoly.

95. *Semana Mercantil* directly challenged assertions that the government would play a large role in railroad development after nationalization ("El ferrocarril interoceánico," *Semana Mercantil*, 5 January 1903, 3; "El control del gobierno sobre los ferrocarriles," *Semana Mercantil*,

10 February 1908, 75–76; and "La unión de los ferrocarriles," *Semana Mercantil*, 2 March 1908, 116–17). Carlos Díaz Dufoo expressed the same general idea, maintaining that railroad nationalization could not be equated with "state socialism, [where the state] was a businessman and exploiter of determined industries" (*Limantour*, 169). See also *El Economista Mexicano*, 11 July 1908, 293–94.

96. Liberals were divided over the impact smallholding would have on the size of the labor pool. See Castellanos, *Algunos problemas*, 95.

97. Carreño, *Problemas indígenas*, 51–62; Romero, *Mexico and the United States*, 518.

98. "Horizonte mexicano: Presente y porvenir," *El Progreso Latino*, 21 July 1906, 65.

99. Sierra, *Educación nacional*, 109.

100. Ibid. Sierra employed similar rhetoric in a later battle in Congress against Cosmes and other federalist critics of his proposal for state-sponsored obligatory national education for the indigenous population (ibid., 223). He had articulated a social Darwinist position over a decade earlier, claiming national "instruction" would make Mexico "better armed for the battle of life" (Sierra, *México social y político*, 28–29).

101. "La educación industrial del pueblo," *El Consultor*, 1 October 1902, reprinted in Eguiarte Sacar, ed., *Hacer ciudadanos*, 157.

102. "Enseñaza industrial," *El Consultor*, 1 September 1899, reprinted in ibid., 149. On another occasion, the paper attributed similar powers to technical education, asserting that with education Mexicans "are going to acquire arms to fight . . . and save Mexican society" (F. M. Ortiz, "La educación industrial del pueblo," *El Consultor*, 1 October 1902, reprinted in ibid., 157–59). Other analysts depicted technical education in nationalist terms, even if they did not use such explicit social Darwinist rhetoric. See "La educación del obrero," *El Imparcial*, 11 November 1902, 1; "La raza indígena y la agricultura," *El Progreso Latino*, 28 November 1905, 603–4. On the importance of technical education to the Mexicanization of the workforce in the railroad industry, see González Roa, *El problema ferrocarrilero*.

103. Molina Enríquez, *Los grandes problemas nacionales*, 361.

104. Ibid., 363.

105. Sierra, *Educación nacional*, 329.

106. On the domestic emphasis of women's education in Porfirian Mexico, see Macías, *Against All Odds*, 10–13; and Vaughan, *The State, Education, and Social Class*, 202–4. This domestic emphasis in women's education in Mexico was in keeping with a general Latin American trend. See Miller, *Latin American Women*, 53.

107. On Porfirian separate spheres ideology, see Radkau, *Por la debilidad de nuestro ser*. On the discourse of domesticity, see Franco, *Plotting Women;* and Ramos Escandón, "Señoritas porfirianas." Not only the bourgeoisie but also some artisans adhered to a separate spheres ideology. See Vaughan, *The State, Education, and Social Class*, 202. This position was not unique to Mexico. Even Latin American feminists emphasized the domestic roles of women. On Latin American feminism, see Miller, *Latin American Women*, 74.

108. Molina Enríquez referred to the family unit as an organism and invoked the authority of biological differences between the sexes to support his contentions. He defined women's central role as reproduction: "The woman is the organ that has become the distinct being whose function is reproduction." Men's role was "complementary," for it was the public realm: "The man . . . has become the distinct being . . . whose function is to provide food for the total

organism." These separate roles, according to Molina Enríquez, were determined biologically and hence were "irreversible." Molina Enríquez invoked the "law of the division of labor" to support his argument (*Los grandes problemas nacionales,* 361). The father of positivism, Auguste Comte, asserting that men were rational and women were moral, stressed the differences between men and women (*Auguste Comte and Positivism,* 267–70).

109. See the following *Semana Mercantil* articles: "La exportación y la importación de Europa y México," 20 May 1907, 266–67; "El henequén en Europa," 3 June 1907, 293–94; "Los puertos del golfo y el tráfico europeo," 15 June 1908, 323–24; "El comercio con Europa," 9 August 1909, 436–37.

110. On Central America, see "Nuestro tráfico con Centro América," *Semana Mercantil,* 27 July 1908, 407; "Nuestra exportación a Centro y Sur-América," *El Progreso Latino,* 14 October 1906, 435–36; "Nuestras relaciones comerciales con Guatemala," *El Economista Mexicano,* 15 August 1908, 403.

111. On expanding the merchant marine, see especially *El Progreso Latino.* The journal strongly advocated developing Mexico's merchant marine, contending that without it Mexican "exports are at the mercy of the foreign merchant marine" ("Horizonte México," 28 February 1906, 226–27). From the same journal, see "Caminos y puertos: Vida, más vida nacional," 7 July 1905, 5; "Deficiencia de nuestros medios de comunicación marítima: Asunto de vital importancia para la nación," 7 December 1905, 633–34; "Deficiencia de nuestros medios de comunicación marítima," 21 December 1905, 712–13; "Los fletes y los terrestres: Differencia onerosa," 14 January 1906, 40; "La marina mercante," 28 February 1906, 233–34; "Marina mercante nacional: Expediente y rutinas," 14 April 1906, 420–21; "El movimiento marítima," 21 October 1906; "Nuestra industria naviera: Otro problema nacional," 28 December 1906, 829–30. For a detailed argument in favor of stationing Mexican trade agents in foreign countries, see Padilla, "Proyecto." It is worth noting that *Semana Mercantil* argued against commercial agents, maintaining that foreign countries were already well aware of what Mexico exported. See the following: "Agentes comerciales en el extranjero," 18 October 1909, 575–76; "Agentes comerciales de México en el extranjero," 24 January 1910, 41–42; "Los agentes comerciales, II," 31 January 1910.

Chapter 4. "Egotistical Capitalism"

1. Sánchez Santos championed increased agricultural productivity as opposed to land redistribution. See his article "El problema agrícola." Proponents of land redistribution advocated taxing unproductive lands to encourage redistribution. The Catholic periodical *El Tiempo* strongly opposed taxation ("El impuesto sobre las tierras," *El Tiempo,* 5 November 1908, 1; "La contribución sobre terrenos," *El Tiempo,* 11 November 1908, 2).

2. Misner, *Social Catholicism,* 190–200.

3. Ketteler, *The Social Teachings,* 325–32.

4. On the influence of the encyclical, see Misner, *Social Catholicism,* 213–26; Moody, "Leo XIII and the Social Crisis," 65–88; Murphy, "Rerum Novarum (1891)," 1–26.

5. León XIII, *Encíclicas: Rerum Novarum.*

6. Supporting this contention, he complained that during "obscure" times interest rates

were 6 percent but that in modern times they were as high as "12 percent, 18 percent, and 30 percent" ("¿Somos más felices?" *El País,* 8 May 1901, 1).

7. Ibid.

8. "La nueva campaña," *El País,* 2 January 1901, 1.

9. "Las 'ideas modernas' y sus frutos," *El País,* 23 June 1900, 1.

10. *El País,* 29 April 1903, 1.

11. "Las 'ideas modernas' y sus frutos."

12. "La 'materialización' de la ciencia," *El País,* 11 September 1906, 1. *El País* quoted from Ingram's popular text, *A History of Political Economy.* Ingram was a well-known economist who began attacking laissez-faire economics in the 1870s. For an analysis of his economic ideas, see Boylan and Foley, *Political Economy and Colonial Ireland,* 138–44.

13. Dumont, *From Mandeville to Marx.*

14. "Las 'ideas modernas' y sus frutos." This association between Anglo ideas and materialism was by no means unique to Sánchez Santos. For the most well-known critique of Anglo materialism, see Rodó, *Ariel.*

15. León XIII, *Encíclicas: Rerum Novarum.* The pope took a middle position regarding the state's role, for there were currents in social Catholicism that advocated both more and less intervention than he did. See Misner, *Social Catholicism.*

16. "¿Somos más felices?" *El País,* 8 May 1901, 1.

17. "Reversión a la barbarie," *El País,* 7 September 1906, 1.

18. "Las grandes cuestiones sociales," *El País,* 24 August 1901, 1.

19. "Notas editoriales: Algo que deben meditar los capitalistas—la idea cristiana previene los antagonismos," *El Tiempo,* 16 January 1907, 2.

20. "La caridad y el egoísmo," *El País,* 16 April 1903, 1. Sánchez Santos identified the author he quoted as "Isern." He was probably the Spanish writer Damian Isern, who wrote on related subjects. See, for example, his work *Del desastre nacional y sus causas.*

21. *El País,* 16 April 1903, 1; *El País,* 29 April 1903, 1.

22. "El hombre máquina de los economistas: Errores y errores; necesidad de su corrección dentro de la ciencia—texto de John Kells Ingram," *El País,* 29 April 1903, 1.

23. León XIII, *Encíclicas: Rerum Novarum,* 45.

24. "La caridad y el egoísmo," *El País,* 16 April 1903, 1.

25. "La cuestión obrero—sus causas y remedios," *El Tiempo,* 30 January 1907, 2.

26. "El anarquismo y sus factores económicos," *El País,* 29 July 1906, 1.

27. "El verdadero origen del socialismo y el anarquismo," *El País,* 29 August 1906, 1.

28. "El anarquismo y sus factores económicos," *El País,* 29 July 1906, 1.

29. Sánchez Santos, *Obras selectas,* 1: 101. He made a similar claim in another essay he wrote that dealt with the conflict between capital and labor (*Trinidad Sánchez Santos: Discursos,* 113).

30. León XIII, *Encíclicas: Rerum Novarum,* 39.

31. "Frailes y tiranos," *Regeneración,* 29 October 1910.

32. Sánchez Santos, "El problema agrícola," 3–4.

33. Sánchez Santos, *Obras selectas,* 1: 86.

34. León XIII, *Encíclicas: Rerum Novarum,* 22–23, 45.

35. Sánchez Santos, "El problema agrícola," 4–8.

36. "La caridad y el egoísmo." Isern was not credited in the 16 April article; however, he was subsequently credited for it in a related article published in *El País* on 29 April 1903, 1.

37. Sánchez Santos, *Trinidad Sánchez Santos: Discursos,* 283–84.

38. Gould, *The Mismeasure of Man,* 39–42.

39. Ibid., 73–112.

40. "Un abismo de males señalado por 'El Imparcial,'" *El País,* 19 December 1899, 1; "El fiasco de la prosperidad," *El País,* 7 January 1908, 1; Sánchez Santos, *Obras selectas,* 1: 123.

41. "Únicos medios de promover el alza de los salarios," *El País,* 16 June 1910.

42. "El gobierno y los salarios," *El Imparcial,* 8 August 1906, 1.

43. León XIII, *Encíclicas: Rerum Novarum,* 14.

44. Ibid., 47.

45. The journal went on to define this "necessity" as sufficient wages to provide for the family's moral and physical needs. See "Las grandes cuestiones sociales," originally published in the Madrid publication *Revista Católica de las Cuestiones Sociales,* directed by José Ignacio Urbina and reprinted in *El País,* 24 August 1901, 1.

46. "Únicos medios de promover el alza de los salarios."

47. Hart, *Revolutionary Mexico.*

48. For this aspect of Thomist thought, see Ceballos Ramírez, *El catolicismo social,* 46.

49. "Causas del actual desequilibrio económico: La depreciación de la plata y la especulación," *El País,* 13 June 1903, 1; "El actual desequilibrio económico," *El País,* 6 June 1899, 1; "El desequilibrio económico," *El País,* 13 July 1899, 1; "El abismo del desequilibrio económico: El enemigo a la vista," *El País,* 13 February 1900, 1; "El desequilibrio económico y las tarifas ferrocarriles," *El País,* 16 May 1900, 1.

50. "La paz y el progreso: La mejor labor. Primero lo necesario, después lo útil y luego lo superfluo," *El País,* 3 May 1902, 1.

51. "El actual desequilibrio económico."

52. Ibid. For a similar argument, see also "Las tarifas de los ferrocarriles: El poder de las empresas," *El País,* 24 May 1900, 1.

53. On epidemics, see "Causas del actual desequilibrio económico: La depreciación de la plata y la especulación," *El País,* 13 June 1903, 1. On infant mortality, see "Los alquileres de las casas: Graves peligros para mejico," *El País,* 21 November 1899, 1. On marriage, see "El abismo del desequilibrio económico: El enemigo a la vista," *El País,* 13 February 1900, 1.

54. "El actual desequilibrio económico," *El País,* 6 June 1899, 1.

55. "Causas del actual desequilibrio económico."

56. "Dos factores del actual desequilibrio económico: Las tarifas y el impuesto sobre ventas," *El País,* 20 December 1900, 1.

57. "El hombre máquina de los economistas: Errores y errores; necesidad de su corrección dentro de la ciencia—texto de John Kells Ingram," *El País,* 29 April 1903, 1.

58. "Causas del actual desequilibrio económico."

59. "Egoísmo reinante: Falsa apariencia de prosperidad," *La Voz de México,* 1 December 1907, 1.

60. León XIII, *Encíclicas: Rerum Novarum,* 26. Sánchez Santos adhered to the pope's position regarding equality (*Obras selectas,* 1: 101).

61. León XIII, *Encíclicas: Rerum Novarum,* 31, 36, 38, 39.

62. Bulnes, *El porvenir,* 107.

63. Partido Liberal Mexicano, "Manifiesto," 140.

Chapter 5. From "Tyranny" to "Slavery"

1. It needs to be stressed, however, that anarchist thought was disseminated in Mexico well before the PLM's movement. For the history of anarchism in nineteenth-century Mexico, see Hart, *Anarchism;* García Cantú, *El socialismo en México.* See also Cappelletti, "Anarquismo latinoamericano." For anarchism in postrevolutionary Mexico, see Hodges, *Mexican Anarchism.*

2. For a discussion of social liberalism during the early nineteenth century, see Reyes Heroles, *El liberalismo mexicano,* 3: 539–681.

3. For instance, the PLM's 1906 manifesto explicitly maintained that Mexicans experienced both economic and political forms of oppression and that both needed to be addressed. The PLM defined the former as "misery" and the latter as "tyranny" (Partido Liberal Mexicano, "Programa y manifiesto," 191).

4. This classic liberal political discourse was strongly articulated in the PLM's 1906 manifesto. Church-state relations, for example, were discussed extensively. Not only did two sections of the document focus on this issue, but there was also a special section on the Catholic Church in the PLM's reform proposals (ibid., 170–74, 184).

5. See, for example, "Tengamos valor," *Regeneración,* 4 July 1901; "La tiranía científica," *El Colmillo Público,* 31 December 1905; "Iniciativa de la junta organizadora del Partido Liberal: Bases que se ponen a discusión," *El Colmillo Público,* 11 March 1906.

6. My investigation has revealed that the famous liberal opposition paper, *El Diario del Hogar,* stressed political themes.

7. "El programa del Partido Liberal," *El Colmillo Público,* 11 March 1906.

8. Partido Liberal Mexicano, "Programa y manifiesto," 174.

9. See "Manifiesto del Club Liberal Ponciano Arriaga," *El Hijo del Ahuizote,* 1 March 1903; "Obrero mexicano," *El Colmillo Público,* 11 February 1906; Partido Liberal Mexicano, "Programa y manifiesto," sec. 5.

10. *El Colmillo Público* revealed the contradictions in the celebrated "Porfirian progress" by contending on a regular basis that the masses remained impoverished. See, for example, the following articles in *El Colmillo Público:* "¿Donde está nuestro progreso?" 24 December 1905; "Nuestro progreso económico," 1 January 1906; "Obrero mexicano," 11 February 1906; "Cómo se nos denigra," 1 July 1906.

11. Partido Liberal Mexicano, "Programa y manifiesto," sec. 5.

12. "El progreso material," *El Colmillo Público,* 11 February 1906. For the journal's ties to the PLM, see Cockcroft, *Intellectual Precursors,* 118.

13. The PLM's 1906 manifesto prescribed a significant mediating and redistributive role to the state in the realm of capital-labor relations. It called for the minimum wage, worker protection, the eight-hour day, and outlawing different coercive labor practices in the countryside such as the company store and debt peonage. The party also advocated state intervention to lower the prices on basic necessities. The PLM promoted reduced taxes on "necessities" and increased taxes on luxury items to provide workers with greater access to basic goods (Partido Liberal Mexicano, "Programa y manifiesto," 175–78, 185–87). On state tax policies,

see also "Nuestras primeras necesidades y los impuestos," *El Colmillo Público,* 12 March 1905; "Consejos a los carnívoros," *El Colmillo Público,* 19 June 1904. For a general discussion of Porfirian tax policy, see Carmagnani, "El liberalismo."

14. Partido Liberal Mexicano, "Programa y manifiesto," 174.

15. Partido Liberal Mexicano, "Iniciativa de la junta organizadora del Partido Liberal: Bases que se ponen a discusión," *El Colmillo Público,* 11 March 1906.

16. *El Colmillo Público,* 31 December 1905, 829–30.

17. See *El Hijo del Ahuizote,* 20 April 1902, 1250. (*El Hijo del Ahuizote* was directed by members of the PLM at this time.) See also Enrique Flores Magón, "Valle nacional," in Bartra, ed., *Regeneración,* 171–72.

18. "La esclavitud en Yucatán," *Regeneración,* 31 January 1901. Labor conditions in Yucatán were notoriously harsh. On labor conditions, see Wells, *Yucatán's Gilded Age* and "Henequen." See also Joseph and Wells, *Summer of Discontent.* For a different analysis of labor conditions in Yucatán, see Tutino, *From Insurrection.*

19. For a reference to "Indian tribes," see Partido Liberal Mexicano, "Programa y manifiesto," sec. 7. The liberal opposition periodical *El Nigromante* expressed a similar position in an article entitled "El exterminio del Yaqui: Afrenta y compromete a la nación; ya es hora de que cese," 13 February 1905. For a regional analysis of the indigenous communities during the Porfiriato, see Tutino, *From Insurrection.*

20. "La guerra del yanqui," *El Colmillo Público,* 16 May 1904. However, in a later discussion of the same issue the periodical did not explain the motivations behind expropriating the Yaqui Indians. See "El llamado bandolerismo Yaqui," *El Colmillo Público,* 30 July 1906.

21. Partido Liberal Mexicano, "Programa y manifiesto," 178.

22. "El programa del Partido Liberal," *El Colmillo Público,* 11 March 1906, 143–44.

23. Partido Liberal Mexicano, "Programa y manifiesto," 178–79.

24. See "Manifiesto," *El Colmillo Público,* 1 March 1903.

25. See, for example, Partido Liberal Mexicano, "Manifiesto," sec. 4, art. 18. On Porfirian policy vis-à-vis church lands, see Knowlton, *Church Property.*

26. Partido Liberal Mexicano, "Programa y manifiesto," 177–80.

27. Ibid., 179.

28. Ibid., 177–78.

29. Ibid., 179.

30. See especially "Manifiesto," *El Hijo del Ahuizote,* 1 March 1903.

31. Partido Liberal Mexicano, "Programa y manifiesto," sec. 8.

32. "El gobierno de México y los extranjeros," *El Colmillo Público,* 2 April 1905, 210–11. Porfirian historiography also stresses American domination of Mexican property. See, for example, Hart, *Revolutionary Mexico,* chap. 5.

33. On this issue, see the following articles in *El Colmillo Público:* "La muerte del Gral. Díaz: ¿Traerá una revolución?" 1 January 1905; "¿A donde vamos?" 7 January 1906; "El crédito nacional," 14 January 1906; "Todavía es tiempo," 24 June 1906.

34. Partido Liberal Mexicano, "Programa y manifiesto," 191.

35. On this issue, see d'Olwer, "Las inversiones extranjeras," 1029–53.

36. Partido Liberal Mexicano, "Programa y manifiesto," sec. 3, art. 52; "Iniciativa de la

junta organizadora del Partido Liberal: Bases que se ponen a discusión," *El Colmillo Público,* 1 March 1906, sec. 5.

37. Raigosa, *El problema fundamental.*

38. "Del estudio del señor licenciado Raigosa (1)," *Regeneración,* 15 January 1901.

39. It advocated the rejection of Chinese immigration, a position it justified by asserting that Asian workers had a depressing effect on Mexicans' wages. There was clearly a nationalist element in this formulation, but unlike the PLM's commentary on Raigosa's essay, its nationalism was tempered a bit by a class analysis. The importation of Asian workers weakened Mexican workers' position vis-à-vis capital (Partido Liberal Mexicano, "Programa y manifiesto," sec. 3, art. 16).

40. "Todavía es tiempo," *El Colmillo Público,* 24 June 1906.

41. On the PLM's experience in the United States, see MacLachlan, *Anarchism.*

42. On the power struggle, see Cockcroft, *Intellectual Precursors.*

43. There is extensive debate about exactly when Ricardo Flores Magón first adopted an anarchist philosophy. Hart, for instance, dates Flores Magón's introduction to anarchism earlier than most scholars (*Revolutionary Mexico,* 90–94). Albro, on the other hand, argues for a later date (*Always a Rebel,* 28–30).

44. Albro, *Always a Rebel,* 122.

45. Partido Liberal Mexicano, "Manifiesto."

46. Despite the fact that former members of the PLM such as Soto y Gama joined the Zapatistas and the PLM reported favorably on Zapata's movement after it broke out, it is clear that there were some tensions between the two movements. Zapata, for example, had poor relations with the anarchist-influenced group Casa del Obrero Mundial (Hart, *Anarchism,* 130–33).

47. See, for example, the following articles in *Regeneración:* "Regeneración," 3 September 1910; "La cadena de los libres," 22 October 1910; "Impossible," 15 April 1911.

48. "La cadena de los libres."

49. Partido Liberal Mexicano, "Manifiesto."

50. "El gobierno y la revolución económica," *Regeneración,* 9 September 1911.

51. Partido Liberal Mexicano, "Manifiesto."

52. "Libertad política," *Regeneración,* 12 November 1910.

53. "Order Means Harmony," *Regeneración,* reprinted in Poole, ed., *Land and Liberty,* 82–83.

54. "Para después del triunfo," *Regeneración,* 28 January 1911.

55. Articulating this internationalist position, the PLM asserted that "humanity is split into two classes whose interests are diametrically opposed—the capitalist class and the working class" (Partido Liberal Mexicano, "Manifiesto").

56. "Manifiesto a todos los trabajadores del mundo," *Regeneración,* 3 April 1911.

57. Partido Liberal Mexicano, "Manifiesto a los trabajadores de todos los países," 10 May 1909, reprinted in Guerrero, *Vocación de libertad,* 80–85.

58. "La repercusión de un linchamiento," *Regeneración,* 12 November 1910.

59. Along these lines, the group promoted the creation of a pan-American labor organization. See "Programa de la Liga Panamericana de Trabajo," *Regeneración,* 22 October 1910. The

article titled "Hacia la unión," *Regeneración,* 12 November 1910, advocated creating bonds between the U.S. and Mexican labor movements. On linking the Mexican labor movement to an international workers movement, too, see "Los consejos del amigo," *Regeneración,* 5 November 1910; and "Labour's Solidarity Should Know neither Race nor Color," *Regeneración,* 29 April 1911, reprinted in Poole, ed., *Land and Liberty,* 88–90. For the PLM's links to U.S. labor and radical movements, see MacLachlan, *Anarchism.*

60. The PLM also cited the French example to support its assertion that it was fruitless to try and change the system through legal means and that only a workers movement would be successful. See "La revolución continúa en todo el país," *Regeneración,* 10 December 1910.

61. Partido Liberal Mexicano, "Manifiesto."

62. "La revolución continúa en todo el país." For a similar analysis, see the following articles in *Regeneración:* "El Partido Liberal y la revolución de Madero," 3 December 1910; "Carne de cañon," 15 October 1910; "La revolución," 19 November 1910. See also Partido Liberal Mexicano, "Manifiesto."

63. See the following articles in *Regeneración:* "A la mujer," 24 September 1910; "Hacia la unión," 12 November 1910; "El espíritu de rebeldía," 5 December 1910. For secondary works that discuss the PLM's position on women, see Deutsch, "Gender and Sociopolitical Change," 262–71; and Soto, *Emergence of the Modern Mexican Worker,* 19–26, 41–43.

64. On Guerrero, see Albro, *To Die on Your Feet.*

65. "La mujer," *Regeneración,* 12 December 1910.

66. "¿A quién amais, mujeres?" *Punto Rojo,* 29 August 1909.

67. "Solidaridad," *Regeneración,* 29 October 1910.

68. "El interés verdadero del burgués y del proletario," *Regeneración,* 2 September 1910.

69. "La revolución continúa en todo el país," *Regeneración,* 10 December 1910.

70. Kropotkin, *Mutual Aid.* See especially the introduction and chaps. 3 and 4. For an analysis of Kropotkin's ideology, see Thompson, *The Market and Its Critics,* 273–80; and Cahm, *Kropotkin.*

71. "Solidaridad," *Regeneración,* 28 October 1910; "Hacia la unión," *Regeneración,* 12 November 1910; "Despierta proletario," *Regeneración,* 24 December 1910.

72. Obviously, there were important differences also. Two salient divides were Flores Magón's support of agrarian revolution and the fact that he did not advocate waiting for the correct "objective conditions" before revolting. Marx, in contrast, viewed industrial workers as the vanguard. Marx did not necessarily argue that the correct "objective conditions" needed to be present before the revolution began. Nevertheless, the fact that he placed primacy on industrial workers suggests that a certain level of industrial development was necessary (Marx, *Capital,* vol. 1).

73. "Manifiesto," *El Hijo del Ahuizote,* 1 April 1903, sec. 3; Partido Liberal Mexicano, "Manifiesto," secs. 3 and 4, arts. 10, 11, 12, 13, 14, and esp. 20.

74. "La cadena de los libres," *Regeneración,* 22 October 1910.

75. See "Impulsemos la enseñanza racionalista," *Regeneración,* 1 October 1910. On Ferrer's radical educational philosophy, see *The Origins and Ideals of the Modern School.*

76. "La cadena de los libres," *Regeneración,* 22 October 1910.

77. See, for example, "¿Está resuelto el problema del hambre?" *Regeneración,* 8 July 1911; "El pueblo mexicano es apto para el comunismo," *Regeneración,* 2 September 1911.

78. See, for example, "Carne de cañon," *Regeneración,* 15 October 1910.

79. See the following articles in *Regeneración:* "La revolución," 19 November 1910; "La revolución maderista," 26 November 1910; "El Partido Liberal y la revolución maderista," 3 December 1910.

80. Social Catholics, too, invoked "natural law" but for the entirely different end of sanctioning private property. Despite the fact that the PLM's call for communal property contrasted with social Catholics' and liberals' support for private property, the three groups shared certain assumptions. They all represented humans (and particularly men) as nature's master. Developmentalist liberals repeatedly emphasized that man needed to control, dominate, and even improve upon nature to realize wealth. In the PLM's discourse, too, workers were masters of nature, for the group's revolutionary discourse repeatedly called for laborers to "possess" the land. The only difference in the discourses, then, was whether Mexicans ruled land and nature individually or communally. See, for example, "La revolución," *Regeneración,* 19 November 1910.

81. On these positive attributes of communal land, see the following articles in *Regeneración:* "Carne de cañon," 15 October 1910; "Solidaridad," 19 November 1910; "El Partido Liberal y la revolución de Madero," 3 December 1910; "El espíritu de rebeldía," 3 December 1910.

82. Kropotkin, *Fields, Factories, and Workshops*.

83. Partido Liberal Mexicano, "Manifiesto." The most detailed discussion of this issue was in the 1911 manifesto, but it was also mentioned in passing on other occasions. See the following *Regeneración* articles: "Tierra," 1 October 1910; "Solidaridad," 29 October 1910; "Hacia la unión," 12 November 1910; "La revolución maderista," 26 November 1910.

Bibliography

Periodicals

El Alacrán
Boletín de la Asociación Financiera Internacional
Boletín de la Bolsa Mercantil de México
Boletín de la Secretaría de Fomento
Boletín de la Sociedad Agrícola Mexicana
El Colmillo Público
El Diario
El Diario del Hogar
El Economista Mexicano
El Ferrocarrilero
El Florecimiento de México
El Fomento Industrial
Haciendas y Ranchos
El Heraldo Agrícola
El Hijo del Ahuizote
El Imparcial
Mexican Financier
Mexican Herald
México Industrial
El Nigromante
El País
El Paladín
El Progreso Latino

Punto Rojo
Regeneración
La Revista de Legislación y Jurisprudencia
Semana Mercantil
Los Sucesos
El Tiempo
La Voz de México

Primary and Secondary Sources

Adame Goddard, Jorge. *El pensamiento político y social de los católicos mexicanos.* Mexico City: Universidad Nacional Autónoma de México, 1981.

Agnew, Jean Christopher. *Worlds Apart: The Market and Theater in Anglo-American Thought, 1550–1750.* Cambridge: Cambridge University Press, 1986.

Aguilar Plata, Blanca. "El Imparcial: Su oficio y su negocio." *Revista Mexicana de Ciencias Políticas,* no. 109 (1982).

Alamán, Lucas. *Historia de Méjico.* 5 vols. Mexico City: Editorial Jus, 1942.

Albro, Ward. *Always a Rebel: Ricardo Flores Magón and the Mexican Revolution.* Fort Worth: Texas Christian University Press, 1992.

———. *To Die on Your Feet: The Life, Times, and Writings of Práxedis G. Guerrero.* Fort Worth: Texas Christian University Press, 1996.

Altman, Roger C. "Global Markets' Massive Extraterritorial Power." *Los Angeles Times,* 7 December 1997, M1.

Amariglio, Jack L. "The Body, Economic Discourse, and Power: An Economist's Introduction to Foucault." *History of Political Economy* 20, no. 4 (1988): 583–613.

Anderson, Rodney. *Outcasts in Their Own Land: Mexican Industrial Workers, 1906–1911.* De Kalb: Northern Illinois University Press, 1976.

Armstrong, George. *Law and Market Society in Mexico.* New York: Praeger, 1989.

Backhouse, Roger, and Tony Dudley-Evans, eds. *Economics as Language.* London: Routledge; 1993.

Banton, Michael. *Racial Theories.* New York: Cambridge University Press, 1992.

Barrera Fuentes, Florencio, ed. *Historia de la revolución mexicana (etapa precursora).* Mexico City: Instituto Nacional de Estudios Históricos de la Revolución Mexicana, 1955.

Bartra, Armando, ed. *Regeneración: 1900–1918.* Mexico City: Ediciones Era, 1991.

———. "Los indios en la sociología prusiana del siglo XIX: Situados en la piel." *Ojarasca,* no. 32 (December 1999). www.jornada.unam.mx/1999/dic99/991214/oja-sitiados/=sitiados.

Bastian, Jean Pierre. "Las sociedades protestantes y la oposición a Porfirio Díaz, 1877–1911." *Historia Mexicana* 37 (1988): 469–512.

Bazant, Jan. *Alienation of Church Wealth in Mexico: Social and Economic Aspects of the Liberal Revolution, 1856–1875.* Cambridge: Cambridge University Press, 1971.

———. *Cinco haciendas mexicanas.* Mexico City: El Colegio de México, 1975.

Bazant, Milda. *Historia de la educación durante el porfiriato.* Mexico City: El Colegio de México, 1995.

————. "Prólogo." In Milda Bazant, ed., *Debate pedagógico durante el porfiriato*, 9–13. Mexico City: Secretaría de Educación Pública, 1985.

Beatty, Edward. "Commercial Policy in Porfirian Mexico: The Structure of Protection." In Stephen Haber and Jeffrey Bortz, eds., *The Mexican Economy, 1870–1930: Essays on the Economic History of Institutions, Revolution, and Growth*, 205–54. Stanford, Calif.: Stanford University Press, 2002.

————. "The Impact of Foreign Trade on the Mexican Economy: Terms of Trade and the Rise of Industry, 1880–1923." *Journal of Latin American Studies* 32, no. 2 (May 2000): 399–434.

————. *Institutions and Investment: The Political Basis of Industrialization in Mexico before 1911*. Stanford, Calif.: Stanford University Press, 2001.

Beaulieu, Leroy. "La depreciación de la plata." Trans. Emilio Pardo. *Boletín de Sociedad Agrícola Mexicana* 10 (August 1886–June 1887).

Bellamy, Edward. *Looking Backward: 2000–1887*. New York: Penguin Books, 1960.

Bernecker, Walther. "Foreign Interests, Tariff Policy and Early Industrialization in Mexico, 1821–1848." *Ibero-Amerikanisches Archiv* 14, no. 1 (1988): 61–102.

Bernstein, Marvin. *The Mexican Mining Industry, 1850–1950*. Albany: State University of New York Press, 1964.

Bertola, Elisabetta, Marcello Carmagnani, and Paolo Riguzzi. "Federación y estados: Espacios políticos y relaciones de poder en México (siglo XIX)." In Jaime E. Rodríguez O., ed., *The Evolution of the Mexican Political System*, 117–36. Wilmington, Del.: Scholarly Resources, 1993.

Blanquel, Eduardo. *Ricardo Flores Magón*. Mexico City: Terra Nova, 1985.

Blomström, Magnus, and Björn Hettne. *Development Theory in Transition*. 2nd ed. London: Zed Books, 1987.

Bobadilla González, Leticia. "La opinión pública en México frente a la guerra hispano-cubano-americano de 1898." Licenciada thesis, Universidad Nacional Autónoma de México, Mexico City, 1994.

Borja Martínez, Francisco. *La reforma monetaria de 1905*. Mexico City: Miguel Ángel Porrúa, 1990.

Borosage, Robert L. "Global Economy: The Coming Fight over Free Trade." *Los Angeles Times*, 21 June 1998, 1M.

Boylan, Thomas, and Timothy Foley. *Political Economy and Colonial Ireland*. London: Routledge, 1992.

Bravo Ugarte, José. *Periodistas y periódicos mexicanos*. Mexico City: Jus, 1966.

Bringas, Guillermina, and David Mascareño. *Esbozo histórico de la prensa obrera en México*. Mexico City: Universidad Nacional Autónoma de México, 1988.

Brown, Jonathan. *Domestic Politics and Foreign Investment: British Development of Mexican Petroleum*. Pre-Publication Working Papers of the Institute of Latin American Studies, University of Texas.

————. "The Structure of the Foreign-Owned Petroleum Industry in Mexico, 1880–1938." In Alan Knight and Jonathan Brown, eds., *The Mexican Petroleum Industry in the Twentieth Century*, 1–35. Austin: University of Texas Press, 1992.

————. "Trabajadores nativos y extranjeros en el México porfiriano." *Siglo XIX* 9 (May–August 1994): 7–49.

Brown, Jonathan, and Peter Linder. "Oil." In Steven Topik and Allen Wells, eds., *The Second Conquest of Latin America*, 125–87. Austin: University of Texas Press, 1998.

Buchanan, Patrick. *The Great Betrayal: How American Sovereignty and Social Justice Are Sacrificed to the Gods of the Global Economy*. Boston: Little, Brown, 1998.

Bulnes, Francisco. "Estudio sobre la debatida cuestión de la depreciación de la plata." In *La crisis monetaria: Estudios sobre la crisis mercantil y la depreciación de la plata*, 131–83. Mexico City: Secretaría de Fomento, 1886.

————. *El porvenir de las naciones latinoamericanas ante las recientes conquistas de Europa y Norteamerica*. 1899. Mexico City: El Pensamiento Vivo de América, n.d.

————. *The Whole Truth about Mexico: The Mexican Revolution and President Wilson's Part Therein, as Seen by a Científico*. New York: M. Bulnes Book Company, 1916.

Burns, E. Bradford. *The Poverty of Progress*. Berkeley: University of California Press, 1980.

Cahm, Caroline. *Kropotkin and the Rise of Revolutionary Anarchism, 1872–1886*. Cambridge: Cambridge University Press, 1989.

Calderón, Francisco. "Los ferrocarriles." In Daniel Cosío Villegas, ed., *Historia moderna de México. El porfiriato. La vida económica (primera parte)*, 7: 483–634. 3rd ed. Mexico City: Editorial Hermes, 1985.

Cámara de Diputados. *Diario de los debates de la Cámara de Diputados*. Vol. 1. 20th legislature. Mexico City: Imprenta de la Cámara de Diputados, n.d.

————. *Los presidentes de México ante la nación, 1821–1984: Informes, manifestos y documentos, de 1821 a 1984*. 2nd ed. 52nd legislature. Mexico City: Quetzal, 1985.

Camarillo Carbajal, María Teresa. *El sindicato de periodistas, una utopía mexicana: Agrupaciones de periodistas en la ciudad de México (1872–1929)*. Mexico City: Universidad Nacional Autónoma de México, 1988.

Cappelletti, Ángel J. "Anarquismo latinoamericano." In Ángel J. Cappelletti and Carlos Rama, eds., *El anarquismo en América latina*, ix–ccxvi. Caracas: Biblioteca Ayacucho, 1990.

Carmagnani, Marcello. *Estado y mercado*. Mexico City: El Colegio de México, 1994.

————. "El liberalismo, los impuestos internos y el estado federal mexicano, 1857–1911." *Historia Mexicana* 38, no. 3 (1989): 471–98.

Carreño, Alberto María. *Problemas indígenas: Collección de obras diversas*. Vol. 1. Mexico City: Ediciones Victoria, 1935.

————. *Temas económicos*. Mexico City: Editorial Jus, 1962.

————. *Temas económicos. Primera parte: Collección de obras diversas*. Vol. 6. Mexico City: Ediciones Victoria, 1938.

Carrier, James, ed. *Meanings of the Market: The Free Market in Western Culture*. New York: Berg Publishers, 1997.

Castellanos, Maqueo. *Algunos problemas nacionales*. Mexico City: Eusebio Gómez de la Puente, 1909.

Ceballos Dosamantes, Jesús. *Jesuitas y pseudo-científicos*. Mexico City: Carranza e Hijos, 1911.

Ceballos Ramírez, Manuel. *El catolicismo social: Un tercero en discordia, rerum novarum, la "cuestión social" y la movilización de los católicos mexicanos (1891–1911)*. Mexico City: El Colegio de México, 1991.

Ceceña, José Luis. *México en la órbita imperial: Las empresas transnacionales.* 16th ed. Mexico City: El Caballito, 1970.

Cerutti, Mario. *Burguesía, capitales e industria en el norte de México.* Mexico City: Alianza Editorial, 1992.

Charlton, William, Tatiana Mallison, and Robert Oakeshott. *The Christian Response to Industrial Capitalism.* London: Sheed and Ward, 1986.

Chevalier, François. *Land and Society in Colonial Mexico: The Great Hacienda.* Trans. Alvin Eustis. Berkeley: University of California Press, 1963.

————. Preface to François-Xavier Guerra, *México: Del antiguo régimen a la revolución,* 1: 7–15. Mexico City: Fondo de Cultura Económica, 1988.

Coatsworth, John. *Growth against Development: The Economic Impact of the Railroads in Mexico.* De Kalb: Northern Illinois University Press, 1981.

————. *Los orígenes del atraso.* Trans. Juan José Trujilla. Mexico City: Alianza Editorial, 1990.

Coatsworth, John, and Alan Taylor, eds. *Latin America and the World Economy since 1800.* Cambridge, Mass.: Harvard University, David Rockefeller Center for Latin American Studies, 1998.

Cockcroft, James. *Intellectual Precursors of the Mexican Revolution, 1900–1913.* Austin: University of Texas Press, 1976.

Colegio de México. *Estadísticas económicas del porfiriato: Comercio exterior de México, 1876–1911.* Mexico City: El Colegio de México, 1960.

Comisión monetaria México: Datos para el estudio de la cuestión monetaria en México. Mexico City: Tipografía de la Oficina Impresora de Estampillas, Palacio Nacional, 1903.

Comte, Auguste. *Auguste Comte and Positivism: The Essential Writings.* Ed. Gertrude Lenzer. New York: Harper and Row, 1975.

Conant, Charles. *The United States and the Orient: The Nature of the Economic Problem.* New York: Kinnikat Press, 1971.

Constable, Pamela, and Arturo Valenzuela. *A Nation of Enemies.* New York: Norton, 1991.

Cora, Moreno. "Reseña histórica de la propiedad territorial en la República Mexicana." In Aniceto Villamar, ed., *Las leyes vigentes sobre tierras, bosques, aguas, ejidos, colonización y el gran registro de la propiedad,* 8–102. 9th ed. Mexico City: Herrero Hermanos.

Córdova, Arnaldo. "El pensamiento social y político de Andrés Molina Enríquez." In Andrés Molina Enríquez, *Los grandes problemas nacionales,* 11–68. Mexico City: Ediciones Era, 1991.

Correa, Alberto. "La nueva ley de instrucción primaria." In Mílda Bazant, ed., *Debate pedagógico durante el porfiriato,* 47–51. Mexico City: Secretaría de Educación Pública, 1985.

Cosío, José L. *Cómo y por quiénes se ha monopolizado la propiedad rústica en México.* 2nd ed. Mexico City: Editorial Jus, 1966.

Cosío Villegas, Daniel. *American Extremes.* Austin: University of Texas Press, 1964.

————. "Séptima llamada particular." In Daniel Cosío Villegas, ed., *Historia moderna de México. El porfiriato. La vida económica (primera parte),* 7: xi–xxviii. 3rd ed. Mexico City: Editorial Hermes, 1985.

Cosío Villegas, Daniel, ed. *Historia moderna de México. El porfiriato. La vida política interior (segunda parte).* Vol. 9. Mexico City: Editorial Hermes, 1972.

Cott, Kennett. "Porfirian Investment Policies, 1876–1910." Ph.D. diss., University of Michigan, 1980.

Covarrubias, José. *Varios informes sobre tierras y colonización*. Mexico City: Secretaría de Fomento, 1912.

Covo, Jacqueline. *Las ideas de la Reforma en México (1855–1861)*. Trans. María Francisca Mourier-Martínez. Mexico City: Universidad Nacional Autónoma de México, 1983.

Creel, Enrique C. "La cuestión de la plata." In *Comisión monetaria México: Datos para el estudio de la cuestión monetaria en México*. Mexico City: Tipografía de la Oficina Impresora de Estampillas, Palacio Nacional, 1903.

Crespo y Martínez, Gilbert. "Evolución minera." In Justo Sierra, ed., *México, su evolución social*, 2: 49–97. Mexico City: J. Ballescá, 1902.

La crisis monetaria: Estudios sobre la crisis mercantil y la depreciación de la plata. Mexico City: Secretaría de Fomento, 1886.

Cuervo, Ulpiano B. "Arbitraje obligatorio y tratado de comercio." *El Paladín*, 5 January 1903, 1.

Deutsch, Sandra McGee. "Gender and Sociopolitical Change in Latin America." *Hispanic American Historical Review* 71, no. 2 (1991): 259–306.

Díaz, Bernal. *The Conquest of New Spain*. Trans. J. M. Cohen. London: Penguin, 1963.

Díaz Dufoo, Carlos. "La evolución industrial." In Justo Sierra, ed., *México, su evolución social*, 2: 99–158. Mexico City: J. Ballescá y Compañía, 1901.

———. *Limantour*. 2nd ed. Mexico City: Imprenta Victoria, 1922.

———. *México y los capitales extranjeros*. Mexico City: C. Bouret, 1918.

Dilley, Roy, ed. *Contesting Markets: Analyses of Ideology, Discourse and Practice*. Edinburgh: Edinburgh University Press, 1992.

Directorio profesional, industrial y de comercio. Mexico City, 1899.

Domínguez, Ángel M. *Relaciones comerciales entre las repúblicas latino-americanas, México y Chile*. Mexico City: Imp. de José M. Mellado, 1899.

Dumas, Claude. "El discurso de oposición en la prensa clerical conservadora de México en la época de Porfirio Díaz." *Historia Mexicana* 39, no. 1 (July–September 1989): 243–56.

Dumont, L. *From Mandeville to Marx: The Genesis and Triumph of Economic Ideology*. Chicago: University of Chicago Press, 1977.

Duncan, Robert. "For the Good of the Country: State and Nation Building during Maximilian's Mexican Empire, 1864–67." Ph.D. diss., University of California, Irvine, 2001.

Eguiarte Sakar, Estela, ed. *Hacer ciudadanos: Educación para el trabajo manufacturero en México en siglo XIX (antología)*. Mexico City: Impresora Galve, 1989.

Ely, Richard T. *The Past and Present of Political Economy*. Baltimore, Md.: John Murphy and Company, 1884.

Escobar, Rómulo. "La emigración de nuestros peones." *Boletín de la Secretaría de Fomento*, no. 1 (August 1906): 28–41.

Farriss, Nancy. *Crown and Clergy in Colonial Mexico: 1759–1821*. London: Athlone Press, 1968.

Ferrer, Francisco. *The Origins and Ideals of the Modern School*. 1913. Trans. Joseph McCabe. New York: Arno Press, 1972.

Flores Magón, Ricardo. *Antología*. Mexico City: Universidad Nacional Autónoma de México, 1970.

———. *Artículos políticos, 1910*. Mexico City: Ediciones Antorcha, 1980.

————. *Artículos políticos, 1911*. Mexico City: Ediciones Antorcha, 1980.

————. *Semilla libertaria*. 2nd ed. Mexico City: Liga de Economistas Revolucionarios, 1975.

————. *Testimonio carcelario*. Mexico City: Secretaría de Gobernación, 1977.

Flores Magón, Ricardo, and Jesús Flores Magón. *Batalla a la dictadura (textos políticos)*. Mexico City: Empresas Editoriales, 1948.

Forget, Evelyn. "Disequilibrium Trade as a Metaphor for Disorder in the Work of Jean-Baptiste Say." In Mary Morgan and Neil De Marchi, eds., *Higgling*, 135–48. Durham, N.C.: Duke University Press, 1994.

Foucault, Michel. *The History of Sexuality*. Vol. 1, *An Introduction*. New York: Vintage, 1980.

————. *The Order of Things: An Archaeology of the Human Sciences*. New York: Vintage, 1973.

Franco, Jean. *Plotting Women: Gender and Representation in Mexico*. New York: Columbia University Press, 1989.

Frank, André Gunder. *Capitalism and Underdevelopment in Latin America*. New York: Monthly Review Press, 1967.

Friedrich, Paul. *Agrarian Revolt in a Mexican Village*. New Jersey: Prentice-Hall, 1970.

Gamboa, Leticia. "La comunidad obrera de León, 1899–1909." In *Comunidad, cultura, y vida social: Ensayos sobre la formación de la clase obrera*. Mexico City: Instituto Nacional de Antropología e Historia, 1991.

————. "Mercado de bolsa de trabajo e industria textil en el centro oriente." *Siglo XIX*, no. 1 (1991): 9–36.

García, Genaro. *Nociones de economía política*. 1902. Mexico City: Universidad Nacional Autónoma de México, 1989.

García Cantú, Gastón. *El socialismo en México: Siglo XIX*. Mexico City: Ediciones Era, 1969.

Gayol, Roberto. *Dos problemas de vital importancia para México: La colonización y el desarrollo de la irrigación*. Mexico City: Tipografía El Popular de Francisco Montes de Oca, 1906.

Gide, Charles. *Curso de economía política*. 3rd ed. Buenos Aires: El Ateneo, 1959.

Gide, Charles, and Charles Rist. *A History of Economic Doctrines*. Trans. R. Richards. 2nd ed. Boston: D. C. Heath and Company, 1948.

González, Luis. *San José de Gracia*. Trans. John Upton. Austin: University of Texas Press, 1974.

González Navarro, Moisés. *La colonización de México, 1877–1910*. Mexico City: Talleres de Impresión de Estampillas y Valores, 1960.

————. *Los extranjeros en México y los mexicanos en el extranjero, 1821–1970*. Vol. 2. Mexico City: El Colegio de México, 1994.

————. *Historia moderna de México. El porfiriato. La vida social*. 5th ed. Mexico City: Editorial Hermes, 1990.

————. *Las huelgas textiles en el porfiriato*. Puebla: Editorial José M. Cajica Jr., 1970.

————. "Las ideas raciales de los científicos, 1890–1910." *Historia Mexicana* 37 (1988): 565—83.

————. "Las tierras ociosas." In Margarita Menegus Bornemann, ed., *Problemas agrarios y propiedad en México, siglos XVIII y XIX*, 190–226. Mexico City: El Colegio de México, 1995.

González Ramírez, Manuel, ed. "Manifiesto de la Convención Nacional Liberal a favor de reelección." In *Manifiestos políticos, 1892–1911*. Mexico City: Fondo de Cultura Económica, 1957.

————. "Manifiesto de los oaxaqueños residentes en el Distrito Federal a favor de la reelección." In *Manifiestos políticos, 1892–1911*. Mexico City: Fondo de Cultura Económica, 1957.

González Roa, Fernando. *El problema ferrocarrilero y la compañía de los ferrocarriles nacionales de México*. 2nd ed. Mexico City: Ediciones de la Liga de Economistas Revolucionarios de la República Mexicana, 1975.

Gootenberg, Paul. *Imagining Development: Economic Ideas in Peru's "Fictitious Prosperity" of Guano, 1840–1880*. Berkeley: University of California Press, 1993.

Gould, Stephen. *The Mismeasure of Man*. New York: Norton, 1981.

Gray, John. *False Dawn: The Delusions of Global Capitalism*. London: Granta Books, 1998.

Greenfield, Gerald. "The Great Drought and Elite Discourse in Imperial Brazil." *Hispanic American Historical Review* 72, no. 3 (1992): 375–400.

Guerra, François-Xavier. *México: Del antiguo régimen a la revolución*. 2 vols. Mexico City: Fondo de Cultura Económica, 1988.

————. "El soberano y su reino. Reflexiones sobre la génesis del ciudadano en América Latina." In Hilda Sabato, ed., *Ciudadanía política y formación de la naciones*, 33–61. Mexico City: El Colegio de México, 1999.

Guerrero, Práxedis G. *Vocación de libertad*. Guanajuato: Ediciones del Gobierno del Estado de Guanajuato, 1977.

Haber, Stephen. "Industrial Concentration and Capital Markets: A Comparative Study of Brazil, Mexico, and the United States, 1830–1930." *Journal of Economic History* 51, no. 3 (1991): 559–80.

————. *Industry and Underdevelopment: The Industrialization of Mexico, 1890–1940*. Stanford, Calif.: Stanford University Press, 1989.

Haber, Stephen, ed. *How Latin America Fell Behind*. Stanford, Calif.: Stanford University Press, 1997.

Hale, Charles. "José María Luis Mora and the Structure of Mexican Liberalism." *Hispanic American Historical Review* 45, no. 2 (1965): 196–227.

————. *Mexican Liberalism in the Age of Mora, 1821–1853*. New Haven, Conn.: Yale University Press, 1968.

————. "Political and Social Ideas in Latin America, 1870–1930." In Leslie Bethell, ed., *The Cambridge History of Latin America*, 4: 367–441. Cambridge: Cambridge University Press, 1985.

————. *The Transformation of Liberalism in Late Nineteenth-Century Mexico*. Princeton, N.J.: Princeton University Press, 1989.

Hall, Stuart. "Variants of Liberalism." In James Donald and Stuart Hall, eds., *Politics and Ideology*, 34–69. Philadelphia: Open University Press, 1986.

Hall, Stuart, and James Donald. "Introduction." In James Donald and Stuart Hall, eds., *Politics and Ideology*, ix–xx. Philadelphia: Open University Press, 1986.

Hart, John. *Anarchism and the Mexican Working Class, 1860–1931*. Austin: University of Texas Press, 1978.

————. *Empire and Revolution: The Americans in Mexico since the Civil War*. Berkeley: University of California Press, 2002.

————. *Revolutionary Mexico*. Berkeley: University of California Press, 1987.

Haskell, Thomas, and Richard Teichgraeber III, eds. *The Culture of the Market: Historical Essays*. Cambridge: Cambridge University Press, 1993.

Helg, Aline. "Race in Argentina and Cuba, 1880–1930: Theory, Policies, and Popular Reaction." In R. Graham, ed., *The Idea of Race in Latin America, 1870–1940*, 37–69. Austin: University of Texas Press, 1990.

Hernández Chávez, Alicia. *La tradición republicana del buen gobierno*. Mexico City: El Colegio de México, 1993.

Hilferding, Rudolph. *Finance Capital: A Study of the Late Phase of Capitalist Development*. Trans. Morris Watnich and Sam Gordon. London: Routledge, 1981.

Himmelfarb, Gertrude. *Victorian Minds*. New York: Alfred A. Knopf, 1968.

Hirschman, Albert O. *The Passions and the Interests: Political Arguments for Capitalism before Its Triumph*. Princeton, N.J.: Princeton University Press, 1977.

———. *Rival Views of Market Society and Other Recent Essays*. New York: Viking, 1986.

Hobsbawm, E. J. *The Age of Empire, 1875–1914*. London: Weidenfeld and Nicolson, 1987.

Hobson, J. A. *Imperialism: A Study*. Ann Arbor: University of Michigan Press, 1972.

Hodges, Donald C. *Mexican Anarchism after the Revolution*. Austin: University of Texas Press, 1995.

Holden, Robert. *Mexico and the Survey of Public Lands*. De Kalb: Northern Illinois University Press, 1994.

Holy, Ladislav. "Culture, Market Ideology and Economic Reform in Czechoslovakia." In Roy Dilley, ed., *Contesting Markets: Analyses of Ideology, Discourse and Practice*, 231–43. Edinburgh: Edinburgh University Press, 1992.

Humboldt, Alexander von. *Political Essay on the Kingdom of New Spain*. 4 vols. 1811. Trans. John Black. New York: AMS Press, 1966.

Ingram, John Kells. *A History of Political Economy*. London: A. and C. Black, 1915.

Isern, Damián. *Del desastre nacional y sus causas*. Madrid: Imprenta de la Viuda de M. Minuesa de los Ríos, 1899.

Islas García, Luis. "Biografía." In Trinidad Sánchez Santos, *Trinidad Sánchez Santos*, 11–118. Mexico City: Editorial Jus, 1945.

James, Emile. *Historia del pensamiento económico en el siglo XX*. Mexico City: Fondo de Cultura Económica, 1957.

Jameson, Fredric. *Postmodernism; or, The Cultural Logic of Late Capitalism*. Durham, N.C.: Duke University Press, 1991.

Jenks, Jeremías. "Problemas monetarios en el Oriente." In *Comisión monetaria México: Datos para el estudio de la cuestión monetaria en México*, 105–8. Mexico City: Tipografía de la Oficina Impresora de Estampillas, Palacio Nacional, 1903.

Joseph, Gilbert, and Allen Wells. *Summer of Discontent, Seasons of Upheaval: Elite Politics and Rural Insurgency in Yucatán, 1876–1915*. Stanford, Calif.: Stanford University Press, 1996.

Kahn, Joel. "Demons, Commodities, and the History of Anthropology." In James Carrier, ed., *Meanings of the Market: The Free Market in Western Culture*, 69–98. New York: Berg Publishers, 1997.

———. "Towards a History of the Critique of Economism: The Nineteenth Century German Origins of the Ethnographer's Dilemma." *Man* 25, no. 2 (June 1990): 230–49.

Katz, Friedrich. "Mexico: Restored Republic and the Porfiriato, 1867–1910." In Leslie Bethell, ed., *The Cambridge History of Latin America,* 5: 3–78. Cambridge: Cambridge University Press, 1984.

—————. *The Secret War in Mexico: Europe, the United States, and the Mexican Revolution.* Chicago: University of Chicago Press, 1983.

—————. *La servidumbre agraria en México en la época porfiriana.* Mexico City: Ediciones Era, 1991.

Kaufman, David. *The Business of Common Life: Novels and Classical Economics between Revolution and Reform.* Baltimore, Md.: Johns Hopkins University Press, 1995.

Ketteler, Wilhelm Emmanuel von. *The Social Teachings of Wilhelm Emmanuel von Ketteler.* Trans. Rupert J. Ederer. Washington, D.C.: University Press of America, 1981.

Kizca, John. *Colonial Entrepreneurs: Families and Businesses in Bourbon Mexico.* Albuquerque: University of New Mexico Press, 1983.

Klamer, Arjo, Donald McCloskey, and Robert Solow, eds. *The Consequences of Economic Rhetoric.* Cambridge: Cambridge University Press, 1988.

Knight, Alan. "El liberalismo Mexicano desde la reforma hasta la revolución (una interpretación)." *Historia Mexicana* 35, no. 1 (1985): 59–91.

—————. *The Mexican Revolution.* 2 vols. Lincoln: University of Nebraska Press, 1990.

—————. "Racism, Revolution, and Indigenismo: Mexico, 1910–1940." In Richard Graham, ed., *The Idea of Race in Latin America,* 71–113. Austin: University of Texas Press, 1990.

—————. *U.S.–Mexican Relations, 1910–1940: An Interpretation.* La Jolla, Calif.: Center for U.S.–Mexican Studies, University of California, San Diego, 1987.

Knowlton, Robert. *Church Property and the Mexican Reform, 1856–1910.* De Kalb: Northern Illinois University Press, 1976.

Kourí, Emilio. "Interpreting the Expropriation of Indian Pueblo Lands in Porfirian Mexico: The Unexamined Legacies of Andrés Molina Enríquez." *Hispanic American Historical Review* 82, no. 1 (February 2002): 69–117.

Kroeber, Clifton. *Man, Land, and Water: Mexico's Farmlands Irrigation Policies, 1885–1911.* Berkeley: University of California Press, 1983.

Kropotkin, Peter. *Fields, Factories, and Workshops.* 2nd ed. London: Thomas Nelson and Sons, 1912.

—————. *Mutual Aid: A Factor of Evolution.* Boston: Extending Horizons Books, 1955.

Kuntz Ficker, Sandra. *Empresa extranjera y mercado interior: El ferrocarril central mexicano, 1880–1907.* Mexico City: El Colegio de México, 1996.

León XIII. *Encíclicas: Rerum Novarum.* Mexico City: La Prensa, 1961.

Limantour, José Yves. *Apuntes sobre mi vida pública.* Mexico City: Editorial Porrúa, 1965.

—————. *Breves apuntes para un proyecto de abolición de las aduanas interiores de la República.* Mexico City: J. F. Jens, 1891.

—————. "Discurso pronunciado por el Sr. Lic. José I. Limantour, secretario de hacienda en la ceremonia de clausura del Concurso Científico Nacional." *Revista Positiva,* 1 February 1901, 54–63. Reprinted in Dirk Raat, "Positivism in Díaz Mexico, 1876–1910." Ph.D. diss., University of Utah, 1967, app. 3.

—————. *The Railway Merger: Being a Report Submitted to Congress in November 1908.* Trans. L. U. Simmons. Mexico City, 1908.

López-Portillo y Rojas, José. *Elevación y caída de Porfirio Díaz*. Mexico City: Editorial Librería Española, 1921.

López Rosado, Diego G. *Historia y pensamiento económico de México*. 4 vols. Mexico City: Universidad Nacional Autónoma de México, 1968–71.

López y Parra, R. "Agricultura y minería." *Boletín de la Sociedad Agrícola Mexicana,* 17 February 1900, 124–27.

Love, Joseph. *Crafting the Third World: Theorizing Underdevelopment in Rumania and Brazil.* Stanford, Calif.: Stanford University Press, 1998.

Love, Joseph, and Nils Jacobsen, eds. *Guiding the Invisible Hand: Economic Liberalism and the State in Latin American History*. New York: Praeger, 1988.

Love Brown, Susan. "The Free Market as Salvation from Government: The Anarcho-Capitalist View." In James Carrier, ed., *Meanings of the Market: The Free Market in Western Culture*, 99–128. New York: Berg Publishers, 1997.

Lustig, Jeffrey. *Corporate Liberalism: The Origins of Modern American Political Theory, 1890–1920*. Berkeley: University of California Press, 1982.

Macedo, Pablo. "Comunicaciones y obras públicas." In Justo Sierra, ed., *México, su evolución social*, 2: 250–325. Mexico City: J. Ballescá y Compañía, 1901.

————. *La evolución mercantil; comunicaciones y obras públicas; la hacienda pública*. 1905. Mexico City: Universidad Nacional Autónoma de México, 1989.

————. "La hacienda pública." In Justo Sierra, ed., *México, su evolución social*, 2: 328–413. Mexico City: J. Ballescá y Compañía, 1901.

Macías, Anna. *Against All Odds: The Feminist Movement in Mexico to 1940*. Westport, Conn.: Greenwood Press, 1981.

MacLachlan, Colin. *Anarchism and the Mexican Revolution: The Political Trials of Ricardo Flores Magón in the United States*. Berkeley: University of California Press, 1991.

Madero, Francisco. *La sucesión presidencial en 1910*. 2nd ed., 1911. De Kalb: Northern Illinois University Press, 1978.

Mandel, Ruth, and Caroline Humphrey, eds. *Markets and Moralities*. Oxford: Berg, 2002.

Marichal, Carlos. "Obstacles to the Development of Capital Markets in Nineteenth Century Mexico." In Stephen Haber, ed., *How Latin America Fell Behind*, 118–45. Stanford, Calif.: Stanford University Press, 1997.

Márquez, Octaviano. "Sánchez Santos, periodista." In Trinidad Sánchez Santos, *Obras selectas: Discursos*, 1: 5–57. Mexico City: Editorial Jus.

Martínez Baca, Eduardo. *Reseña histórica de la legislación minera en México*. Mexico City: Oficina Tipográfica de la Secretaría de Fomento, 1901.

Martínez Sobral, Enrique. *Principio de economía*. 2nd ed. Mexico City: Sociedad de Ediciones y Librería Franco-Americana, 1926.

Marx, Karl. *Capital*. Vol. 1. Trans. Ben Fowkes. New York: Vintage, 1977.

McCloskey, Donald. *The Rhetoric of Economics*. Madison: University of Wisconsin Press, 1985.

McNally, David. *Against the Market: Political Economy, Market Socialism, and the Marxist Critique*. New York: Verso, 1993.

Mead, Walter Russell. "Markets Pose the Biggest Threat to Peace." *Los Angeles Times,* 23 August 1998, M1.

————. "A Real Crisis Looms, but World Looks Other Way." *Los Angeles Times*, 20 September 1998, M2.

Memoria presentada al Congreso de la Unión por el Secretario de Estado y del Despacho de Fomento, Colonización, Industria y Comercio de la República Mexicana, Carlos Pacheco, diciembre 1877–diciembre 1882. Vol. 1. Mexico City: Imprenta de la Secretaría de Fomento, 1885.

Memoria presentada al Congreso de la Unión por el Secretario de Estado y del Despacho de Fomento, Colonización, Industria y Comercio de la República Mexicana. 1892–1896. Mexico City: Tipografía de la Secretaría de Fomento, 1897.

Memoria presentada al Congreso de la Unión por el Secretario de Estado y del Despacho de Fomento, Colonización, Industria y Comercio de la República Mexicana. 1897–1900. Mexico City: Tipografía de la Secretaría de Fomento, 1908.

Memoria presentada al Congreso de la Unión por el Secretario de Estado y del Despacho de Fomento, Colonización e Industria, 1908–1909. Mexico City: Fototipia de la Secretaría de Fomento, 1910.

Memoria presentada al Congreso de la Unión por el Secretario de Estado y del Despacho de Fomento, Colonización e Industria, Rafael Hernández, 1910–1911. Mexico City: Tipografía de la Secretaría de Fomento, 1910.

Memoria que presentó el Secretario de Hacienda al Congreso de la Unión. 1894–1895. Mexico City: Tipografía de la Impresora de Estampillas, 1895.

Memoria que presentó el Secretario de Hacienda al Congreso de la Unión. 1898–1899. Mexico City: Tipografía de la Impresora de Estampillas, 1902.

Memoria que presentó el Secretario de Hacienda al Congreso de la Unión. 1903–1904. Mexico City: Tipografía de la Impresora de Estampillas, 1909.

Mendez, Luis. "Academia central mexicana de legislación y jurisprudencia: Alocución del Presidente Don Luis Mendez, en la sesión inaugural del benio de 1906–1907, tenida el 24 de febrero de 1906." *Revista de Legislación y Jurisprudencia* 29 (July–December 1905).

Meyer, Jean. *The Cristero Rebellion*. Trans. Richard Southern. Cambridge: Cambridge University Press, 1976.

Miller, Francesca. *Latin American Women and the Search for Justice*. Hanover: University Press of New England, 1991.

Minowitz, Peter. *Profits, Priests, and Princes: Adam Smith's Emancipation of Economics from Politics and Religion*. Stanford, Calif.: Stanford University Press, 1993.

Misner, Paul. *Social Catholicism in Europe: From the Onset of Industrialization to the First World War*. New York: Crossroad, 1991.

Molina Enríquez, Andrés. *Los grandes problemas nacionales*. 6th ed. Mexico City: Ediciones Era, 1991.

Mommsen, Wolfgang J. *Theories of Imperialism*. Trans. P. S. Falla. Chicago: University of Chicago Press, 1980.

Moody, Joseph N. "Leo XIII and the Social Crisis." In Edward T. Gargan, ed., *Leo XIII and the Modern World*, 65–88. New York: Sheed and Ward, 1961.

Moody, Joseph N., ed. *Church and Society: Catholic Social and Political Thought and Movements, 1789–1950*. New York: Arts, 1953.

Mora, José María Luis. *México y sus revoluciones*. Vol. 1. Mexico City: Editorial Porrúa, 1950.

Moreno, Roberto. "Mexico." In Thomas Glick, ed., *The Comparative Reception of Darwinism,* 346–74. Austin: University of Texas Press, 1974.

Murphy, William. "Rerum Novarum (1891)." In George Weigel and Robert Royal, eds., *A Century of Catholic Social Thought,* 1–26. Lanham, Md.: Ethics and Public Policy Center, 1991.

Nava Oteo, Guadalupe. "La minería." In Daniel Cosío Villegas, ed., *Historia moderna de México. El porfiriato. La vida económica (primera parte),* 7: 179–310. 3rd ed. Mexico City: Editorial Hermes, 1985.

Nederveen Pieterse, Jan. *Empire and Emancipation.* London: Pluto Press, 1990.

Nelson, Robert. "Economics as Religion." In H. Geoffrey Brennan and A. M. C. Waterman, eds., *Economics and Religion: Are They Distinct?* 227–36. Boston: Kluwer, 1994.

————. *Reaching for Heaven on Earth: The Theological Meaning of Economics.* Savage, Md.: Rowman and Littlefield Publishers, 1991.

Novo, Salvador, ed. *El periodismo en México: 450 años de historia.* Mexico City: Editorial Tradición, 1974.

Oakley, Allen. *Classical Economic Man.* Brookfield, Vt.: Edward Elgar, 1994.

d'Olwer, Luis Nicolau. "Las inversiones extranjeras." In Daniel Cosío Villegas, ed., *Historia moderna de México. El porfiriato. La vida económica (segunda parte),* 7: 973–1185. 3rd ed. Mexico City: Editorial Hermes, 1985.

Orozco, Luis. *Los ejidos de los pueblos.* Mexico City: Ediciones El Caballito, 1975.

Padilla, Federico G. "Proyecto para la creación de agentes comerciales." Monterrey: La Europa, 1908.

Palacios, Leopoldo. *El problema de la irrigación.* Mexico City: Secretaría de Fomento, 1909.

Parlee, Lorena May. "Porfirio Díaz, Railroads, and Development in Northern Mexico: A Study of Government Policy Towards the Central and National Railroads, 1876–1910." Ph.D. diss., University of California at San Diego, 1981.

Parrini, Carl, and Martin Sklar. "New Thinking about the Market, 1896–1904: Some American Economists on Investment and the Theory of Surplus Capital." *Journal of Economic History* 43, no. 3 (September 1983): 559–78.

Partido Liberal Mexicano. "Manifiesto del 23 de septiembre de 1911." In Armando Bartra, ed., *Regeneración, 1900–1918,* 306–12. Mexico City: Ediciones Era, 1991.

————. "Programa y manifiesto del Partido Liberal Mexicano." In Florencio Barrera Fuentes, ed., *Historia de la revolución mexicana (etapa precursura),* 166–93. Mexico City: Instituto Nacional de Estudios Históricos de la Revolución Mexicana, 1955.

Peel, J. D. Y. *Herbert Spencer: The Evolution of a Sociologist.* London: Heinemann, 1971.

Peña, Manuel de la. *Algunos problemas sociales y económicos.* Mexico City: Tip. Vázquez e Hijos, 1907.

Peralta Zamora, Gloria. "La hacienda pública." In Daniel Cosío Villegas, ed., *Historia moderna de México. El porfiriato. La vida económica (segunda parte),* 7: 179–310. 3rd ed. Mexico City: Editorial Hermes, 1985.

Pereyra, Carlos. "Prólogo." In Otto Peust, *La defensa nacional de México,* iiv–viii. Mexico City: Imprenta Central, 1907.

Perry, Laurens B. *Juárez and Díaz: Machine Politics in Mexico.* De Kalb: Northern Illinois University Press, 1978.

Peust, Otto. *La defensa nacional de México.* Mexico City: Imprenta Central, 1907.

————. *Estadista agrícola, razones que determinada la naturaleza de los datos más vigentes para fundamento de la política agraria.* Mexico City: Secretaría de Fomento, 1910. Reprinted in Marta Eugenia García Ugarte, ed., *En torno a la democracia: La política agraria en México, 1893–1921.* Mexico City: Instituto Nacional de Estudios Históricos de la Revolución Mexicana, 1993.

————. *México y el problema obrero rural.* Mexico City: Secretaría de Fomento, 1911.

————. "Situación económica de la agricultura mexicana." In *Boletín de la Sociedad Agrícola Mexicana,* 1 July 1906, 489.

Pimentel, Francisco. "La economía política aplicada a la propiedad territorial en México." In Francisco Pimentel, *Dos obras de Francisco Pimentel.* Mexico City: Consejo Nacional para la Cultura y las Artes, 1995.

————. "Memoria sobre las causas que han originado la situación actual de la raza indígena de México y medios de remediarla." In Francisco Pimentel, *Dos obras de Francisco Pimentel.* Mexico City: Consejo Nacional para la Cultura y las Artes, 1995.

Platt, D. C. M. *Latin America and British Trade, 1806–1914.* New York: Harper and Row, 1973.

Platt, Tristan. "Divine Protection and Liberal Damnation: Exchanging Metaphors in Nineteenth-Century Potosí (Bolivia)." In Roy Dilley, ed., *Contesting Markets: Analyses of Ideology, Discourse and Practice,* 131–58. Edinburgh: Edinburgh University Press, 1992.

Pletcher, David. *Rails, Mines, and Progress: Seven American Promoters in Mexico, 1867–1911.* New York: Cornell University Press, 1958.

Polanyi, Karl. *The Great Transformation: The Political and Economic Origins of Our Time.* Boston: Beacon Press, 1957.

Poole, David, ed. *Land and Liberty: The Anarchist Influences in the Mexican Revolution—Ricardo Flores Magón.* Sanday, England: Cienfuegos Press, 1977.

Potash, Robert. *Mexican Government and Industrial Development in the Early Republic: The Banco de Avío.* Amherst: University of Massachusetts Press, 1983.

Powell, T. G. *El liberalismo y el campesinado en el centro de México (1850 a 1876).* Trans. Roberto Gómez Ciriza. Mexico City: Secretaría de Educación Pública, 1974.

————. "Mexican Intellectuals and the Indian Question." *Hispanic American Historical Review* 48, no. 1 (1968): 19–36.

Prieto, Guillermo. *Economía política.* 1876. Mexico City: Universidad Nacional Autónoma de México, 1989.

Quirk, Robert. *The Mexican Revolution and the Catholic Church, 1910–1929.* Bloomington: Indiana University Press, 1973.

Raat, Dirk. "Ideas and Society in Don Porfirio's Mexico." *Americas* 30 (1973): 32–53.

————. "Los intelectuales, el positivismo, y la cuestión indígena." *Historia Mexicana* 20 (1971): 412–27.

————. "Leopoldo Zea and Positivism: A Reappraisal." *Hispanic American Historical Review* 48 (1968): 1–18.

————. "Positivism in Díaz Mexico: An Essay in Intellectual History." Ph.D. diss., University of Utah, 1967.

————. *El positivismo durante el porfiriato, 1876–1910.* Mexico City: Secretaría de Educación Pública, 1975.

Radkau, Verna. *Por la debilidad de nuestro ser: Mujeres del pueblo en la paz porfiriana.* Mexico City: Secretaría de Educación Pública, 1989.

Raigosa, Genaro. "La evolución agrícola." In Justo Sierra, ed., *México, su evolución social,* 2: 6–48. Mexico City: J. Ballescá y Compañía, 1901.

———. *El problema fundamental de México en siglo XX: La población.* Mexico City: F. P. Hoeck and Company, 1900.

Ramos Escandón, Carmen. "Señoritas porfirianas: Mujer e ideología en el México progresista, 1880–1910." In Carmen Ramos Escandón et al., eds., *Presencia y transparencia: La mujer en la historia de México,* 143–62. Mexico City: El Colegio de México, 1987.

Ramos Lanz, Miguel. *Estudio sobre inmigración y colonización.* Mexico City: El Tiempo, 1897.

Refugio González, María del. "Comercio y comerciante en la legislación y la doctrina mexicana del siglo XIX." In *Anuario mexicano de historia del derecho,* 2: 115–49. Mexico City: Universidad Nacional Autónoma de México, 1990.

Reich, Peter Lester. *Mexico's Hidden Revolution.* Notre Dame, Ind.: University of Notre Dame Press, 1995.

El resurgimiento mexicano: Cuatro opúsculos sobre algunas cuestiones que ha suscitado el ingreso de los católicos a la vida pública. Mexico City: Aguilar Vera, 1913.

Reyes Heroles, Jesús. *El liberalismo mexicano: La integración de las ideas.* 3 vols. Mexico City: Fondo de Cultura Económica, 1974.

Ricardo, David. *Principles of Political Economy and Taxation.* 1817. Ed. R. M. Hartwell. Harmondsworth: Penguin, 1971.

Rice, Jacqueline Ann. "The Porfirian Political Elite: Life Patterns of the Delegates to the Unión Liberal Convention." Ph.D. diss., University of California, Los Angeles, 1979.

Robinson, Ronald, and John Gallagher. "The Imperialism of Free Trade." *Economic History Review,* 2nd ser., 6, no. 1 (1953): 1–15.

Rodó, José Enrique. *Ariel.* Cambridge: Cambridge University Press, 1967.

Rodríguez O., Jaime E. *The Independence of Spanish America.* Cambridge: Cambridge University Press, 1998.

Rojas de Ferro, Christina. "The 'Will to Civilize' and Its Encounter with Laissez-faire." *Review of International Political Economy* 2, no. 1 (winter 1995): 150–73.

Romero, Matías. *Estudio sobre la anexión de México a los Estados Unidos.* Mexico City: Imprenta del Gobierno, 1890.

———. *Mexico and the United States.* New York: G. P. Putnam's Sons, 1898.

———. *Reciprocidad comercial entre México y los Estados Unidos (el Tratado Comercial de 1883).* 1890. Mexico City: Banco Nacional de Comercio Exterior, 1971.

Rosenberg, Emily. "Foundations of United States' International Financial Power: Gold Standard Diplomacy 1900–1905." *Business History Review* 59 (summer 1985): 169–202.

Rosensweig, Fernando. "El comercio exterior." In Daniel Cosío Villegas, ed., *Historia moderna de México. El porfiriato. La vida económica (segunda parte),* 7: 635–729. 3rd ed. Mexico City: Editorial Hermes, 1985.

———. "Moneda y bancos." In Daniel Cosío Villegas, ed., *Historia moderna de México. El porfiriato. La vida económica (segunda parte),* 7: 789–885. 3rd ed. Mexico City: Editorial Hermes, 1985.

Safford, Frank. "Política, ideología y sociedad." In Leslie Bethell, ed., *América Latina independiente: Historia de América Latina*, 6: 42–104. Barcelona: Editorial Crítica, 1991.

Salvatore, Ricardo. "Market Oriented Reforms and the Language of Popular Protest: Latin America from Charles III to the IMF." *Social Science History* 17, no. 4 (winter 1993): 485–523.

———. "The Normalization of Economic Life: Representations of the Economy in Golden Age Buenos Aires, 1890–1913." *Hispanic American Historical Review* 81, no. 1 (February 2001): 1–44.

———. "The Strength of Markets in Latin America's Sociopolitical Discourse, 1750–1850: Some Preliminary Observations." *Latin American Perspectives* 26, no. 1 (January 1999): 22–43.

Samuels, William, ed. *Economics as Discourse*. Boston: Kluwer, 1990.

Sánchez, Manuel León, ed. *Trinidad Sánchez Santos: Editoriales de "El País" en 1910, 1911, y 1912*. Mexico City: Ediciones León Sánchez, 1923.

Sánchez Santos, Trinidad. *Obras selectas de Trinidad Sánchez Santos*. Vol. 1, *Discursos*. Mexico City: Editorial Jus, 1961.

———. "El problema agrícola de la República Mexicana como problema nacional." *Boletín de la Secretaría de Fomento*, no. 1 (August 1906): 1–11.

———. *Trinidad Sánchez Santos: Discursos*. Mexico City: Tip. de la Comp. E. Católica, 1902.

Schell, William, Jr. *Integral Outsiders: The American Colony in Mexico City, 1876–1911*. Wilmington, Del.: Scholarly Resources, 2001.

Schmitt, Karl. "Catholic Adjustment to the Secular State: The Case of Mexico, 1877–1911." *Catholic Historical Review* 48 (July 1962): 182–204.

———. "The Díaz Conciliation Policy on State and Local Levels, 1876–1911." *Hispanic American Historical Review* 40 (November 1960): 513–32.

Schumpeter, Joseph. *History of Economic Analysis*. New York: Oxford University Press, 1954.

Sellers, Charles. *The Market Revolution*. Oxford: Oxford University Press, 1991.

Shadle, Stanley. *Andrés Molina Enríquez: Mexican Land Reformer of the Revolutionary Era*. Tucson: University of Arizona Press, 1994.

Sierra, Justo. *Educación nacional*. Vol. 8 of *Obras completas*. Mexico City: Universidad Nacional Autónoma de México, 1991.

———. *Evolución política del pueblo mexicano*. Vol. 12 of *Obras completas*. Mexico City: Universidad Nacional Autónoma de México, 1991.

———. *México social y político*. 1885. Mexico City: Dirección General de Prensa, Memoria, Bibliotecas y Publicaciones, 1960.

Sierra, Justo, ed. *Mexico, Its Social Evolution*. 3 vols. Mexico City: J. Ballescá y Compañía, 1900–1904.

———. *México, su evolución social*. 3 vols. Mexico City: J. Ballescá y Compañía, 1900–1902.

Silva Herzog, Jesús. *Nueve estudios mexicanos*. Mexico City: Imprenta Universitaria, 1953.

———. *El pensamiento económico, social y político de México 1810–1964*. Mexico City: Instituto Mexicano de Investigación Económica, 1964.

Sinkin, Richard. *The Mexican Reform, 1855–1876: A Study in Liberal Nation Building*. Austin: University of Texas Press, 1979.

————. "Modernization and Reform in Mexico, 1855–76." Ph.D. diss., University of Michigan, 1971.

Skidmore, Thomas, and Peter Smith. *Modern Latin America*. 4th ed. New York: Oxford University Press, 1997.

Sklar, Martin. *The Corporate Reconstruction of American Capitalism, 1890–1916*. Cambridge: Cambridge University Press, 1988.

Smith, Adam. *The Wealth of Nations*. New York: Random House, 1994.

Soros, George. *The Crisis of Global Capitalism: Open Society Endangered*. New York: BBS/Public Affairs, 1998.

Soto, Shirlene. *Emergence of the Modern Mexican Worker*. Denver: Arden Press, 1990.

Stabb, Martin. "Indigenism and Racism in Mexican Thought: 1857–1911." *Journal of Inter-American Studies* 1 (1959): 405–23.

Stevens, Donald Fithian. "Agrarian Policy and Instability in Porfirian Mexico." *Americas* 39, no. 2 (October 1982): 153–66.

Stubbs, Michael. *Discourse Analysis: The Sociolinguistic Analysis of Natural Language*. Oxford: B. Blackwell, 1983.

Tannenbaum, Frank. *Peace by Revolution: Mexico after 1910*. New York: Columbia University Press, 1966.

Taylor, Overton. *A History of Economic Thought*. New York: McGraw Hill, 1960.

Teichgraeber, Richard. *Sublime Thoughts/Penny Wisdom: Situating Emerson and Thoreau in the American Market*. Baltimore, Md.: Johns Hopkins University Press, 1995.

Tenenbaum, Barbara. *The Politics of Penury: Debts and Taxes in Mexico, 1821–1856*. Albuquerque: University of New Mexico Press, 1986.

Tenorio-Trillo, Mauricio. *Mexico at the World's Fair: Crafting a Modern Nation*. Berkeley: University of California Press, 1996.

Terdiman, Richard. *Discourse/Counterdiscourse: The Theory and Practice of Symbolic Resistance in Nineteenth-Century France*. Ithaca, N.Y.: Cornell University Press, 1985.

Thompson, Guy. "Protectionism and Industrialization in Mexico, 1821–1854: The Case of Puebla." In Christopher Abel and Colin Lewis, eds., *Latin America: Economic Imperialism and the State*, 125–46. London: University of London Press, 1985.

Thompson, Noel. *The Market and Its Critics: Socialist Political Economy in Nineteenth Century Britain*. London: Routledge, 1988.

Topik, Steven. "The Economic Role of the State in Liberal Regimes: Brazil and Mexico Compared, 1888–1910." In Joseph L. Love and Nils Jacobsen, eds., *Guiding the Invisible Hand: Economic Liberalism and the State in Latin American History*, 117–44. New York: Praeger, 1988.

————. "The Emergence of Finance Capital in Mexico." In Virginia Guedea and Jaime Rodríguez, ed., *Five Centuries of Mexican History/México en el medio milenio*, 445–71. Mexico City: Instituto Mora and Universidad Nacional Autónoma de México, 1993.

————. "Exports under the Porfiriato." Paper, University of California, Irvine, 1992.

————. "La revolución, el estado y el desarrollo económico en México." *Historia Mexicana* 40, no. 1 (1990): 79–142.

Topik, Steven, and Allen Wells, eds. *The Second Conquest of Latin America: Coffee, Henequen, and Oil during the Export Boom, 1850–1930*. Austin: University of Texas Press, 1998.

Tribe, Keith. *Land, Labour and Economic Discourse*. London: Routledge, 1978.

Trotter, David. *Circulation*. London: Macmillan, 1988.

Turner, John Kenneth. *Barbarous Mexico*. Chicago: S. H. Kern, 1911.

Tutino, John. *From Insurrection to Revolution in Mexico*. Princeton, N.J.: Princeton University Press, 1986.

Ulloa, Ambrosio. "La baja de la plata." In *Boletín de la Escuela de Ingenieros*. Reprinted in *El Economista Mexicano*, 30 August 1902, 425–28.

Urías Horcasitas, Beatríz. "El pensamiento económico moderno en México." In Jaime E. Rodríguez O., ed., *The Independence of Mexico and the Creation of the New Nation*, 265–74. Los Angeles: University of California Latin American Center Publications, 1989.

Valdés, Juan Gabriel. "Changing Paradigms in Latin America: From Dependency to Neoliberalism in the International Context." In Joseph Tulchin, ed., *The Consolidation of Democracy in Latin America*, 127–38. Boulder, Colo.: Lynne Rienner Publishers, 1995.

Vanderwood, Paul. *Disorder and Progress: Bandits, Police, and Mexican Development*. Lincoln: University of Nebraska Press, 1981.

Van Young, Eric. *Hacienda and Market in Eighteenth-Century Mexico: The Rural Economy in the Guadalajara Region, 1675–1820*. Berkeley: University of California Press, 1981.

Vasconcelos, José. "The Latin American Basis of Mexican Civilization." In Manuel Gamio and José Vasconcelos, eds., *Aspects of Mexican Civilization*, 3–102. Chicago: University of Chicago Press, 1926.

Vaughan, Mary K. *The State, Education, and Social Class in Mexico, 1880–1928*. De Kalb: Northern Illinois University Press, 1982.

Vera Estañol, Jorge. "Juridical Evolution." In Justo Sierra, ed., *Mexico, Its Social Evolution*. Mexico City: J. Ballescá, 1902.

Villoro, Luis. *Los grandes momentos del indigenismo en México*. Mexico City: Secretaría de Educación Pública, 1987.

Viner, Jacob. *Religious Thought and Economic Society*. Durham, N.C.: Duke University Press, 1978.

————. *The Role of Providence in the Social Order: An Essay in Intellectual History*. Philadelphia: American Philosophical Society, 1972.

Walker, David. *Business, Kinship and Politics*. Austin: University of Texas Press, 1986.

Weaver, Frederick Stirton. *Latin America in the World Economy*. Boulder, Colo.: Westview Press, 2000.

Weiner, Richard. "Battle for Survival: Porfirian Views of the International Marketplace." *Journal of Latin American Studies* 32, pt. 3 (2000): 645–70.

————. "Challenges to Porfirian Visions of Progress." Paper presented at the Ninth Conference of Mexican and North American Historians, Mexico City, October 1994.

————. "Competing Market Discourses in Porfirian Mexico." *Latin American Perspectives* 26, no. 1 (1999): 44–64.

————. "Rich Colony, Poor Nation: The Labor Theory of Value and Porfirian Agriculture." Paper presented at El Primer Congreso Nacional de Historia Económica, Mexico City, October 2001.

————. "Trinidad Sánchez Santos: Voice of the Catholic Opposition in Porfirian Mexico." *Mexican Studies/Estudios Mexicanos* 17, no. 2 (2001): 321–48.

Wells, Allen. "Henequen." In Allen Wells and Steven Topik, eds., *The Second Conquest of Latin America: Coffee, Henequen, and Oil during the Export Boom, 1850–1930*, 85–124. Austin: University of Texas Press, 1998.

————. *Yucatán's Gilded Age: Haciendas, Henequen, and International Harvester, 1860–1915*. Albuquerque: University of New Mexico Press, 1985.

Wiener, Martin. "Market Culture, Reckless Passion, and the Victorian Reconstruction of Punishment." In Thomas Haskell and Richard Teichgraeber III, eds., *The Culture of the Market: Historical Essays*, 136–60. Cambridge: Cambridge University Press, 1993.

Wilkins, Mira. *The Emergence of Multinational Enterprise: American Business Abroad from the Colonial Era to 1914*. Cambridge, Mass.: Harvard University Press, 1970.

Wilson, Irma. *Mexico: A Century of Educational Thought*. Westport, Conn.: Greenwood Press, 1974.

Woodward, Ralph Lee, ed. *Positivism in Latin America, 1850–1900*. Lexington, Mass.: D. C. Heath and Company, 1971.

Zayas Enríquez, Rafael de. *Los Estados Unidos Mexicanos, sus progresos en veinte años de paz, 1877–1897. Estudio histórico y estadístico, fundado en los datos oficiales más recientes y completos*. New York: H. A. Rost, 1898.

Zea, Leopoldo. *El positivismo en México: Nacimiento, apogeo y decadencia*. Mexico City: Fondo de Cultura Económica, 1968.

Index

About the Author

Richard Weiner received his Ph.D. in history from the University of California at Irvine in 1999. Currently, he is an assistant professor of history at Indiana University—Purdue University at Fort Wayne. His articles have appeared in *Journal of Latin American Studies*, *Mexican Studies/Estudios Mexicanos*, and *Latin American Perspectives*. He is an associate editor of *Latin American Perspectives*. He and Raúl Galoppe are coeditors of *A Fine Line: Explorations in Subjectivity, Borders, and Demarcation*, a multidisciplinary volume about the construction of boundaries in Latin America that is near completion. His current research focuses on conceptions of Mexico's wealth. By exploring underlying cultural values about what constituted wealth, he hopes to gain insights into why perceptions of Mexico's economy have changed so dramatically over time. His work-in-progress is provisionally called *Narratives of Wealth and Poverty: A Cultural History of the Mexican Economy.*